More Praise for *Lost Connections*

"Like a secular oracle, Johann Hari stands on the periphery observing what is coming. This book is a prescient and compassionate Rosetta Stone for those trying to understand mental illness. Beautiful."

—Russell Brand

"An exquisitely lucid treatise on why no person is, has been, or ever should be an island. This book is the most exciting thing I've read this year. From slightly seedy to suicidal—however you are feeling—read this book and it will honestly help you to understand which roads we must walk if we want to see true, lasting change."

—Emma Thompson, Oscar-winning actress and screenwriter

"This is one of those extraordinary books that you want all your friends to read immediately—because the shift in worldview is so compelling and dramatic that you wonder how you'll be able to have conversations with them otherwise. A highly personal book, written with humility, humor, and candor, it nonetheless heralds a crucial new discussion about our mental health—and health of the world we've created for ourselves. I haven't been so gripped for ages . . . I honestly couldn't put it down. What a stunning piece of work."

—Brian Eno

"A special writer, a great researcher, and a great wordsmith . . . This look at depression will change everything you think about it."

—Touré

"*Lost Connections* is an important, convention-challenging, provocative, and supremely timely read. It is about time we looked at mental health through the prism of society rather than, simply, medicine. This brilliant book helps us to do that." —Matt Haig, author of *Reasons to Stay Alive*

Lost Connections

Chasing the Scream: The First and Last Days of the War on Drugs

Lost Connections

*Why You're Depressed
and How to Find Hope*

Johann Hari

BLOOMSBURY PUBLISHING
NEW YORK • LONDON • OXFORD • NEW DELHI • SYDNEY

BLOOMSBURY PUBLISHING
Bloomsbury Publishing Inc.
1385 Broadway, New York, NY 10018, USA

BLOOMSBURY, BLOOMSBURY PUBLISHING, and the Diana logo are
trademarks of Bloomsbury Publishing Plc

First published in the United States 2018
This paperback edition published 2019

ISBN: HB: 978-1-63286-830-5; eBook: 978-1-63286-832-9; PB: 978-1-63286-831-2

Library of Congress Cataloging-in-Publication Data is available

2 4 6 8 10 9 7 5 3 1

Typeset by Westchester Publishing Services
Printed and bound in the U.S.A. by Berryville Graphics Inc., Berryville, Virginia

To find out more about our authors and books visit www.bloomsbury.com and
sign up for our newsletters.

Bloomsbury books may be purchased for business or promotional use. For information
on bulk purchases please contact Macmillan Corporate and Premium Sales Department
at specialmarkets@macmillan.com.

For Barbara Bateman, John Bateman, and Dennis Hardman

You can hear the audio for the interviews in this book at www.thelostconnections.com.

CONTENTS

PART III: RECONNECTION. OR, A DIFFERENT
KIND OF ANTIDEPRESSANT

Prologue: The Apple

One evening in the spring of 2014, I was walking down a small side street in central Hanoi when, on a stall by the side of the road, I saw an apple. It was freakishly large and red and inviting. I'm terrible at haggling, so I paid three dollars for this single piece of fruit, and carried it into my room in the Very Charming Hanoi Hotel. Like any good foreigner who's read his health warnings, I washed the apple diligently with bottled water, but as I bit into it, I felt a bitter, chemical taste fill my mouth. It was the flavor I imagined, back when I was a kid, that all food was going to have after a nuclear war. I knew I should stop, but I was too tired to go out for any other food, so I ate half, and then set it aside, repelled.

Two hours later, the stomach pains began. For two days, I sat in my room as it began to spin around me faster and faster, but I wasn't worried: I had been through food poisoning before. I knew the script. You just have to drink water and let it pass through you.

On the third day, I realized my time in Vietnam was slipping away in this sickness-blur. I was there to track down some survivors of the war for another book project I'm working on, so I called my translator, Dang Hoang Linh, and told him we should drive deep into the countryside in the south as we had planned all along. As we traveled around—a trashed hamlet here, an Agent Orange victim there—I was starting to feel steadier on my feet. The next morning, he took me to the hut of a tiny eighty-seven-year-old woman. Her lips were dyed bright red from the herb she was chewing, and she pulled herself toward me across the floor on a wooden plank that somebody had managed to attach some wheels to. Throughout the war, she explained, she had spent nine years wandering from bomb to bomb, trying to keep her kids alive. They were the only survivors from her village.

As she was speaking, I started to experience something strange. Her voice seemed to be coming from very far away, and the room appeared to be moving around me uncontrollably. Then—quite unexpectedly—I started to explode, all over her hut, like a bomb of vomit and feces. When—some time later—I became aware of my surroundings again, the old woman was looking at me with what seemed to be sad eyes. "This boy needs to go to a hospital," she said. "He is very sick."

No, no, I insisted. I had lived in East London on a staple diet of fried chicken for years, so this wasn't my first time at the E. coli rodeo. I told Dang to drive me back to Hanoi so I could recover in my hotel room in front of CNN and the contents of my own stomach for a few more days.

"No," the old woman said firmly. "The hospital."

"Look, Johann," Dang said to me, "this is the only person, with her kids, who survived nine years of American bombs in her village. I am going to listen to her health advice over yours." He dragged me into his car, and I heaved and convulsed all the way to a sparse building that I learned later had been built by the Soviets decades before. I was the first foreigner ever to be treated there. From inside, a group of nurses—half-excited, half-baffled—rushed to me and carried me to a table, where they immediately started shouting. Dang was yelling back at the nurses, and they were shrieking now, in a language that had no words I could recognize. I noticed then that they had put something tight around my arm.

I also noticed that in the corner, there was a little girl with her nose in plaster, alone. She looked at me. I looked back. We were the only patients in the room.

As soon as they got the results of my blood pressure—dangerously low, the nurse said, as Dang translated—they started jabbing needles into me. Later, Dang told me that he had falsely said that I was a Very Important Person from the West, and that if I died there, it would be a source of shame for the people of Vietnam. This went on for ten minutes, as my arm got heavy with tubes and track marks. Then they started to shout questions at me about my symptoms through Dang. It was a seemingly endless list about the nature of my pain.

As all this was unfolding, I felt strangely split. Part of me was consumed with nausea—everything was spinning so fast, and I kept thinking: stop moving, stop moving, stop moving. But another part of me—below or beneath or beyond this—was conducting a quite rational little monologue. Oh. You are close to death. Felled by a poisoned apple. You are like Eve, or Snow White, or Alan Turing.

Then I thought—Is your last thought really going to be *that* pretentious?

Then I thought—If eating half an apple did this to you, what do these chemicals do to the farmers who work in the fields with them day in, day out, for years? That'd be a good story, some day.

Then I thought—You shouldn't be thinking like this if you are on the brink of death. You should be thinking of profound moments in your life. You should be having flashbacks. When have you been truly happy? I pictured myself as a small boy, lying on the bed in our old house with my grandmother, cuddling up to her and watching the British soap opera *Coronation Street*. I pictured myself years later when I was looking after my little nephew, and he woke me up at seven in the morning and lay next to me on the bed and asked me long and serious questions about life. I pictured myself lying on another bed, when I was seventeen, with the first person I ever fell in love with. It wasn't a sexual memory—just lying there, being held.

Wait, I thought. Have you only ever been happy lying in bed? What does this reveal about you? Then this internal monologue was eclipsed by a heave. I begged the doctors to give me something that would switch off this extreme nausea. Dang talked animatedly with the doctors. Then he told me finally: "The doctor says you need your nausea. It is a message, and we must listen to the message. It will tell us what is wrong with you."

And with that, I began to vomit again.

Many hours later, a doctor—a man in his forties—came into my field of vision and said: "We have learned that your kidneys have stopped working. You are extremely dehydrated. Because of the vomiting and diarrhea, you have not absorbed any water for a very long time, so you are like a man who has been wandering in the desert for days." Dang interjected: "He says if we had driven you back to Hanoi, you would have died on the journey."

The doctor told me to list everything I had eaten for three days. It was a short list. An apple. He looked at me quizzically. "Was it a clean apple?" Yes, I said, I washed it in bottled water. Everybody burst out laughing, as if I had served up a killer Chris Rock punch line. It turns out that you can't just wash an apple in Vietnam. They are covered in pesticides so they can stand for months without rotting. You need to cut off the peel entirely—or this can happen to you.

Although I couldn't understand why, all through the time I was working on this book, I kept thinking of something that doctor said to me that day, during my unglamorous hour of poisoning.

You need your nausea. It is a message. It will tell us what is wrong with you.

It only became clear to me why in a very different place, thousands of miles away, at the end of my journey into what really causes depression and anxiety—and how we can find our way back.

Introduction: A Mystery

I was eighteen years old when I swallowed my first antidepressant. I was standing in the weak English sunshine, outside a pharmacy in a shopping center in London. The tablet was white and small, and as I swallowed, it felt like a chemical kiss.

That morning I had gone to see my doctor. I struggled, I explained to him, to remember a day when I hadn't felt a long crying jag judder its way out of me. Ever since I was a small child—at school, at college, at home, with friends—I would often have to absent myself, shut myself away, and cry. They were not a few tears. They were proper sobs. And even when the tears didn't come, I had an almost constant anxious monologue thrumming through my mind. Then I would chide myself: It's all in your head. Get over it. Stop being so weak.

I was embarrassed to say it then; I am embarrassed to type it now.

In every book about depression or severe anxiety by someone who has been through it, there is a long stretch of pain-porn in which the author describes—in ever more heightened language—the depth of the distress they felt. We needed that once, when other people didn't know what depression or severe anxiety felt like. Thanks to the people who have been breaking this taboo for decades now, I don't have to write that book all over again. That is not what I am going to write about here. Take it from me, though: it hurts.

A month before I walked into that doctor's office, I found myself on a beach in Barcelona, crying as the waves washed into me, when, quite suddenly, the explanation—for why this was happening, and how to find my way back—came to me. I was in the middle of traveling across Europe with a friend, in the summer before I became the first person in my family to go to a fancy university. We had bought cheap student rail passes, which meant for a month we could travel on any train in Europe for free, staying in youth hostels along the way. I had visions of yellow beaches and high culture—the Louvre, a spliff, hot Italians. But just before we left, I had been rejected by the first person I had ever really been in love with, and I felt emotion leaking out of me, even more than usual, like an embarrassing smell.

The trip did not go as I planned. I burst into tears on a gondola in Venice. I howled on the Matterhorn. I started to shake in Kafka's house in Prague.

For me, it was unusual, but not *that* unusual. I'd had periods in my life like this before, when pain seemed unmanageable and I wanted to excuse myself from the world. But then in Barcelona, when I couldn't stop crying, my friend said to me—You realize most people don't do this, don't you?

And then I experienced one of the very few epiphanies of my life. I turned to her and said: "I am depressed! It's not all in my head! I'm not unhappy, I'm not weak—I'm depressed!"

This will sound odd, but what I experienced at that moment was a happy jolt—like unexpectedly finding a pile of money down the back of your sofa. There is a term for feeling like this! It is a medical condition, like diabetes or irritable bowel syndrome! I had been hearing this, as a message bouncing through the culture, for years, of course, but now it clicked into place. They meant me! And there is, I suddenly recalled in that moment, a solution to depression: antidepressants. So that's what I need! As soon as I get home, I will get these tablets, and I will be normal, and all the parts of me that are not depressed will be unshackled. I had always had drives that have nothing to do with depression—to meet people, to learn, to understand the world. They will be set free, I said, and soon.

The next day, we went to the Parc Güell, in the center of Barcelona. It's a park designed by the architect Antoni Gaudí to be profoundly strange—everything is out of perspective, as if you have stepped into a funhouse mirror. At one point you walk through a tunnel in which everything is at a rippling angle, as though it has been hit by a wave. At another point, dragons rise close to buildings made of ripped iron that almost appears to be in motion. Nothing looks like the world should. As I stumbled around it, I thought—this is what my head is like: misshapen, wrong. And soon it's going to be fixed.

Like all epiphanies, it seemed to come in a flash, but it had in fact been a long time coming. I knew what depression was. I had seen it play out in soap operas, and had read about it in books. I had heard my own mother talking about depression and anxiety, and seen her swallowing pills for it. And I knew about the cure, because it had been announced by the global media just a few years before. My teenage years coincided with the Age of Prozac—the dawn of new drugs that promised, for the first time, to be able to cure depression without crippling side effects. One of the best-selling books of the decade explained that these drugs actually make you "better than well"—they make you stronger and healthier than ordinary people.

I had soaked all this up, without ever really stopping to think about it. There was a lot of talk like that in the late 1990s; it was everywhere. And now I saw—at last—that it applied to me.

My doctor, it was clear on the afternoon when I went to see him, had absorbed all this, too. In his little office, he explained patiently to me why

I felt this way. There are some people who naturally have depleted levels of a chemical named serotonin in their brains, he said, and this is what causes depression—that weird, persistent, misfiring unhappiness that won't go away. Fortunately, just in time for my adulthood, there was a new generation of drugs—Selective Serotonin Reuptake Inhibitors (SSRIs)—that restore your serotonin to the level of a normal person's. Depression is a brain disease, he said, and this is the cure. He took out a picture of a brain and talked to me about it.

He was saying that depression was indeed all in my head—but in a very different way. It's not imaginary. It's very real, and it's a brain malfunction.

He didn't have to push. It was a story I was already sold on. I left within ten minutes with my script for Seroxat (or Paxil, as it's known in the United States).

It was only years later—in the course of writing this book—that somebody pointed out to me all the questions my doctor didn't ask that day. Like: Is there any reason you might feel so distressed? What's been happening in your life? Is there anything hurting you that we might want to change? Even if he had asked, I don't think I would have been able to answer him. I suspect I would have looked at him blankly. My life, I would have said, was good. Sure, I'd had some problems; but I had no reason to be unhappy—certainly not *this* unhappy.

In any case, he didn't ask, and I didn't wonder why. Over the next thirteen years, doctors kept writing me prescriptions for this drug, and none of them asked either. If they had, I suspect I would have been indignant, and said—If you have a broken brain that can't generate the right happiness-producing chemicals, what's the point of asking such questions? Isn't it cruel? You don't ask a dementia patient why they can't remember where they left their keys. What a stupid thing to ask me. Haven't you been to medical school?

The doctor had told me it would take two weeks for me to feel the effect of the drugs, but that night, after collecting my prescription, I felt a warm surge running through me—a light thrumming that I was sure consisted of my brain synapses groaning and creaking into the correct configuration. I lay on my bed listening to a worn-out mix tape, and I knew I wasn't going to be crying again for a long time.

I left for the university a few weeks later. With my new chemical armor, I wasn't afraid. There, I became an evangelist for antidepressants. Whenever a friend was sad, I would offer them some of my pills to try, and I'd tell them to get some from the doctor. I became convinced that I was not merely nondepressed, but in some better state—I thought of it as "antidepression." I was, I told myself, unusually resilient and energetic. I could feel some physical side effects from the drug, it was true—I was putting on a lot of weight, and I would find myself sweating unexpectedly. But that was a small price to pay to stop hemorrhaging sadness on the people around me. And—look!—I could do anything now.

Within a few months, I started to notice that there were moments of welling sadness that would come back to me unexpectedly. They seemed inexplicable, and manifestly irrational. I returned to my doctor, and we agreed that I needed a higher dose. So my 20 milligrams a day was upped to 30 milligrams a day; my white pills became blue pills.

And so it continued, all through my late teens, and all through my twenties. I would preach the benefits of these drugs; after a while, the sadness would return; so I would be given a higher dose; 30 milligrams became 40; 40 became 50; until finally I was taking two big blue pills a day, at 60 milligrams. Every time, I got fatter; every time, I sweated more; every time, I knew it was a price worth paying.

I explained to anyone who asked that depression is a disease of the brain, and SSRIs are the cure. When I became a journalist, I wrote articles in newspapers explaining this patiently to the public. I described the sadness returning to me as a medical process—clearly there was a running down of chemicals in my brain, beyond my control or comprehension. Thank God these drugs are remarkably powerful, I explained, and they work. Look at me. I'm the proof. Every now and then, I would hear a doubt in my head—but I would swiftly dismiss it by swallowing an extra pill or two that day.

I had my story. In fact, I realize now, it came in two parts. The first was about what causes depression: it's a malfunction in the brain, caused by serotonin deficiency or some other glitch in your mental hardware. The second was about what solves depression: drugs, which repair your brain chemistry.

I liked this story. It made sense to me. It guided me through life.

I only ever heard one other possible explanation for why I might feel this way. It didn't come from my doctor, but I read it in books and saw it discussed on TV. It said depression and anxiety were carried in your genes. I knew my mother had been depressed and highly anxious before I was born (and after), and that we had these problems in my family running further back than that. They seemed to me to be parallel stories. They both said—it's something innate, in your flesh.

I started work on this book three years ago because I was puzzled by some mysteries—weird things that I couldn't explain with the stories I had preached for so long, and that I wanted to find answers to.

Here's the first mystery. One day, years after I started taking these drugs, I was sitting in my therapist's office talking about how grateful I was that antidepressants exist and were making me better. "That's strange," he said. "Because to me, it seems you are still really quite depressed." I was perplexed. What could he possibly mean? "Well," he said, "you are emotionally distressed a lot of the time. And it doesn't sound very different, to me, from how you describe being before you took the drugs."

I explained to him, patiently, that he didn't understand: depression is caused by low levels of serotonin, and I was having my serotonin levels boosted. What sort of training do these therapists get, I wondered?

Every now and then, as the years passed, he would gently make this point again. He would point out that my belief that an increased dose of the drugs was solving my problem didn't seem to match the facts, since I remained down and depressed and anxious a lot of the time. I would recoil, with a mixture of anger and prissy superiority.

It was years before I finally heard what he was saying. By the time I was in my early thirties, I had a kind of negative epiphany—the opposite of the one I had that day on a beach in Barcelona so many years before. No matter how high a dose I jacked up my antidepressants to, the sadness would always outrun it. There would be a bubble of apparently chemical relief, and then that sense of prickling unhappiness would return. I would start once again to have strong recurring thoughts that said: life is pointless; everything you're doing is pointless; this whole thing is a fucking waste of time. It would be a thrum of unending anxiety.

So the first mystery I wanted to understand was: How could I still be depressed when I was taking antidepressants? I was doing everything right, and yet something was still wrong. Why?

~

A curious thing has happened to my family over the past few decades.

From when I was a little kid, I have memories of bottles of pills laid out on the kitchen table, waiting, with inscrutable white medical labels on them. I've written before about the drug addiction in my family, and how one of my earliest memories was of trying to wake up one of my relatives and not being able to. But when I was very young, it wasn't the banned drugs that were dominant in our lives—it was the ones handed out by doctors: old-style antidepressants and tranquilizers like Valium, the chemical tweaks and alterations that got us through the day.

That's not the curious thing that happened to us. The curious thing is that as I grew up, Western civilization caught up with my family. When I was small and I stayed with friends, I noticed that nobody in their families swallowed pills with their breakfast, lunch, or dinner. Nobody was sedated or amped up or antidepressed. My family was, I realized, unusual.

And then gradually, as the years passed, I noticed the pills appearing in more and more people's lives, prescribed, approved, recommended. Today they are all around us. Some one in five U.S. adults is taking at least one drug for a psychiatric problem; nearly one in four middle-aged women in the United States is taking antidepressants at any given time; around one in ten boys at American high schools is being given a powerful stimulant to make them focus; and addictions to legal and illegal drugs are now so widespread that the life expectancy of white men is declining for the first time in the entire peacetime history of the United States. These effects have radiated out across the Western world: for example, as you read this, one in three French people is taking a legal psychotropic drug such as an antidepressant, while the UK has almost the highest use in all of Europe. You can't escape it: when scientists test the water supply of Western countries, they always find it is laced with antidepressants, because so many of us are taking them and excreting them that they simply can't be filtered out of the water we drink every day. We are literally awash in these drugs.

What once seemed startling has become normal. Without talking about it much, we've accepted that a huge number of the people around us are so distressed that they feel they need to take a powerful chemical every day to keep themselves together.

So the second mystery that puzzled me was: Why were so many more people apparently feeling depressed and severely anxious? What changed?

~

Then, when I was thirty-one years old, I found myself chemically naked for the first time in my adult life. For almost a decade, I had been ignoring my therapist's gentle reminders that I was still depressed despite my drugs. It was only after a crisis in my life—when I felt unequivocally terrible and couldn't shake it off—that I decided to listen to him. What I had been trying for so long wasn't—it seemed—working. And so, when I flushed away my final packs of Paxil, I found these mysteries waiting for me, like children on a train platform, waiting to be collected, trying to catch my eye. Why was I still depressed? Why were there so many people like me?

And I realized there was a third mystery, hanging over all of it. Could something *other* than bad brain chemistry have been causing depression and anxiety in me, and in so many people all around me? If so—what could it be?

Still, I put off looking into it. Once you settle into a story about your pain, you are extremely reluctant to challenge it. It was like a leash I had put on my distress to keep it under some control. I feared that if I messed with the story I had lived with for so long, the pain would be like an unchained animal, and would savage me.

Over a period of several years, I fell into a pattern. I would begin to research these mysteries—by reading scientific papers, and talking to some of the scientists who wrote them—but I always backed away, because what they said made me feel disoriented, and more anxious than I had been at the start. I focused on the work for another book—*Chasing the Scream: The First and Last Days of the War on Drugs*—instead. It sounds ridiculous to say I found it easier to interview hit men for the Mexican drug cartels than to look into what causes depression and anxiety, but messing with my story about my emotions—what I felt, and why I felt it—seemed more dangerous, to me, than that.

And then, finally, I decided I couldn't ignore it any longer. So, over a period of three years, I went on a journey of over forty thousand miles. I conducted more than two hundred interviews across the world, with some of the most important social scientists in the world, with people who had been through the depths of depression and anxiety, and with people who had recovered. I ended up in all sorts of places I couldn't have guessed at in the beginning—an Amish village in Indiana, a Berlin housing project rising up in rebellion, a Brazilian city that had banned advertising, a Baltimore laboratory taking people back through their traumas in a totally unexpected way. What I learned forced me to radically revise my story—about myself, and about the distress spreading like tar over our culture.

~

I want to flag up, right at the start, two things that shape the language I am going to use all through the book. Both were surprising to me.

I was told by my doctor that I was suffering from both depression and acute anxiety. I had believed that those were separate problems, and that is how they were discussed for the thirteen years I received medical care for them. But I noticed something odd as I did my research. Everything that causes an increase in depression also causes an increase in anxiety, and the other way around. They rise and fall together.

It seemed curious, and I began to understand it only when, in Canada, I sat down with Robert Kohlenberg, a professor of psychology. He, too, once thought that depression and anxiety were different things. But as he studied it—for over twenty years now—he discovered, he says, that "the data are indicating they're not that distinct." In practice, "the diagnoses, particularly depression and anxiety, overlap." Sometimes one part is more pronounced than the other—you might have panic attacks this month and be crying a lot the next month. But the idea that they are separate in the way that (say) having pneumonia and having a broken leg are separate isn't borne out by the evidence. It's "messy," he has proved.

Robert's side of the argument has been prevailing in the scientific debate. In the past few years, the National Institutes of Health—the main body funding medical research in the United States—has stopped funding studies that present depression and anxiety as different diagnoses. "They want something more realistic that corresponds to the way people are in actual clinical practice," he explains.

I started to see depression and anxiety as like cover versions of the same song by different bands. Depression is a cover version by a downbeat emo band, and anxiety is a cover version by a screaming heavy metal group, but the underlying sheet music is the same. They're not identical, but they are twinned.

~

The second comes from something else I learned as I studied these nine causes of depression and anxiety. Whenever I wrote about depression and anxiety in the past, I started by explaining one thing: I am *not* talking about unhappiness. Unhappiness and depression are totally different things. There is nothing more infuriating to a depressed person than to be told to cheer up, or to be offered jolly little solutions as if they were merely having a bad week. It feels like being told to cheer yourself up by going out dancing after you've broken both your legs.

But as I studied the evidence, I noticed something that I couldn't ignore.

The forces that are making some of us depressed and severely anxious are, at the same time, making even more people unhappy. It turns out there *is* a continuum between unhappiness and depression. They're still very different—in the same way that losing a finger in a car accident is different from losing an arm, and falling over in the street is different from falling off a cliff. But they are connected. Depression and anxiety, I was going to learn, are only the sharpest edges of a spear that has been thrust into almost everyone in our culture. That's why even people who are not depressed or severely anxious will recognize a lot of what I'm about to describe.

~

As you read this book, please look up and read the scientific studies I'm referencing in the endnotes as I go, and try to look at them with the same skepticism that I brought to them. Kick the evidence. See if it breaks. The stakes are too high for us to get this wrong. Because I have come to believe something that would have shocked me at the start.

We have been systematically misinformed about what depression and anxiety are.

I had believed two stories about depression in my life. For the first eighteen years of my life, I had thought of it as "all in my head"—meaning it was not real, imaginary, fake, an indulgence, an embarrassment, a weakness. Then, for the next thirteen years, I believed it was "all in my head" in a very different way—it was due to a malfunctioning brain.

But I was going to learn that neither of these stories is true. The primary cause of all this rising depression and anxiety is not in our heads. It is, I discovered, largely in the world, and the way we are living in it. I learned there are at least nine proven causes of depression and anxiety (although nobody had brought them together like this before), and many of them are rising all around us—causing us to feel radically worse.

This wasn't an easy journey for me. As you will see, I clung to my old story about my depression being caused by my brain being broken. I fought for it. I refused for a long time to see the evidence they were presenting to me. This wasn't a warm slide into a different way of thinking. It was a fight.

But if we continue with the errors we have been making for so long, we will remain trapped in these states, and they will continue to grow. I know it might seem daunting to read about the causes of depression and anxiety at first, because they run very deep in our culture. It daunted me. But as I pressed on through the journey, I realized what was on the other side of it: the real solutions.

When I finally understood what was happening—to me, and to so many people like me—I learned there are real antidepressants waiting for us. They don't look like the chemical antidepressants that have worked so poorly for so many of us. They aren't something you buy, or swallow. But they might hold the beginning of a true path out of our pain.

PART I

The Crack in the Old Story

CHAPTER I

The Wand

Dr. John Haygarth was puzzled. All across the English city of Bath—and in several scattered pockets around the Western world—something extraordinary was happening. People who had been paralyzed with pain for years were clambering out of their sickbeds and walking once again. It didn't matter whether you had been crippled by rheumatism, or by hard physical work—the word was spreading that there was hope. You could rise. Nobody had ever seen anything like it.

John knew that a company founded by an American named Elisha Perkins, from Connecticut, had announced several years before that they had discovered the solution to all kinds of pain—and there was only one way to get it: you had to pay for the use of a thick metal rod they had patented, which the company named a "tractor." It had special qualities that the company explained they sadly couldn't tell you about, because then their competitors would copy them and take all their profit. But if you needed help, one of the people trained to use the tractor would come to you at home, or to your hospital bed, and explain somberly that, just like a lightning rod draws lightning, the tractor will draw the sickness out of your body and expel it into the air. They would then run the tractor over your body without its ever touching you.

You will feel a hot sensation, perhaps even a burning. Steadily, they said, the pain is being pulled away. Can't you feel it?

And once this procedure was over—it worked. Many people tortured by pain really did rise. Their agony really did recede. Lots of apparently hopeless cases were set free—at first.

What Dr. John Haygarth couldn't understand was how. Everything he had learned in his medical training suggested that the claim that pain was a disembodied energy that could just be expelled into the air was nonsense. But here were the patients, telling him it worked. Only a fool, it seemed, would doubt the power of the tractor now.

So John decided to conduct an experiment. At the Bath General Hospital, he took a plain long piece of wood and disguised it inside some old metal. He had created a fake "tractor"—one that had none of the secret qualities of the official one. He then went to the five patients in his hospital who had been disabled by chronic pain, including rheumatism, and explained that he had one of the now-famous Perkins wands, which might help them. And so, on the seventh of January 1799, with five distinguished doctors there as witnesses, he ran the wand over them. Out of the five, he wrote a little later, "four of the patients believed themselves immediately, and three remarkably, relieved by the false Tractors." A man whose knee had been unbearably painful, for example, started to walk freely—and showed it to the doctors with glee.

John wrote to a friend of his, a distinguished doctor in Bristol, to ask him to try the same experiment. The friend wrote back not long after, explaining to his amazement that his false tractor—also just a stick covered with metal—had produced the same remarkable effects. For example, a forty-three-year-old patient named Robert Thomas had such bad rheumatic pain in his shoulder that he hadn't been able to lift his hand from his knee for years—it was like it had been nailed there. But within four minutes of the wand being waved over him, he raised his hand several inches. They continued to treat him with the wand over the next few days, and before long he could touch the mantelpiece. Within eight days of treatment with the wand, he could touch a wooden board that was fully a foot above the mantelpiece.

It happened with patient after patient. So they wondered: Could there be some special property in a stick they hadn't known before? They tried to vary the experiment by wrapping an old bone in metal. It worked just the same. They tried wrapping an old tobacco pipe in metal. "With the same success," he noted drily. "To a more curious farce I never was witness; we were almost afraid to look each other in the face," another doctor who repeated the experiment wrote to him. And yet the patients looked at the doctors and said sincerely: "God bless you, sir."

Mysteriously, though, it was noted with some of the patients that the effect did not last. After the initial miracle, they became crippled again.

What could possibly be going on?

~

At the start of my research for this book, I spent a long time reading the scientific debate about antidepressants that has been playing out in medical journals for more than two decades now. I was surprised to discover that nobody seems to know quite what these drugs do to us, or why—including the scientists who most strongly support them. There is a huge argument among scientists, and no consensus. But one name kept appearing in this discussion more than any other, so far as I could see— and when I read about his findings, in his scientific papers and in his book *The Emperor's New Drugs*, I had two responses.

First, I scoffed; his claims seemed absurd, and contrary to my own direct experience in all sorts of ways. And then I became angry. He seemed to be kicking away the pillars on which I had built a story about my own depression. He was threatening what I knew about myself. His name was

Professor Irving Kirsch, and by the time I went to see him in Massachusetts, he was associate director of a leading program at Harvard Medical
School.

~

In the 1990s, Irving Kirsch sat in his book-lined office and told his
patients they should take antidepressants. He is a tall gray-haired man
with a soft voice, and I can imagine the sense of relief they felt. Sometimes, he noticed, the drugs worked, and sometimes they didn't, but he
had no doubt why the successes came: depression was caused by low serotonin levels, and these drugs boosted your serotonin levels. So he wrote
books in which he described the new antidepressants as a good, effective
treatment, which should be paired with therapy to also treat any psychological issues that are going on. Irving believed the huge body of scientific
research that had been published, and he could see the positive effects
with his own eyes when his patients walked back through the door feeling
better.

But Irving was also one of the leading experts in the world in a field of
science that began right back in Bath when John Haygarth first waved his
false wand. At that time, the English doctor had realized that when you
give a patient a medical treatment, you are really giving her two things.
You are giving her a drug, which will usually have a chemical effect on her
body in some way. And you are giving her a story—about how the treatment will affect her.

As amazing as it seems, Haygarth realized, the story you tell is often
just as important as the drug. How do we know this? Because if you offer
the patient nothing but a story—like, say, by telling them this old bone
wrapped in metal will cure your pain—it works an extraordinary amount
of the time.

This came to be known as the placebo effect, and in the two centuries
since, the scientific evidence for it has become enormous. Scientists like

Irving Kirsch have shown remarkable effects from placebos. They are not only able to change how we feel—they can actually have physical effects in our bodies. For example, a placebo can make an inflamed jaw go back to normal. A placebo can cure a stomach ulcer. A placebo can soothe—at least a little—most medical problems to some degree. If you expect it to work, for many of us it will work.

Scientists kept stumbling across this effect for years and being baffled by it. For example: as the Allied troops fended off the Nazis during World War II, there were so many terrible wounds among the men that the medical teams often ran out of opiate-based painkillers. An American anesthetist named Henry Beecher—posted on the front lines—was worried he would kill his soldiers by inducing heart failure if he tried to operate on them without anything to numb them. So, because he didn't know what else to do, he tried an experiment. He told the soldiers he was giving them morphine, when in fact he was giving them nothing but a saltwater drip with no painkiller in it at all. The patients reacted just as if they had been given morphine. They didn't scream, or howl, and they didn't go into full-blown shock. It worked.

By the mid-1990s, Irving understood this science better than almost anyone else alive, and he was about to become a leading figure in the program investigating it at Harvard. But he knew that the new antidepressant drugs worked *better* than a placebo—that they had a real chemical effect. He knew this for a simple reason. If you want to sell a drug to the public, you have to go through a rigorous process. Your drug has to be tested on two groups: one is given the real drug, and the other is given a sugar pill (or some other placebo). Then the scientists compare these groups. You are allowed to sell the drug to the public only if it does significantly better than the placebo.

So when one of his graduate students—a young Israeli named Guy Sapirstein—approached Irving with a proposal, he was intrigued, but not wildly excited. Guy explained that he was curious to investigate something. Whenever you take a drug, there's always *some* placebo effect, on top of the effects of the chemicals. But how much? With powerful drugs, it's always assumed to be a minor element. Guy thought the new antidepressants were an interesting place to try to figure this out—to see what small percentage of the effect is down to our belief in the drugs themselves. Irving and Guy both knew that if they started exploring this, they'd certainly find that most of the effect was chemical, but it would be intellectually interesting to look at the more minor placebo effect, too.

So they started with a pretty simple plan. There's an easy way to separate out how much of the effect of any drug you take is caused by the chemicals it contains and how much is caused by your belief in them. The investigators have to carry out one particular kind of scientific study. They split the people taking part into three groups. If you are in the first group, they tell you they are giving you a chemical antidepressant—but in fact, they simply give you a placebo: a sugar pill, as effective as John Haygarth's wand. If you are in the second group, you are told you were being given a chemical antidepressant—and you actually get one. And if you are in the third group, you aren't given anything—no drug, and no sugar pill; you are just followed over time.

The third group, Irving says, is really important—although almost all studies leave it out. "Imagine," he explains, "that you are investigating a new remedy for colds." You give people either a placebo or a drug. Over time, everyone gets better. The success rate seems amazing. But then you remember: lots of people with a cold recover within a few days anyway. If you don't factor that in, you'll get a really misleading impression about how well a cold remedy works—it would look like the drug was curing people who were just recovering naturally. You need the third group to test the rate that people will simply get better on their own, without any help.

So Irving and Guy started to compare the results for antidepressants from these three groups, in every study that had ever been published. To find out the chemical effects of the drug, you do two things. First, you subtract all the people who would have just gotten better anyway. Then you subtract all the people who got better when they were given a sugar pill. What's left is the real effect of the drug.

But when they added up the figures from all the publicly available scientific studies on antidepressants, what they found baffled them.

The numbers showed that 25 percent of the effects of antidepressants were due to natural recovery, 50 percent were due to the story you had been told about them, and only 25 percent to the actual chemicals. "That surprised the hell out of me," Irving told me in the front room of his home in Cambridge, Massachusetts. They assumed they had gotten their numbers wrong—that there was some mistake in their calculations. Guy was sure, he told me later, "there's got to be something wrong with this data," and so they kept going over it, again and again, for months. "I got so sick of looking at spreadsheets and data and analyzing it every which way possible," he said, but they knew there must be a mistake somewhere. They couldn't find any errors—so they published their data, to see what other scientists made of it.

As a result, one day, Irving received an e-mail—one that suggested he may have, in fact, only scratched the surface of a much more shocking scandal. This was, I think, the moment when Irving turned into the Sherlock Holmes of antidepressants.

～

In the e-mail, a scientist named Thomas J. Moore explained he had been struck by Irving's finding, and he believed there was a way to move this investigation forward—to get to the bottom of what was really going on.

Almost all the scientific studies Irving had looked at up to now, the e-mail explained, had a catch. The vast majority of research into whether drugs work or not is funded by big pharmaceutical companies, and they do this research for a specific reason: they want to be able to market those

drugs so they can make a profit out of them. That's why the drug companies conduct their scientific studies in secret, and afterward, they only
publish the results that make their drugs look good, or that make their
rivals' drugs look worse. They do this for exactly the same reasons that
(say) KFC would never release information telling you that fried chicken
isn't good for you.

This is called "publication bias." Of all the studies drug companies
carry out, 40 percent are never released to the public, and lots more are
only released selectively, with any negative findings left on the cutting
room floor.

So, this e-mail explained to Irving, you have, up to now, been looking
only at the parts of the scientific studies that the drug companies want us
to see. But Thomas Moore said there is a way beyond this. He explained to
Irving that there was actually a way he could get access to all the data the
drug companies don't want us to see. Here's how. If you want to release a
drug onto the U.S. market, you have to apply to the Food and Drug
Administration (FDA), the official drug regulator. As part of your appli-
cation, you have to submit all the trials you have conducted, in full—
whether they're good or bad for your profit margin. It's like when you take
selfies, and you snap yourself twenty times, only to discard the nineteen
in which you look double-chinned or bleary-eyed. You post to Facebook
or Instagram only the one where you look hot (or, in my case, least
hideous). But the drug companies have to—by law—send the FDA the
equivalent of all their selfies, even the ones that make them look fat.

If you apply through the Freedom of Information Act for it, the e-mail
said, you will be able to see everything. Then we can figure out what's
really going on.

Intrigued, Irving joined Thomas in requesting the information
submitted by the drug companies for the six most widely used antidepressants in the United States at that time—Prozac, Paxil (the drug I was
taking), Zoloft, Effexor, Duronin, and Celexa. Several months later, the

data was released to them, and Irving began to go over it with the scientific equivalent of Sherlock Holmes's magnifying glass.

He learned right away that the drug companies had—for years—been selectively publishing research, and to a greater degree than he expected. For example, in one trial for Prozac, the drug was given to 245 patients, but the drug company published the results for only twenty-seven of them. Those twenty-seven patients were the ones the drug seemed to work for.

Irving and Guy realized—using these, the real figures—they could calculate how much better the people on antidepressants were doing than the people on sugar pills. Scientists measure the depth of someone's depression using something named the Hamilton scale, which was invented by a scientist named Max Hamilton in 1959. The Hamilton scale ranges from 0 (where you're skipping along merrily) to 51 (where you're jumping in front of trains). To give you a yardstick: you can get a six-point leap in your Hamilton score if you improve your sleeping patterns.

What Irving found is that, in the real data that hadn't been run through a PR filter, antidepressants *do* cause an improvement in the Hamilton score—they do make depressed people feel better. It's an improvement of 1.8 points.

Irving furrowed his brow. That's a third less than getting better sleep. It was absolutely startling. If this was true, it suggested the drugs were having almost no meaningful effect at all, at least for the average patient—that like John Haygarth's patients back in Bath, the story made them feel better for a time, but then they would sink back as the real underlying problem reasserted itself.

Yet the data showed something else. The side effects of the drugs, by contrast, were very real. They make many people gain weight, or develop sexual dysfunction, or start to sweat a lot. These are real drugs, with a real effect. But when it came to the effects they are intended to have—on depression and anxiety? They are highly unlikely to solve the problem for most people.

Irving didn't want this to be true—it contradicted his own published work—but he told me, "One thing I do pride myself on is looking at the data, and allowing my mind to be changed when the data's different than I expected." He had promoted these drugs to patients when all he had to go on was the drug companies' handpicked studies. Now he had the unvarnished science, and he was starting to realize he couldn't continue as he had before.

∼

When Irving published these figures in a scientific journal, he expected a big fightback from the scientists who had produced all this data. But in fact, in the months that followed, he found there was—if anything—a feeling of shamefaced relief from many of them. One group of researchers wrote that it had been a "dirty little secret" in the field for a long time that the effects of these drugs on depression itself were in reality tiny. Irving thought, before he published, that he had a scoop, a previously unknown shocker. In fact, he had only discovered what many people in the field had privately known all along.

∼

One day, after these revelations had got a lot of press coverage, Guy—the grad student Dr. Watson—was at a family party when one of his relatives came up to him. She had been taking antidepressants for years. She burst into tears, and told him she felt that he was saying everything she had experienced on antidepressants—her most basic emotions—were false.

"I'm absolutely not," he said to her. "The fact that most of [the effect] is placebo just means that your brain is the most incredible, incredible part of your being—and your brain is doing a terrific job of making you feel better." It's not that the way you feel isn't real, he said. It's that it has a different cause than the one you have been told about.

She wasn't convinced. She didn't speak to him again for years.

~

A short while later, Irving was handed another leaked study. This one struck me especially hard when I read about it, because it was talking directly about a situation I had been in.

Not long before I started taking Seroxat (also marketed as Paxil), the drug's manufacturers, GlaxoSmithKline, had secretly conducted three clinical trials into whether Seroxat should be given to teenagers like me. One study discovered the placebo worked *better*; one study showed no difference between the drug and placebo; and one study showed mixed results. None showed a success. Yet, in a partial publication of the results, they announced: "Paroxetine [another name for the drug] is effective for major depression in adolescents."

The internal discussion within the company from this time was also later leaked. A company insider had warned: "It would be commercially unacceptable to include a statement that efficacy has not been demonstrated, as this would undermine the profile of Paroxetine." In other words—we can't say it doesn't work, because we'll make less money. So they didn't.

In the end, in court, they were forced to pay $2.5 million in New York State for the lie after New York attorney general Eliot Spitzer sued them. But I had been prescribed the drug as a teenager by then, and I had continued to take it for more than a decade. Later, one of the world's leading medical journals, the *Lancet*, conducted a detailed study of the fourteen major antidepressants that are given to teenagers. The evidence—from the unfiltered, real results—showed that they simply didn't work, with a single exception, where the effect was very small. The journal concluded they shouldn't be prescribed to teenagers any more.

Reading this was a turning point for me. Here was the drug I started taking as a teenager, and here was the company that manufactured it, saying, in their own words, that it didn't work for people like me—but they were going to carry on promoting it anyway.

As I read their words, I realized I couldn't continue to dismiss what Irving Kirsch was saying quite so easily. But this was only the first of his revelations. The most shocking was still to come.

CHAPTER 2

Imbalance

The year after I swallowed my first antidepressant, Tipper Gore—the wife of Vice President Al Gore—explained to the newspaper *USA Today* why she had recently become depressed. "It was definitely a clinical depression, one that I was going to have to have help to overcome," she said. "What I learned about is your brain needs a certain amount of serotonin and when you run out of that, it's like running out of gas." Tens of millions of people—including me—were being told the same thing.

When Irving Kirsch discovered that these serotonin-boosting drugs were not having the effects that everyone was being sold, he began—to his surprise—to ask an even more basic question. What's the evidence, he began to wonder, that depression is caused primarily by an imbalance of serotonin, or any other chemical, in the brain? Where did it come from?

∿

The serotonin story began, Irving learned, quite by accident in a tuberculosis ward in New York City in the clammy summer of 1952, when some patients began to dance uncontrollably down a hospital corridior. A new drug named Marsilid had come along that doctors thought might help TB patients. It turned out it didn't have much effect on TB—but the doctors noticed it did something else entirely. They could hardly miss it. It made the patients gleefully, joyfully euphoric—some began to dance frenetically.

So it wasn't long before somebody decided, perfectly logically, to try to give it to depressed people—and it seemed to have a similar effect on them, for a short time. Not long after that, other drugs came along that seemed to have similar effects (also for short periods)—ones named Ipronid and Imipramine. So what, people started to ask, could these new drugs have in common? And whatever it was—could it hold the key to unlocking depression?

Nobody really knew where to look, and so for a decade the question hung in the air, tantalizing researchers. And then in 1965, a British doctor called Alec Coppen came up with a theory. What if, he asked, all these drugs were increasing levels of serotonin in the brain? If that were true, it would suggest that depression might be caused by low levels of serotonin. "It's hard to overstate just how far out on a limb these scientists were climbing," Dr. Gary Greenberg, who has written the history of this period, explains. "They really had no idea what serotonin was doing in the brain." To be fair to the scientists who first put forward the idea, he says, they put it forward tentatively—as a suggestion. One of them said it was "at best a reductionist simplification," and said it couldn't be shown to be true "on the basis of data currently available."

But a few years later, in the 1970s, it was finally possible to start testing these theories. It was discovered that you can give people a chemical brew that lowers their serotonin levels. So if this theory was right—if low serotonin caused depression—what should happen? After taking this brew, people should become depressed. So they tried it. They gave people a drug to lower their serotonin levels and watched to see what would happen. And—unless they had already been taking powerful drugs—they didn't become depressed. In fact, in the vast majority of patients, it didn't affect their mood at all.

I went to see one of the first scientists to study these new antidepressants in Britain, Professor David Healy, in his clinic in Bangor, a town in the north of Wales. He has written the most detailed history of antidepressants we have. When it comes to the idea that depression is caused by low serotonin, he told me: "There was never any basis for it, ever. It was just marketing copy. At the time the drugs came out in the early 1990s, you couldn't have got any decent expert to go on a platform and say, 'Look, there's a lowering of serotonin in the brains of people who are depressed' . . . There wasn't ever any evidence for it." It hasn't been discredited, he said, because "it didn't ever get 'credited,' in a sense. There wasn't ever a point in time when 50 percent of the field actually believed it." In the biggest study of serotonin's effects on humans, it found no direct relationship with depression. Professor Andrew Skull of Princeton has said attributing depression to low serotonin is "deeply misleading and unscientific."

It had been useful in only one sense. When the drug companies wanted to sell antidepressants to people like me and Tipper Gore, it was a great metaphor. It's easy to grasp, and it gives you the impression that what antidepressants do is restore you to a natural state—the kind of balance that everyone else enjoys.

Irving learned that once serotonin was abandoned by scientists (but certainly not by drug company PR teams) as an explanation for depression and anxiety, there was a shift in scientific research. Okay, they said: if it's not low serotonin that's causing depression and anxiety, then it must be the lack of some other chemical. It was still taken for granted that these problems are caused by a chemical imbalance in the brain, and antidepressants work by correcting that chemical imbalance. If one chemical turns out not to be the psychological killer, they must start searching for another one.

But Irving began to ask an awkward question. If depression and anxiety are caused by a chemical imbalance, and antidepressants work by fixing that imbalance, then you have to account for something odd that he kept finding. Antidepressant drugs that increase serotonin in the brain have the same modest effect, in clinical trials, as drugs that *reduce* serotonin in the brain. And they have the same effect as drugs that increase *another* chemical, norepinephrine. And they have the same effect as drugs that increase *another* chemical, dopamine. In other words—no matter what chemical you tinker with, you get the same outcome.

So Irving asked: What do the people taking these different drugs actually have in common? Only, he found, one thing: the belief that the drugs work. It works, Irving believes, largely for the same reason that John Haygarth's wand worked: because you believe you are being looked after and offered a solution.

∽

After twenty years researching this at the highest level, Irving has come to believe that the notion depression is caused by a chemical imbalance is just "an accident of history," produced by scientists initially misreading what they were seeing, and then drug companies selling that misperception to the world to cash in.

And so, Irving says, the primary explanation for depression offered in our culture starts to fall apart. The idea you feel terrible because of a "chemical imbalance" was built on a series of mistakes and errors. It has come as close to being proved wrong, he told me, as you ever get in science. It's lying broken on the floor, like a neurochemical Humpty Dumpty with a very sad smile.

∽

I had traveled a long way with Irving on his journey—but I stopped there, startled. Could this really be true? I am trained in the social sciences, which is the kind of evidence that I'll be discussing in the rest of this book. I'm not trained in the kind of science he is a specialist in. I wondered if I was misunderstanding him, or if he was a scientific outlier. So I read all that I could, and I got as many other scientists to explain it to me as possible.

"There's no evidence that there's a chemical imbalance" in depressed or anxious people's brains, Professor Joanna Moncrieff—one of the leading experts on this question—explained to me bluntly in her office at the University College of London. The term doesn't really make any sense, she said: we don't know what a "chemically balanced" brain would look like. People are told that drugs like antidepressants restore a natural balance to your brain, she said, but it's not true—they create an artificial state. The whole idea of mental distress being caused simply by a chemical imbalance is "a myth," she has come to believe, sold to us by the drug companies.

The clinical psychologist Dr. Lucy Johnstone was more blunt still. "Almost everything you were told was bullshit," she said to me over coffee. The serotonin theory "is a lie. I don't think we should dress it up and say, 'Oh, well, maybe there's evidence to support that.' There isn't."

~

Yet it seemed wildly implausible to me that something so huge—one of the most popular drugs in the world, taken by so many people all around me—could be so wrong. Obviously, there are protections against this happening: huge hurdles of scientific testing that have to take place before a drug gets to our bathroom cabinets. I felt as if I had just landed in a flight from JFK to LAX, only to be told that the plane had been flown by a monkey the whole way. Surely there are procedures in place to stop something like this from happening? How could these drugs have gotten through the procedures in place, if they were really as limited as this deeper research suggested?

I discussed this with one of the leading scientists in this field, Professor John Ioannidis, who the *Atlantic Monthly* has said "may be one of the most influential scientists alive." He says it is not surprising that the drug companies could simply override the evidence and get the drugs to market anyway, because in fact it happens all the time. He talked me through how these antidepressants got from the development stage to my mouth. It works like this: "The companies are often running their own trials on their own products," he said. That means they set up the clinical trial, and they get to decide who gets to see any results. So "they are judging their own products. They're involving all these poor researchers who have no other source of funding . . . [and who] have little control over . . . how the [results] will be written up and presented." Once the scientific evidence is gathered, it's not even the scientists who write it up much of the time. "Typically, it's the company people who write up the [published scientific] reports."

This evidence then goes to the regulators, whose job is to decide whether to allow the drug onto the market. But in the United States, 40 percent of the regulators' wages are paid by the drug companies (while in Britain, it's 100 percent). When a society is trying to figure out which drug is safe to put on the market, there are meant to be two teams: the drug company making the case for it, and a referee working for us, the public, figuring out if it properly works. But Professor Ioannidis was telling me that in this match, the referee is paid by the drug company team, and that team almost always wins.

The rules they have written are designed to make it extraordinarily easy to get a drug approved. All you have to do is produce two trials—any time, anywhere in the world—that suggest *some* positive effect of the drug. If there are two, and there is some effect, that's enough. So you could have a situation in which there are one thousand scientific trials, and 998 find the drug doesn't work at all, and two find there is a tiny effect—and that means the drug will be making its way to your local pharmacy.

"I think that this is a field that is seriously sick," Professor Ioannidis told me. "The field is just sick and bought and corrupted, and I can't describe it otherwise." I asked him how it made him feel to have learned all of this. "It's depressing," he said. That's ironic, I replied. "But it's not depressing," he responded, "to the severe extent that I would take SSRIs [antidepressants]."

I tried to laugh, but it caught in my throat.

~

Some people said to Irving—so what? Okay, so say it's a placebo effect. Whatever the reason, people still feel better. Why break the spell? He explained: the evidence from the clinical trials suggests that the antidepressant effects are a largely a placebo, but the side effects are mostly the result of the chemicals themselves, and they can be very severe.

"Of course," Irving says, there's "weight gain." I massively ballooned, and saw the weight fall off almost as soon as I stopped. "We know that SSRIs [the new type of antidepressants] in particular contribute to sexual dysfunction, and the rates for most SSRIs are around 75 percent of treatment-engendered sexual dysfunction," he continued. Though it's painful to talk about, this rang true for me, too. In the years I was taking Paxil, I found my genitals were a lot less sensitive, and it took a really long time to ejaculate. This made sex painful and it reduced the pleasure I took from it. It was only when I stopped taking the drug and I started having more pleasurable sex again that I remembered regular sex is one of the best natural antidepressants in the world.

"In young people, [these chemical antidepressants] increase the risk of suicide. There's a new Swedish study showing that it increases the risk of violent criminal behavior," Irving continued. "In older people it increases the risk of death from all causes, increases the risk of stroke. In everybody, it increases the risk of type 2 diabetes. In pregnant women, it increases the risk of miscarriage [and] of having children born with autism or physical deformities. So all of these things are known." And if you start experiencing these effects, it can be hard to stop—about 20 percent of people experience serious withdrawal symptoms.

So, he says, "if you want to use something to get its placebo effect, at least use something that's safe." We could be giving people the herb St. John's Wort, Irving says, and we'd have all the positive placebo effects and none of these drawbacks. Although—of course—St. John's Wort isn't patented by the drug companies, so nobody would be making much profit off it.

By this time, Irving was starting, he told me softly, to feel "guilty" for having pushed those pills for all those years.

~

In 1802, John Haygarth revealed the true story of the wands to the public. Some people are really recovering from their pain for a time, he explained, but it's not because of the power in the wands. It's because of the power in their minds. It was a placebo effect, and it likely wouldn't last, because it wasn't solving the underlying problem.

This message angered almost everyone. Some felt duped by the people who had sold the expensive wands in the first place—but many more felt furious with Haygarth himself, and said he was clearly talking rubbish. "The intelligence excited great commotions, accompanied by threats and abuse," he wrote. "A counter-declaration was to be signed by a great number of very respectable persons"—including some leading scientists of the day—explaining that the wand worked, and its powers were physical, and real.

Since Irving published his early results, and as he has built on them over the years, the reaction has been similar. Nobody denies that the drug companies' own data, submitted to the FDA, shows that antidepressants have only a really small effect over and above placebo. Nobody denies that my own drug company admitted privately that the drug I was given, Paxil, was not going to work for people like me, and they had to make a payout in court for their deception.

But some scientists—a considerable number—do dispute many of Kirsch's wider arguments. I wanted to study carefully what they say. I hoped the old story could still—somehow—be saved. I turned to a man who—more than anyone else alive—successfully sold antidepressants to the wider public, and he did it because he believed it: he never took a cent from the drug companies.

~

In the 1990s, Dr. Peter Kramer was watching as patient after patient walked into his therapy office in Rhode Island, transformed before his eyes after they were given the new antidepressant drugs. It's not just that they seemed to have improved; they became, he argued, "better than well"—they had *more* resilience and energy than the average person. The book he wrote about this, *Listening to Prozac*, became the bestselling book ever about antidepressants. I read it soon after I started taking the drugs. I was sure the process Peter described so compellingly was happening to me. I wrote about it, and I made his case to the public in articles and interviews.

So when Irving started to present his evidence, Peter—by then a professor at Brown Medical School—was horrified. He started taking apart Irving's critique of antidepressants, at length, in public—both in books and in a series of charged public debates.

His first argument is that Irving is not giving antidepressants enough time. The clinical trials he has analyzed—almost all the ones submitted to the regulator—typically last for four to eight weeks. But that isn't enough. It takes longer for these drugs to have a real effect.

This seemed to me to be an important objection. Irving thought so, too. So he looked to see if there were any drug trials that had lasted longer, to find their results. It turns out there were two—and in the first, the placebo did the same as the drug, and in the second, the placebo did *better*.

Peter then pointed to another mistake he believed Irving had made. The antidepressant trials that Irving is looking at lump together two groups: moderately depressed people and severely depressed people. Maybe these drugs don't work much for moderately depressed people, Peter concedes—but they do work for severely depressed people. He's seen it. So when Irving adds up an average for everyone, lumping together the mildly depressed and the severely depressed, the effect of the drugs looks small—but that's only because he's diluting the real effect, as surely as Coke will lose its flavor if you mix it with pints and pints of water.

Again, Irving thought this was a potentially important point, and one he was keen to understand, so he went back over the studies he had drawn his data from. He discovered that, with a single exception, he had looked *only* at studies of people classed as having very severe depression.

This then led Peter to turn to his most powerful argument. It's the heart of his case against Irving and for antidepressants.

~

In 2012, Peter went to watch some clinical trials being conducted, in a medical center that looked like a beautiful glass cube, and gazed out over expensive houses. When the company there wants to conduct trials into antidepressants, they have two headaches. They have to recruit volunteers who will swallow potentially dangerous pills over a sustained period of time, but they are restricted by law to paying only small amounts: between $40 and $75. At the same time, they have to find people who have very specific mental health disorders—for example, if you are doing a trial for depression, they have to have *only* depression and no other complicating factors. Given all that, it's pretty difficult for them to find anyone who will take part, so they often turn to quite desperate people, and they have to offer other things to tempt them. Peter watched as poor people were bused in from across the city to be offered a gorgeous buffet of care they'd never normally receive at home—therapy, a whole community of people who'd listen to them, a warm place to be during the day, medication, and money that could double their poverty-level income.

As he watched this, he was struck by something. The people who turn up at this center have a strong incentive to pretend to have any condition they happen to be studying there—and the for-profit companies conducting the clinical trials have a strong incentive to pretend to believe them. Peter looked on as both sides seemed to be effectively bullshitting each other. When he saw people being asked to rate how well the drugs had worked, he thought they were often clearly just giving the interviewer whatever answer they wanted.

So Peter concluded that the results from clinical trials of antidepressants—all the data we have—are meaningless. That means Irving is building his conclusion that their effect is very small (at best) on a heap of garbage, Peter declared. The trials themselves are fraudulent.

~

It's a devastating point, and Peter has proved it quite powerfully. But it puzzled Irving when he heard it, and it puzzled me. The leading scientific defender of antidepressants, Peter Kramer, is making the case for them by saying that the scientific evidence for them is junk.

When I spoke to Peter, I told him that if he is right (and I think he is), then that's not a case *for* the drugs. It's a case *against* them. It means that— by law—they should never have been brought to market.

When I started to ask about this—in a friendly tone—Peter became quite irritable, and said even bad trials can yield usable results. He soon changed the subject. Given that he puts so much weight on what he's seen with his own eyes, I asked Peter what he would say to the people who claimed that John Haygarth's wand worked—because they, too, were just believing what they saw with their own eyes. He said that in cases like that, "the collection of experts isn't as expert or as numerous as what we're talking about here. I mean—this would be [an] orders-of-magnitude bigger scandal if these were [like] just bones wrapped in cloth."

Shortly after, he said: "I think I want to cut off this conversation."

~

Even Peter Kramer had one note of caution to offer about these drugs. He stressed to me that the evidence he has seen only makes the case for prescribing antidepressants for six to twenty weeks. Beyond that, he said, "I think that the evidence is thinner, and my dedication to the arguments is less as you get to long-term use. I mean—does anyone really know about what fourteen years of use does in terms of harm and benefit? I think the answer is we don't really know." I felt anxious as he said that—I had already told him that I used the drugs for almost that long.

Perhaps because he sensed my anxiety, he added: "Although I do think we've been reasonably lucky. People like you come off and function."

~

Very few scientists now defend the idea that depression is simply caused by low levels of serotonin, but the debate about whether chemical antidepressants work—for some other reason we don't fully understand—is still ongoing. There is no scientific consensus. Many distinguished scientists agree with Irving Kirsch; many agree with Peter Kramer. I wasn't sure what to take away from all of this, until Irving led me to one last piece of evidence. I think it tells us the most important fact we need to know about chemical antidepressants.

~

In the late 1990s, a group of scientists wanted to test the effects of the new SSRI antidepressants in a situation that wasn't just a lab, or a clinical trial. They wanted to look at what happens in a more everyday situation, so they set up something called the Star-D Trial. It was pretty simple. A normal patient goes to the doctor and explains he's depressed. The doctor talks through the options with him, and if they both agree, he starts taking an antidepressant. At this point, the scientists conducting the trial start to monitor the patient. If the antidepressant doesn't work for him, he's given another one. If that one doesn't work, he's given another one—and on and on until he gets one that feels as though it works. This is how it works for most of us out there in the real world: a majority of people who get prescribed antidepressants try more than one, or try more than one dosage, until they find the effect they're looking for.

And what the trial found is that the drugs worked. Some 67 percent of patients did feel better, just like I did in those first months.

But then they found something else. Within a year, half of the patients were fully depressed again. Only one in three of the people who stayed on the pills had a lasting, proper recovery from their depression. (And even that exaggerates the effect—since we know many of those people would have recovered naturally without the pills.)

It seemed like my story, played out line by line. I felt better at first; the effect wore off; I tried increasing the dose, and then that wore off, too. When I realized that antidepressants weren't working for me any more, that no matter how much I jacked up the dose, the sadness would still seep back through, I assumed there was something wrong with me.

Now I was reading the Star-D Trial's results, and I realized—I was normal. My experience was straight from the textbook: far from being an outlier, I had the typical antidepressant experience.

This evidence has been followed up several times since—and the proportion of people on antidepressants who continue to be depressed is found to be between 65 and 80 percent.

To me, this seems like the most crucial piece of evidence about anti-depressants of all: most people on these drugs, after an initial kick, remain depressed or anxious. I want to stress—some reputable scientists still believe that these drugs genuinely work for a minority of people who take them, due to a real chemical effect. It's possible. Chemical antidepressants may well be a partial solution for a minority of depressed and anxious people—I certainly don't want to take away anything that's giving relief to anyone. If you feel helped by them, and the positives outweigh the side effects, you should carry on. (And if you are going to stop taking them, then it's essential that you don't do it overnight, because you can experience severe physical withdrawal symptoms and a great deal of panic as a result. I gradually reduced my dose very slowly, over six months, in consultation with my doctor, to prevent this from happening.) But it is impossible, in the face of this evidence, to say they are *enough*, for *a big majority* of depressed and anxious people. I couldn't deny it any longer: for the vast majority we clearly needed to find a different story about what is making us feel this way, and a different set of solutions.

But what—I asked myself, bewildered—could they be?

CHAPTER 3

The Grief Exception

Ironically, learning that depression and anxiety are not caused by a chemical imbalance made me feel unbalanced. Somebody once told me that giving a person a story about why they are in pain is one of the most powerful things you can ever do. Taking away the story for your pain is just as powerful: I felt like I was on a rocky ship and somebody had taken away the railings.

I began searching for another story. It was only some time later, when I first spoke with a woman in Arizona named Joanne Cacciatore, that I began to see the first thread of a different way of thinking about this problem—one that would transform the journey I was about to take.

～

"Oh honey," Joanne's doctor said to her, "you just need some attention." She had been having extremely painful contractions for three weeks, and she thought she needed help. She was very diligent during her pregnancy—she wouldn't even chew gum with aspartame in it because she was worried it might harm her baby. So she kept insisting: "These are really painful contractions—they don't feel normal to me." But the doctor insisted right back to her: "It's normal."

When she finally did go in to the hospital to give birth, "I'd had three other children, so I knew what the labor room was supposed to sound like," she says, and so she sensed quite quickly that there was something wrong. There was chaos all around her, and the medical team was visibly panicked. She would have a contraction that lasted for a minute, then thirty seconds later, she'd have another contraction.

As she pushed as hard as she physically could, they told her that they had lost the baby's heartbeat. She tried to push even more violently and she felt like she was leaving her body, and looking down on herself. "I remember . . . looking at myself. My legs were shaking. Just shaking. I couldn't stop quivering. I had my eyes closed tightly when she was born because . . . I was going to get her out as quickly as I could."

As soon as the baby emerged, the doctors made a decision—without asking Joanne—not to try to revive her. They handed her to Joanne's then-husband, and he said gently to her: "We have a beautiful little girl."

At that moment, "I just sat up," Joanne told me years later. "I became a mother to her in that moment. And I reached my hands out—I said, 'give her to me.' She was perfect. She was eight pounds. She had rolls of fat under her cheeks. Her little wrists had little rolls of fat. And he put her in my arms. She just looked asleep. It was a strange juxtaposition of birth and death that coalesced in a single moment—[and] that would change the course of my life.

"Now I will tell you," she said to me, "I've had a lot of loss in my life. Before I even turned forty, I'd lost both my parents. I lost my best friend." But "I never expected to lose my daughter. That's something I just couldn't have prepared myself for. It's just unfathomable." Three months after her daughter died, Joanne weighed eighty-eight pounds. "I wasn't sure I was going to make it," she said. "It felt like I was dying. Every day, I would open my eyes—if I slept—and say: I don't want to be here. I don't want to be here. I don't want to feel like this any more. I can't do this anymore."

The autopsy was inconclusive. "She didn't have any congenital problems. My best guess is that . . . I think my body was trying to go into labor but I wasn't dilating. The only thing I could think of is that my body killed her—just literally suffocated her to death. So I had a pretty acrimonious relationship with my body for a long time, as you can imagine . . . The only person I had to blame was me. My body. I was supposed to do one thing—give birth to this healthy baby—and she was healthy, so it wasn't her problem. It was my problem. Something in my body failed. I used to call my body Judas, because I felt like it betrayed her, and thus me."

~

Over the years that followed, Joanne trained as a clinical psychologist, and eventually became a professor of social work at Arizona State University. Her specialty was traumatic bereavement—people who have lost loved ones in the worst possible circumstances.

As she treated many people who had gone through experiences like hers, she noticed something peculiar. Very soon after they went through the death of a loved one, lots of her patients were being diagnosed by psychiatrists with clinical depression, and being given very powerful psychiatric drugs. This was becoming routine. So if (say) your child was murdered, you were told you were clinically unwell and needed to have your brain chemistry fixed. For example, one of her patients, whose child had died recently, told her doctor that she sometimes felt her child was speaking to her. It didn't distress her; she felt mildly comforted by it. Yet the patient was immediately diagnosed with psychosis, and given antipsychotic drugs.

Joanne noticed that when her patients were given these diagnoses, they would "start questioning their own feelings, and doubting themselves—and that causes them to hide more."

After seeing this happen more times than she could count, she began to investigate how depression is diagnosed, and to publish scientific papers on one aspect of it in particular. The way doctors are supposed to identify depression is laid out, in the United States, in the *Diagnostic and Statistical Manual* (*DSM*), which has appeared in five different editions now and is written by panels of psychiatrists. This is the Bible used by almost all U.S. general practitioners when they diagnose depression or anxiety, and it's hugely influential across the world. To get a diagnosis of depression, you have to show at least five out of nine symptoms nearly every day: for example, depressed mood, decreased interest in pleasure, or feelings of worthlessness.

But as doctors first started to apply this checklist, they discovered something awkward. Almost everybody who is grieving, it turns out, matches the clinical criteria for depression. If you simply use the checklist, virtually anyone who has lost someone should be diagnosed as having a clear mental illness.

This made many doctors and psychiatrists feel uncomfortable. So the authors of the *DSM* invented a loophole, which became known as "the grief exception."

They said that you are allowed to show the symptoms of depression and *not* be considered mentally ill in one circumstance and one circumstance only—if you have recently suffered the loss of somebody close to you. After you lose (say) a baby, or a sister, or a mother, you can show these symptoms for a year before you are classed as mentally ill. But if you continued to be profoundly distressed after this deadline, you will still be classified as having a mental disorder. As the years passed and different versions of the *DSM* were published, the time limit changed: it was slashed to three months, one month, and eventually just two weeks.

"To me, it's the greatest insult," Joanne told me. "It's not just an insult to grief and to the relationship [with the person who has died], but it's an insult to love. I mean—why do we grieve? [If] my neighbor [across the street] died, and I don't know my neighbor, I might say, 'Oh, that's sad for his family,' but I don't grieve. But when I love the person, I grieve. We grieve because we have loved." To say that if grief lasts beyond an artificial time limit, then it is a pathology, a disease to be treated with drugs, is—she believes—to deny the core of being human.

Joanne had a patient whose daughter was abducted from the park during her first semester at college and burned alive. How can we tell that mother that she has a mental health problem, she asked me, because she is still in agony about it many years later? Yet that is what the *DSM* says.

Far from being irrational, Joanne says, the pain of grief is necessary. "I don't even want to recover from her death," she says about her daughter Chayenne. "Staying connected to the pain of her death helps me to do my work with such a full, compassionate heart," and to live as fully as she can. "I integrated that guilt and shame that I felt, and the betrayal, by serving others," she said to me, with some of the horses she has rescued running in a field behind her. "So in a way my service to others is how I remunerate—it's my way of saying sorry to her every day. I'm sorry I did not bring you safely into the world, and because of that I'm going to bring your love into the world."

It made her understand the pain of others in a way she couldn't before. It "makes me stronger," she says, "even in my vulnerable places."

~

The grief exception revealed something that the authors of the *DSM*—the distillation of mainstream psychiatric thinking—were deeply uncomfortable with. They had been forced to admit, in their own official manual, that it's reasonable—and perhaps even necessary—to show the symptoms of depression, in one set of circumstances.

But once you've conceded that, it invites an obvious follow-up question. Why is a death the only event that can happen in life where depression is a reasonable response? Why not if your husband has left you after thirty years of marriage? Why not if you are trapped for the next thirty years in a meaningless job you hate? Why not if you have ended up homeless and you are living under a bridge? If it's reasonable in one set of circumstances, could there also be other circumstances where it is also reasonable?

But this blasts a hole in the rudder of the boat the psychiatrists writing the *DSM* have been sailing in for so long. Suddenly, life—with all its complexity—starts to flood into diagnosing depression and anxiety. It can't just be a matter of chemical imbalance, as verified by checklists of symptoms. It would have to be seen as a response to your circumstances.

As Joanne Cacciatore researched the grief exception in more detail, she came to believe it revealed a basic mistake our culture is making about pain, way beyond grief. We don't, she told me, "consider context." We act like human distress can be assessed solely on a checklist that can be separated out from our lives, and labeled as brain diseases.

As she said this, I told her that in thirteen years of being handed ever higher doses of antidepressants, no doctor ever asked me if there was any reason why I might be feeling so distressed. She told me I'm not unusual—and it's a disaster. The message my doctors gave me—that our pain is simply a result of a malfunctioning brain—makes us, she told me, "disconnected from ourselves, which leads to disconnection from others."

If we started to take people's actual lives into account when we treat depression and anxiety, Joanne said, it would require "an entire system overhaul." There are many good and decent psychiatrists who want to think in this deeper way, she stressed, and can see the limits of what we are doing right now. Instead of saying our pain is an irrational spasm to be taken away with drugs, they see that we should start to listen to it and figure out what it is telling us.

In most cases, Joanne says, we would have to stop talking about "mental health"—which conjures pictures of brain scans and defective synapses—and start talking about "emotional health." "Why do we call it mental health?" she asked me. "Because we want to scientize it. We want to make it sound scientific. But it's our emotions."

She approaches her patients, she says, not with a checklist, but by saying: "Tell me your story. Oh my gosh—how hard. I'd probably feel the same way if I was in your situation. I'd probably have the same 'set of symptoms.' . . . Let's look at context." Sometimes, all you can do for a person is hold them. The mother whose daughter was burned alive came to see Jo one day howling and screaming with pain. Jo sat on the floor, and held her, and let the pain come out, and after it did, the mother felt some relief, for a time, because she knew she was not alone. Sometimes, that is the most we can do. It's a lot.

And sometimes, when you listen to the pain and you see it in its context, it will point you to a way beyond it—as I learned later.

Our approach today is, Joanne said, "like putting a Band-Aid on an amputated limb. [When] you have a person with extreme human distress, [we need to] stop treating the symptoms. The symptoms are a messenger of a deeper problem. Let's get to the deeper problem."

~

For decades, then, there was a tension at the heart of the psychiatric bible. The public was being told two clashing things. First, that the symptoms of depression are straightforwardly the result of a chemical imbalance in the brain that has to be fixed with drugs. Second, that somehow, and at the same time, there was one unique situation where all the symptoms of depression were, in fact, a response to something terrible happening in your life, and in that one unique case, a chemical imbalance is not the cause, and drugs are not the solution.

This tension unsettled lots of people. It begged too many questions. People like Joanne could use it to force debates onto the table that many people didn't want to have.

So the psychiatrists who wrote the fifth and most recent edition of the *DSM*, which was published in 2015, came up with a solution. They got rid of the grief exception. In the new version, it's not there. There's just the checklist of symptoms, followed by a vague footnote. So now if your baby dies and you go to the doctor the next day and you're in extreme distress, "you can be diagnosed immediately," Joanne explained to me.

And so the model is preserved. Depression is something you can find on a checklist. If you tick the boxes, you're mentally ill. Don't look for context. Look for symptoms. Don't ask what is happening in the person's life.

~

Thinking like this, Joanne told me, makes her believe that "we're such an utterly disconnected culture, we just don't get human suffering." She looked at me, and I thought of everything she has gone through, and the wisdom it has given her. She blinked, and said: "We just don't get it."

~

A long time after I spoke with Joanne—and after I had carried out much more research—I listened again to the audio of my interview with her. I was beginning to think there was something significant about the fact that grief and depression have identical symptoms. Then one day, after interviewing several depressed people, I asked myself: What if depression is, in fact, a form of grief—for our own lives not being as they should? What if it is a form of grief for the connections we have lost, yet still need?

But to understand how I came to ask that question, we need to step back—to a moment when there was a key breakthrough in the scientific understanding of depression and anxiety.

CHAPTER 4

The First Flag on the Moon

In the days after the Second World War, a young woman in her early twenties—fresh from giving birth—walked through the ruins of Kensal Rise. It was a crowded working-class suburb of West London, and parts of it had been reduced by the Nazis to rubble. She was finding her way to the Grand Canal. Once she got there, she threw herself into its dust-choked waters.

In the months and years that followed her suicide, nobody talked about her depression. There was silence. It was taboo to ask why people become desperately distressed in this way.

In a house not far away, there was a teenage boy named George Brown. The woman who died had been a close neighbor, and when he developed a rumbling infection, in a world without antibiotics, she had looked after him for months, in these poor, cramped houses. "She was a very warm person," he told me, seventy-one years later, smiling at her memory. "So this is one of my earliest experiences. There were very strong feelings associated at that time—shame—with depression." He repeated this later: "There was a great deal of shame associated with it."

"It was hushed up, really," he added.

This puzzled him, although he didn't think about it deeply again until he was thirty-six years old, and about to make a remarkable discovery.

~

In the early 1970s, George returned to a working-class London neighborhood, very like the one he had grown up in, to investigate a mystery. Why did so many people like his neighbor sink into deep depression? What causes it?

At the time, there was still a silence hanging not only over this individual victim, but over the whole society. When depression was discussed by professionals, far from the public gaze, there was a split between two contrasting ways of thinking about it. You can picture it crudely as a division between, on one side, a patient lying on a sofa in front of the founder of psychoanalysis, Sigmund Freud, and on the other side, a dissected brain. The Freudians had been arguing for almost a century that the explanation for this kind of distress could only be found in the depressed person's personal life—and particularly in their early childhood. The only way to deal with it was to explore it through one-on-one therapy, through which you would piece together the story of what had happened, and find a better story for the patient to tell about her life.

As a backlash against this way of thinking, many psychiatrists had started to argue in contrast that depression was just something going wrong with a person's brain or body—an internal malfunction—and so searching for deeper reasons in her life story in this way was missing the point. It was clearly a physical problem, with a physical cause.

George had always suspected that there was some truth in both these perspectives but that neither told the whole story. There seemed, he thought, to be more to this question—but what? He had been trained not as a doctor or psychiatrist but as an anthropologist—a profession in which you observe a culture as an outsider and try to figure out how it works. This meant, he told me, that he arrived at the psychiatric treatment center he was going to work out of in South London "completely igno-rant" of what you are supposed to think about something like depression, and he now believes "that was a great advantage. I had no preconceived ideas [so] I was forced to have an open mind."

He started to read over the science that had been carried out up to that point—and it struck him that very little data had been gathered. "It seemed to me," he remembers, "there was a lot of ignorance." The theories were being formulated largely in the dark—they were based either on personal anecdotes or on abstract theories. "The studies [that had already been done] seemed to be fairly inadequate," he said.

By then, the official medical position on depression was to cut the baby in half between these two warring factions. The mainstream scientific community had declared there were two kinds of depression. The first kind was caused by your brain or body starting to spontaneously malfunction: they named this "endogenous depression." But there are also, they said, some forms of depression caused by something bad happening in your personal life, which they named "reactive depression." Yet nobody knew what people with "reactive" depression were meant to be reacting to, or where the line between these two different kinds of depression was—or even if it was a distinction that made any sense.

To find the real story, George concluded, you had to do something that nobody had ever done before on a significant scale. You had to conduct a proper scientific investigation into depressed or highly anxious people, using techniques a little like those you'd use to (say) figure out why cholera spreads, or how pneumonia is contracted. So he began to draw up plans.

~

In the South London district of Camberwell, as George walked through its streets, the thrum of the city seemed a world away. It was only two miles from central London, but the only thing that could convince you of that was the spire of St. Paul's Cathedral in the distance. He would stroll past some beautiful, large Victorian houses, and then through old slum streets that were being abandoned one by one as they were demolished by the government. The working-class row houses he had known as a kid were being cleared out and knocked down to make way for the big concrete high-rise blocks that were starting to pierce the London skyline. As he arrived at one woman's home, she told him she had to have fire engines come to her house three times that week because as the streets were being evacuated, kids were setting fire to the rubble.

Through the local psychiatric services, George had arranged to carry out an unprecedented research project. The plan was that, for many years, he and his team would follow and get to know two different groups of women. The first group consisted of women who had been diagnosed with depression by their psychiatrists. There were 114 of them, and the team's job was to interview them in depth, at home, and gather some key facts about them. In particular, they wanted to look at what happened to them in the year *before* they had become depressed. That period was crucial, for reasons you'll see in a moment.

At the same time, they randomly selected a second group—344 "normal" women from Camberwell, in the same income group, who had *not* been classed as depressed. They repeatedly interviewed them in depth at their homes, too, to see what good and bad things were happening in their lives over a typical year.

The key to figuring out what causes depression, George suspected, would lie in comparing these two groups.

Imagine if you investigated something genuinely random, like being hit by a meteor. If you studied what happened to the people who got hit by meteors in the year leading up to their accident, and compared them to a typical year in the life of people who didn't get hit by meteors, you'd find they were just the same. It has nothing to do with any wider factors in their lives: they are just victims of a rock falling from space. Lots of people thought then—and think now—that depression and anxiety are like that: that it's just a random piece of chemical bad luck, happening inside your skull rather than in your life. This research could prove if they were right. If they were, then George would find no difference between the depressed women's lives and the nondepressed women's lives in that key year leading up to the onset of depression.

But what if there were a difference? If you could find out what the difference was, George knew that would reveal something really important. It could give us clues about what causes depression. Was it only that the early childhoods or personal lives of the depressed women had gone wrong, as the Freudians said? Or was something else going on? If so—what was it?

So George—and his team, including a young researcher and therapist named Tirril Harris—went to all these women's houses and sat with them and got to know them. They interviewed them in great detail. Then when they left, they graded these women's lives very carefully, using complex data-gathering and statistical methods that they had agreed on at the start of the study. They were building up a database of an enormous range of factors—anything they suspected might even conceivably play a role in depression.

One day, Tirril went to see a woman living on the ground floor of a typical two-bedroom house in the neighborhood, named Mrs. Trent. She was married to a van driver, and they lived in this small house with their three kids, who were all under seven. By the time Tirril met her, she said she couldn't concentrate at all—not even long enough to read an article in the morning paper. She was losing her interest in eating, or having sex. Most of the day, she wept. She felt like her body was physically locking up with tension, but she didn't know why. For six weeks, she had just been going to bed during the day, and staying there, inert, hoping the world would go away.

As they got to know Mrs. Trent, they discovered that something had happened, not long before she became depressed. Just after their third kid was born, Mr. Trent had lost his job. His wife wasn't too worried, and he got another job a few weeks later—but then he was abruptly fired, for no apparent reason. She became convinced that his reference from his old boss had come through, and it was bad. He couldn't find another job. Since it was taboo in Camberwell at that time for mothers to work, that meant the family was chronically insecure—how were they going to live? The marriage was "finished," she told George and Tirril, but what could she do? She kept packing her bags and leaving, but she never got beyond the end of the street. Where could she go?

"What I recall was how moving the interviews could be," George told me when I went to see him. "These women on the whole weren't used to talking about themselves. Here was someone who showed interest in them, and someone who had allowed them to talk." He could see "it meant something to the women, on the whole. Also—the stories they told made sense . . . They knew they were suffering, and in trouble."

Many of the women they met were like Mrs. Trent, and neither of the two models of depression that had existed up to then seemed sufficient to describe her. Perhaps there was a problem in her brain or body. There certainly *was* a problem in her personal life. But it seemed likely to George that her depression had been activated by something bigger. But he couldn't be sure how to describe it until he had his results.

～

The first thing they wanted to know about these women was—had they experienced any severe losses, or really negative events, in the year before they became depressed? The women often described going through a whole range of horrible events—from a son going to prison, to a husband being diagnosed as schizophrenic, to a baby being born seriously disabled. George and Tirril were strict about what they classified as "severe" in their data. One woman said her dog had been like a child to her, and she had built her life around him, and he died—but they had not classified the loss of a pet as a severe event, so they left it out.

At the same time they wanted to look at the other things they suspected could affect someone's mental health over time, but don't really count as a one-off event. They divided them into two categories.

They labeled the first category "difficulties"—which they defined as a chronic ongoing problem, which could range from having a bad marriage, to living in bad housing, to being forced to move away from your community and neighborhood.

The second category looked at the exact opposite—"stabilizers," the things that they suspected could boost you and protect you from despair. For that, they carefully recorded how many close friends the women had, and how good their relationships with their partners were.

After years of patiently gathering their evidence, talking to woman after woman and returning to them over long intervals, the team finally sat down and crunched the numbers. They spent months figuring out what the data revealed. As they did this, they felt a weight of responsibility. This was the first time scientific evidence had ever been gathered in this way.

If the story I was told by my doctor when I was a teenager—that depression is caused simply by low serotonin levels in the brain, rather than by anything happening in your life—was true, then there would be no difference between the two groups.

~

Tirril stared at the results.

Among the women who didn't develop depression, some 20 percent had experienced a significant negative event in the preceding year. Among the women who *did* develop depression, some 68 percent of them had experienced a significant negative experience in the year before the depression set in.

It was a gap of 48 percent—far more than could be caused by chance. This showed that experiencing something really stressful can cause depression.

But this was only the first of their findings. It turned out depressed women were *three times* more likely to be facing serious long-term stressors in their lives in the year before they developed their depression than women who didn't get depressed. It wasn't just a bad event that caused depression—it was also long-term sources of stress. And if you had some *positive* stabilizing things in your life, that massively reduced the chances of developing depression. For every good friend you had, or if your partner was more supportive and caring, it reduced depression by a remarkable amount.

So George and Tirril had discovered that two things make depression much more likely—having a severe negative event, and having long-term sources of stress and insecurity in your life. But the most startling result was what happened when these factors were added together. Your chances of becoming depressed didn't just combine: they exploded. For example— if you didn't have any friends, and you didn't have a supportive partner, your chances of developing depression when a severe negative life event came along were 75 percent. It was much more likely than not.

It turned out that every bad thing that happened to you, every source of stress, every lack of support—each one accelerated the risks of depression more and more. It was like putting a fungus in a place that's dark and wet. It wouldn't just grow more than it would in a place that was just dark, or in a place that was just wet. It would balloon bigger than both combined.

George hadn't expected to find such a huge effect. As they tried to absorb these results, they thought back over the women they'd got to know over all these years. They had proved that depression is—in fact— to a significant degree a problem not with your brain, but with your life.

After it was published, one professor—summarizing the general view among scientists—called it "a quantum leap ahead" in our understanding.

~

We are told in our culture that depression is the ultimate form of irrationality: that's how it feels from the inside, and that's how it looks to the outside. But on the contrary, George and Tirril were reaching the conclusion that, as they wrote then, "clinical depression is an understandable response to adversity." Think about Mrs. Trent, trapped in a dead marriage with a man who couldn't get work, scrambling to survive, with no chance of a better life—she was being given a guarantee that her life would be a stressful, joyless scramble forever. Didn't it make more sense, they wondered, to say the "fault" for her depression lay "in the environment, rather than in the person"?

As I read this, I could see the force of their logic. But I had an obvious objection. I wasn't living in a run-down housing project in the worst part of London—not now, nor at any point in my depression. My life had never been like Mrs. Trent's. Most of the people I knew who were depressed weren't living in poverty, either. What did their findings mean for people like us?

As they crunched the numbers, George and Tirril had discovered people living in poverty were more likely to become depressed—but the data showed it was too crude to say the poverty *caused* the depression. No: something more subtle was happening. People in poverty were more likely to become depressed because on average they faced more long-term stress, and because more negative life events happened to them, and because they had fewer stabilizers. But the underlying lessons were true for everyone, rich, middle-class, or poor. We all lose some hope when we're subjected to severe stress, or when something horrible happens to us, but if the stress or the bad events are sustained over a long period, what you get is "the generalization of hopelessness," Tirril told me. It spreads over your whole life, like an oil slick, and you begin to want to give up.

Years later, teams of social scientists used the exact same techniques as George and Tirril to investigate the causes of depression in places as radically different as the Basque country and rural Zimbabwe. What they discovered is that these factors were driving depression—or protecting people from it—everywhere. In rural Spain, depression was extremely low—because there was a strong community protecting people, and few traumatic experiences. In Zimbabwe, depression was extremely high—because people faced traumatic experiences often: for example, if you were a woman and you couldn't have a child, you could just be expelled from your home and your community. (I went to rural Zimbabwe while I was researching this book, and I saw this for myself.)

Wherever you were in the world, researchers were learning, these factors played a crucial role in whether you would become depressed or not. They seemed to have discovered the beginnings of the secret recipe for what is really contained in depression.

And yet, even after all this work, George and Tirril knew there was still something they couldn't see in this picture. What was it?

~

When George and Tirril published their results, there was a rapid response from some psychiatrists. They claimed: We always said some people become depressed because of events in their life. Those are the people with "reactive depression." Okay, so you've refined what we know about them: kudos to you. But there's still a huge category of people who are depressed for internal physical reasons. Those are people with "endogenous depression." All that's happening to them is that something is malfunctioning internally.

But George and Tirril explained that they had, all along, been studying women who had been classified by psychiatrists as having "reactive depression" *and* women classified as having "endogenous depression." And what they found—when they compared the evidence—is there was no difference between them. Both groups had things going wrong in their lives at the same rate. This distinction, they concluded, was meaningless.

"I mean—it seems incredible now, really, to think that we had to convince people that life events were relevant [to depression and anxiety], you know?" Tirril Harris—the coauthor of this research—said to me, in the office where she still practices therapy, in North London. I asked her what she would say to the people who think most depression is solely caused internally, by the brain—as my generation was told by our doctors. She furrowed her brow. "No organism exists without the environment— so it just can't be," she said. "I think they're a bit ignorant, that's all," she said. She smiled at me patiently. "I mean—there are an awful lot of people in the world who have ill-founded opinions, and one gets used to it."

~

Years later, Tirril used the same techniques to carry out a study of anxiety—and found similar results. It wasn't just a problem caused by the brain going wrong. It was caused by life going wrong.

~

George and Tirril believed their research on the streets of South London had only scratched the surface. There was so much more to ask. They were acutely conscious that there were lots of factors in the lives of depressed and anxious people they didn't look at. What should be studied next? They were planting the first flag on the moon of investigating the social causes of depression and anxiety. They expected other spaceships to follow soon, to carry out other probes. And then . . . so far as communicating these ideas to the public went, there was silence. The other spacecraft never came. Their flag was left, in windless space.

The public debate about depression shifted, within a few years, to the discovery of the new antidepressant drugs, and how to prevent depression inside the brain—rather than out here in society. The conversation shifted from figuring out what is making us so unhappy in our lives, to trying to block the neurotransmitters in the brain that allow us to feel it.

Yet, in one limited sense, George and Tirril won. Within a few years, the evidence that environmental factors are a key part of depression and anxiety was steadily building up among academics, until in most scientific circles it became undeniable. These findings soon ended up as a key part of the basis for psychiatric training in many parts of the Western world. Most mainstream training courses began to teach that forms of mental distress such as depression and anxiety have three kinds of cause: biological, psychological, and social. They are all real. This is known as the "bio-psycho-social model." It's simple. All three sets of factors are relevant, and to understand a person's depression and anxiety, you need to look at them all.

But these truer insights remained private, sealed off from a public who could have been helped by them. They weren't explained to the swelling ranks of depressed and anxious people, and they didn't shape the treatment that was offered to them.

~

The public was never told about the biggest implication of this research. George and Tirril had concluded that when it comes to depression and anxiety, "paying attention to a person's environment may turn out to be at least as effective as physical treatment." Nobody asked them—how do we do that? What environmental changes would reduce depression and anxiety?

These questions seemed too big, too revolutionary, to process. They are still ignored today—although later, I began to explore what they could mean.

~

That research in Camberwell—I realize now—was a moment when the whole history of understanding depression could have gone in a radically different direction. Their research was published in 1978, the year before I was born. If the world had listened to George and Tirril, when I went to my doctor eighteen years after the publication of their research he would have had to tell me a very different story about why I was in such pain— and how to find my way back.

~

When I said goodbye to George Brown after one of our long conversations, he told me that he would be spending the rest of the day working on his latest scientific paper, digging further into the causes of depression. By the time I met him, he was eighty-five years old, so, he said, it would probably be his last research project. But he is not stopping. As he walked away, I pictured his neighbor, drowning herself all those years ago in silence. There is so much, George had told me, that we still need to know. Why would he stop now?

PART II

Disconnection: Nine Causes of Depression and Anxiety

CHAPTER 5

Picking Up the Flag
(An Introduction to Part Two)

After learning all this, I began to follow the trail that led from George Brown and Tirril Harris's research out across the world. I wanted to know—who else has studied the seemingly hidden dimensions of depression and anxiety, and what does that mean for how we might reduce them? Over the next few years I found that all across the world, there are social scientists and psychologists who had been picking up George and Tirril's tattered flag. I sat with them from San Francisco to Sydney, from Berlin to Buenos Aires, and I came to think of them as a kind of Depression and Anxiety Underground, piecing together a more complex and truthful story.

It was only a long time into talking with these social scientists that I realized every one of the social and psychological causes of depression and anxiety they have discovered has something in common.

They are all forms of disconnection. They are all ways in which we have been cut off from something we innately need but seem to have lost along the way.

After researching depression and anxiety for several years now, I have been able to identify nine causes. I want to stress that I am not saying these are the *only* causes of depression and anxiety. There will be more that have not yet been discovered (or that I didn't come across in my research). I'm also not saying that every depressed or anxious person will find all of these factors in their lives. For example, I experienced some of them, but not all.

But following this trail was going to change how I thought—about some of my own deepest feelings.

CHAPTER 6

Cause One: Disconnection from Meaningful Work

Joe Phillips was waiting for the day to end. If you had walked into the paint shop in Philadelphia where he worked, and you asked for a gallon of paint in a particular shade, he would ask you to pick it from a chart, and he would prepare it for you. It was always the same. He would put a dash of pigment into the can, and put the can into a machine that looked a bit like a microwave, and the machine would shake it vigorously. This made the color of the paint even. Then he would take your money and say "Thank you, sir." Then he'd wait for the next customer, and do the same thing. Then he would wait for the next customer, and do the same thing. All day. Every day.

Take an order.

Shake paint.

Say "Thank you, sir."

Wait.

Take an order.

Shake paint.

Say "Thank you, sir."

Wait.

And on. And on.

Nobody ever noticed whether Joe did it well or badly. The only thing his boss ever commented on was if he was late, and then he'd get bawled out. As Joe left work, he would always think: "I don't feel like I made a difference in anyone's life." The attitude of his employers, he told me, was: "You're going to do it this way. And you're going to show up at this time. And as long as you do that, you're fine." But he found himself thinking, as he put it to me, "Where's the ability to change? Where's the ability to grow? Where's the ability to really make an impact on this company that I'm working for? Because anyone can just show up on time, do what they tell you to do."

Joe felt like his human thoughts and insights and feelings were almost a defect. But whenever he told me about how his work made him feel, as we ate dinner in a Chinese restaurant, Joe would chastise himself soon afterward. "There's people out there who would die for this job, and I understand that. I'm grateful for that." It was reasonably paid; he could live with his girlfriend in an okay place; he knew plenty of people who didn't have any of that. He felt guilty for feeling this way. But then the feelings kept coming back.

And he shook more paint.

And he shook more paint.

And he shook more paint.

"So the monotony is lying in that fact that you constantly feel like you're doing things you don't want to do," he told me. "Where's the joy at? I'm not intellectual enough to be able to explain it, but there was just an overall feeling . . . [that] you needed something to fill that void. Although you couldn't ever put your finger on what that void really was."

He would leave home at seven in the morning, work all through the day, and get home at seven at night. He began to wonder—you "go through this forty- to fifty-hour workweek, and if you don't really like it, you're just setting yourself up for depression, and anxiety. And questioning—why am I doing this? There's got to be something better than this." He started to feel, he said, that there was "no hope. What's the point?"

"You have to be challenged in a healthy way," he told me, shrugging a little; I think he felt embarrassed to say it. "You have to know that your voice counts. You have to know that if you have a good idea, you can speak up, and change something." He had never had a job like that, and he feared he never would.

If you spend so many of your waking hours deadening yourself to get through the day, it's hard—he explained—to turn that off and be engaged with the people you love when you get home. Joe would have five hours to himself before he had to sleep and then shake paint again. He wanted to just collapse in front of the television, or to be alone. On weekends, all he wanted to do was drink a lot and watch a game.

Joe contacted me one day because he'd listened to some of my speeches online, and he wanted to talk about the subject of my last book, which was (in part) addiction. We arranged to meet and walked through the streets of Philadelphia before we ate. There he told me a story. After years of shaking paint, Joe went one night to a casino with one of his friends, and he was offered a little blue pill by one of them. It was 30 miligrams of the opiate-based painkiller Oxycontin. Joe took it and felt pleasantly numbed. And a few days later, he thought—maybe this would help me at work. When he took it, he felt the fading of those feelings that had been flooding his head. Before long, "I made sure I had them before I went to work, made sure I had enough with me at work to get through work, rationing them out," he says. He would take some more when he got home with some beers, thinking: "I can deal with that bullshit at work knowing that when I come home, I get to do this."

And he shook more paint.

And he shook more paint.

And he shook more paint.

I wondered if this was because the Oxy made him as blank and empty as the job itself. It seemed to dissolve the conflict between his desire to make a difference and the reality of his life. When I started talking to Joe, he thought at first he was telling me a story about addiction. He had been told by the people he went to for help kicking the Oxy that he was "born an addict," and that's the story he told me at first. But when we talked about it some more, he said he'd had periods of pretty heavy drinking, weed smoking, and the odd line of cocaine as a college student, and he'd never felt any urge to use them more than at occasional parties. It was only when he entered a deadening job—and saw it as a dead end—that he started to numb himself.

And when he did kick the Oxy, after a few rough months, his sense that his life was unbearable came back. All the thoughts he had been trying to get away from recurred as he shook the paint again and again.

He knew people need paint, he told me. He added—once again—that he knew he should be grateful. But he said he couldn't stand the thought that his life would be like this for another thirty-five years until he retired. "Like—you like what you do, right?" he said to me. I stopped writing in my notebook for a moment. "When you wake up in the morning, you look forward to your day. When I wake up, I don't look forward to work . . . It's just something I have to do."

∼

Between 2011 and 2012, the polling company Gallup conducted the most detailed study ever carried out of how people across the world feel about their work. They studied millions of workers across 142 countries. They found that 13 percent of us say we are "engaged" in our jobs—which means they are "enthusiastic about, and committed to their work and contribute to their organization in a positive manner."

Against them, 63 percent say they are "not engaged," which is defined as "sleepwalking through their workday, putting time—but not energy or passion—into their work."

And a further 24 percent are "actively disengaged." They, Gallup explained, "aren't just unhappy at work; they're busy acting out their unhappiness. Every day, these workers undermine what their engaged co-workers accomplish . . . Actively disengaged employees are more or less out to damage their company."

That means, taking the Gallup study, that 87 percent of people, if they read Joe's story, could recognize at least a little of themselves in it. Nearly twice as many people hate their jobs as love their jobs.

And this thing that most of us don't like doing—that feels like sleep-walking, or worse—now takes up most of our waking lives. One professor who has studied this in detail writes: "A recent survey has confirmed that nine to five is indeed a relic of the past. Today the average worker checks their work e-mail at 7.42 am, gets to the office at 8.18 am and leaves at 7.19 pm . . . The recent survey found that one in three British workers check their e-mails before 6.30 am, while 80% of British employers consider it acceptable to phone employees out of hours." The concept of "work hours" is vanishing for most people—so this thing that 87 percent of us don't enjoy is spreading over more and more of our lives.

I began to wonder, after my meal with Joe, if all this might be playing a role in the rise of depression and anxiety. A common symptom of depression is something called "derealization"—which is where you feel like nothing you are doing is authentic or real. That seems to me, as I read it, to describe Joe—and it didn't sound irrational. It sounds like a normal human reaction to working at a job like Joe's for your whole life. So I started to search for scientific evidence about how this makes people feel, to see if there was a link to depression and anxiety. I was able to figure it out only when I went to meet a remarkable scientist.

~

One day in the late 1960s, a little Greek woman shuffled into a small outpatient clinic in the suburbs of Sydney, Australia. It was part of a hospital in one of the poorest parts of the city, looking after mostly immigrants from Greece. She explained to the doctor on duty that she was crying all the time. "I feel life is not worth living," she explained. Sitting in front of her were two men—a European psychiatrist with a thick accent, and a trainee who turned out to be a tall young Aussie named Michael Marmot. "When were you last completely well?" the older man asked. She replied: "Oh, doctor. My husband is drinking again and beating me. My son is back in prison. My teenage daughter is pregnant. And I cry most days. Have no energy. Difficulty sleeping."

Michael was seeing a lot of patients like her coming into the ward asking for help. Immigrants to Australia were subjected to a lot of racism, and that first generation in particular had tough, degrading lives. When they became as broken-down as this woman standing before them, they were usually described as having a medical problem. Sometimes they were just given mild white mixtures, as a kind of placebo; sometimes they were drugged more seriously.

To Michael, as a young trainee doctor, that seemed like a weird way to respond. "It seemed startlingly obvious," he wrote years later, "that her depression was related to her life circumstances." Yet "people would come in with problems in their lives, and we would treat them with a bottle of white mixture." He suspected that a lot more of the problems they were seeing—like the men who complained of mysterious stomach pains that appeared to have no cause—were similarly caused by the stress of the lives they were forced to live.

Michael would walk around the hospital wards and think—all this sickness and distress must tell us something about our society, and what we're doing wrong. He tried to discuss this with the other doctors, explaining that he believed that with a woman like this patient, we "should be paying attention to the causes of her depression." The doctors were incredulous. They told him he was talking rubbish. It's not possible for psychological distress to cause physical illnesses, they explained. This was the belief of most medical practitioners across the world at that time. Michael suspected they were wrong—but what did he know? He had no evidence, and it didn't seem like anyone was researching this. He had a hunch; that was all.

One of the doctors gently suggested to him that if that's what he cared about, he should consider going into research rather than practical psychiatry.

~

That's how—a few years later—Michael found himself in London in the chaos of the 1970s. These were the last days when Englishmen went to work in bowler hats, although they passed young women in miniskirts on the streets, as two eras awkwardly evaded each other's gaze. He arrived, in the middle of a freezing winter, in a country that seemed to be falling apart. The electricity had recently been shut off for four days a week in a protracted strike.

Yet at the heart of this fracturing British society, there was a slick, purring machine. The British civil service—with its offices along White-hall, running from Trafalgar Square down to the Houses of Parliament—likes to regard itself as the Rolls-Royce of government bureaucracies. It consists of a vast stream of bureaucrats administering every aspect of the British state, and it is organized as tightly as an army. That meant that every day, thousands of men—they were almost all men when Michael first went there—arrived by tube to work in neatly ordered desks, from which they would administer the British Isles.

For Michael, it seemed like a perfect laboratory to test something he was intensely curious about: How does your work affect your health? You can't really investigate this by comparing very different jobs. If you compare (say) a construction worker, a nurse, and an accountant, there's so much variation that it's hard to figure out what's really going on. Construction workers have more accidents, nurses are exposed to more diseases, accountants sit down more (which is bad for you); you can't disentangle what's really causing anything.

But in the British civil service, nobody is poor; nobody is going home to a damp house; nobody is in physical danger. Everybody does a desk job. But there are real differences in status, and in how much freedom you get at work. British civil servants were divided into grades—strict levels that determined how much they were paid, and how much responsibility they were given at work. Michael wanted to study whether those differences affect your health. He suspected it might tell us something about why so many people in our society were depressed or anxious—the mystery that had been troubling him since Sydney.

At this time, most people thought they already knew the answer, and so this study was pointless. Picture a man running a big government department, and a guy whose job—eleven steps down the pay scale—is to file his papers and type up his notes. Who's more likely to have a heart attack? Who's more likely to be overwhelmed? Who's more likely to become depressed? Almost everyone believed the answer was clear: it was the boss. He has a more stressful job. He has to take really tough decisions, with big consequences. The guy doing his filing has a lot less responsibility; it will weigh on him less; his life will be easier.

Michael and the team he belonged to began the work of interviewing civil servants to gather data about their physical and mental health. It would take them years, and would be broken into two major studies. The civil servants would come in and Michael would talk with each of them for an hour, one on one, about what their jobs involved. The team worked through eighteen thousand civil servants in this way. Michael noticed right away a difference between the different rungs on this social ladder. When he talked with the top-level civil servants, they would lean back and take charge of the conversation, demanding to know what Michael wanted. When he talked with the lower-grade civil servants, they would lean forward and wait for him to tell them what to do.

After years of intensive interviewing, Michael and the team added up the results. It turned out the people at the top of the civil service were *four times less* likely to have a heart attack than the people at the bottom of the Whitehall ladder. The truth was the opposite of what everyone had expected. But then there was a finding that was weirder still.

If you plotted it on a graph, as your position in the civil service rose, your chances of developing depression fell, step by step. There was a very close relationship between becoming depressed and where you stood in the hierarchy. This is what social scientists call a "gradient." "This is really astonishing," Michael wrote. "Why should educated people with good stable jobs have a higher risk of dropping dead [or becoming depressed] than people with a bit more education or slightly higher-status jobs?"

Something about work was making people depressed. But what could it be? When Michael and his team returned to Whitehall to investigate further, they wanted to know: As you rise up the civil service, what actually changes in your work that could explain this shift?

They had one early hypothesis, based on everything they'd seen. Could it be, they wondered, that top civil servants have more control over their work than lower civil servants, and that's why they're less depressed? It seemed like a reasonable guess: "Think about your own life," Michael said to me, when we met in his office in central London. "Just examine your own feelings. Where you feel worst about jobs—and probably life—is when you feel out of control."

There was a way to find out. This time, instead of comparing people at the top, middle, and bottom, they compared people within the same civil service band—but whose jobs differed in how much control they had. They wanted to know—Is someone on the middle band more likely to get depressed, or have a heart attack, than another person on the same middle band who has more control? They returned to conduct more interviews and gather more detailed data.

What Michael found when he did this was even more striking than the first results. It's worth spelling it out.

If you worked in the civil service and you had a higher degree of control over your work, you were a lot less likely to become depressed or develop severe emotional distress than people *working at the same pay level, with the same status, in the same office,* as people with a lower degree of control over their work.

Michael remembers a woman named Marjorie. She worked as a secretary in the typing pool, where she had to type documents all day, every day. It was "heaven," she said, to be allowed to smoke and eat sweets at your desk, but it was "absolutely soul-destroying," she told him, to sit there doing work that was shoveled to you and that you didn't understand. "We were not allowed to talk," she said, so they had to sit in silence, typing up documents that might as well have been in Swedish for all they were told about them, to go to people they did not know, surrounded by people they couldn't talk to. Michael writes: "The thing that characterizes Marjorie's work is not how much demand there is on her, but that she has no discretion to decide anything at all."

By contrast, if you were a top civil servant and you had an idea, you had a good chance of making it happen. That carried through to your whole existence. It informed how you saw the world. If you were a lower-rank civil servant, though, you had to learn to be passive. "Imagine a typical Tuesday morning in a large government department," Michael wrote years later. "Marjorie from the typing pool comes to Nigel, who is eleven levels higher than her in the hierarchy, and says: 'I've been thinking, Nige. We could save a lot of money if we ordered our supplies over the Internet. What do you think?' I've been trying to imagine such a conversation, but my imagination fails me."

You have to shut yourself down inside yourself to get through this—and Michael uncovered evidence that this affected your whole life. The higher up you went in the civil service, he found, the more friends and social activity you had after work. The lower you went, the more that tapered off—the people with boring, low-status jobs just wanted to collapse in front of the television when they got home. Why would that be? "When work is enriching, life is fuller, and that spills over into the things you do outside work," he said to me. But "when it's deadening," you feel "shattered at the end of the day, just shattered."

～

As a result of this research, and the science it opened up, "the notion of what constitutes stress at work has undergone a revolution," Michael explains. The worst stress for people isn't having to bear a lot of responsibility. It is, he told me, having to endure "work [that] is monotonous, boring, soul-destroying; [where] they die a little when they come to work each day, because their work touches no part of them that is them." Joe, then, in his paint shop, by this real standard, had one of the most stressful jobs there is. "Disempowerment," Michael told me, "is at the heart of poor health"—physical, mental, and emotional.

～

A few years ago, long after these Whitehall studies, the British government's tax office had a problem, and they called Michael back to the civil service to ask him to help them—urgently—to find a solution. The staff investigating tax returns kept killing themselves. So Michael spent time in their offices to find out why this was happening.

The staff explained to him that when they got to work, they felt immediately attacked by their in-trays. It felt like it would "engulf them. The greater the height of the in-tray, the greater the threat of feeling like you would never get your head above water." They would work super hard for a whole day—and at the end of it, the pile in the in-tray would be higher than it was at the start. "Holidays made them unhappy," Michael noted, "because the tidal wave of paper would build up so that, on return, they would be engulfed. It wasn't just the ineluctable flow of work that did them in, but the lack of control. No matter how steadily, how hard they worked, they fell further and further behind." And nobody ever thanked them for it—people weren't thrilled to have their tax dodges pointed out.

During the Whitehall studies, Michael had discovered one other factor that turns work into a generator of depression—and he could see it here, too. If these tax inspectors worked really hard and gave it their best, nobody noticed. And if they did a lousy job, nobody noticed, either. Despair often happens, he had learned, when there is a "lack of balance between efforts and rewards." It was the same for Joe in his paint shop. Nobody ever noticed how much effort he put in. The signal you get from the world, in that situation, is—you're irrelevant. Nobody cares what you do.

So Michael explained to the tax office bosses that a lack of control and a lack of balance between efforts and rewards were causing such severe depression that it was leading their staff to suicide.

~

When Michael first suggested—forty years before, in a hospital in the suburbs of Sydney—that how we live can make us depressed, the doctors around him scoffed. Today, nobody seriously disputes the core of the evidence he has uncovered, although we rarely talk about it. He has become one of the leading public health scientists in the world. Yet we are still, it occurred to me, making the mistake those doctors made back then. The Greek woman who came to Michael saying she was crying all day and didn't know how to stop didn't have a problem with her brain; she had a problem with her life. But the hospital gave her a few tablets they knew were just a placebo, and sent her on her way.

∽

Back in Philly, I started to tell Joe about the Whitehall studies and the other scientific evidence I had learned about. He was interested at first, but after a while, he said, a little impatiently: "You can get real in-depth and intellectual with all that stuff, but when it comes down to it—doing anything, and not having a purpose behind it, and then feeling like you don't have any other option except to continue: it's terrible. At least for me, it turns into—well, what's the point?"

∽

There was one last thing about Joe that puzzled me. He hated working in paint, but unlike a lot of people, Joe wasn't trapped: he didn't have kids or any responsibilities; he was still young, and he had an alternative. "I love to fish," he told me. "My goal is to fish all fifty states before I die. I have [done] twenty-seven of them, at [the age of] thirty-two." He's looked into being a fishing guide down in Florida. It pays a lot less than he earns now, but he would love it. He would look forward to work every day. He thought out loud about what that would be like. He asked: "Do you sacrifice your monetary stability to do something you thoroughly enjoy, but, at the same time—the cost of living . . ."

Joe has been thinking about quitting and going to Florida for years. "I can only speak for myself," he said, "that when I leave work every day, I have this overwhelming feeling like—there is no way this is all that's on the horizon for me. There's times when I say to myself—dude, quit your job . . . Move to Florida, and be a fishing guide on a boat, and you'll be happy."

So I asked—why don't you do it, Joe? Why don't you leave? "Right," he said. And he looked hopeful. And then he looked afraid. Later in our conversation, I came back to it. "You could do it tomorrow," I said. "What's stopping you?" There's a part of all of us, he says, that thinks "if I keep buying more stuff, and I get the Mercedes, and I buy the house with the four garages, people on the outside [will] think I'm doing good, and then I can will myself into being happy." He wanted to go. Yet he was being blocked by something neither he nor I fully understood. Ever since then, I've been trying to understand why Joe probably won't go. Something keeps many of us trapped in those situations that's more than just needing to pay the bills. I was going to investigate it soon.

As I said goodbye to Joe, and he began to walk away, I called after him: "Go to Florida!" The moment I said it, I felt foolish. He didn't look back.

CHAPTER 7

Cause Two: Disconnection from Other People

When I was a child, something unexpected happened to my parents. My father grew up in a tiny village in the Swiss mountains called Kandersteg where he could have named every other inhabitant, and my mother grew up in the working-class Scottish tenements where if you raised your voice, all your neighbors heard every word you said. Then, when I was a baby, they moved to a place called Edgware. It is the last tube stop on the Northern Line—a suburban sprawl of detached and semidetached houses, built on what used to be London's green edges. If you fall asleep on a train and find yourself there, you'll see lots of houses, some fast food joints, a park, and lots of decent, likable, alienated people hurrying through them.

When my parents moved in, they tried befriending people in the neighborhood, in just the way they would have in the places they were from. It was as natural an instinct to them as breathing. But when they tried to do this, they were perplexed. In Edgware, people weren't hostile. We knew our neighbors to smile at. But that was it; any attempt at engagement beyond brief chitchat was shut down. Life was meant to happen, my

parents learned slowly, inside your house. I didn't regard this as unusual—
it was all I ever knew—although my mother never got used to it. "Where
is everyone?" she asked me once when I was quite small, looking down
our empty street, baffled.

~

Loneliness hangs over our culture today like a thick smog. More people
say they feel lonely than ever before—and I wondered if this might be
related to our apparent rise in depression and anxiety. As I investigated
this, I learned there were two scientists who have been studying loneliness
for decades—and had made a series of crucial breakthroughs.

~

In the mid-1970s, a young neuroscience researcher named John Cacioppo
was listening to his professors—some of the best in the world—but there
was something he just couldn't understand.

When they tried to explain why human emotions change, they seemed
to focus only on one thing: what happens *inside* your brain. They didn't
look at what was happening in your life, and ask whether that might be
causing any of the changes in the brain they were discovering. It was as if
they thought your brain is an island, cut off from the rest of the world and
never interacting with it.

So John asked himself: What would happen if, instead of studying the
brain as if it were an isolated island, we did it differently? What if we tried
to study it as if it were an island that is connected by a hundred bridges to
the outside world, where things are being carried on and off all the time
as you receive signals from the world?

When he raised these questions, his mentors were puzzled. "You
know," they told him, "even if it were relevant, [the factors outside the
brain] are not fundamental" to changes like depression or anxiety. And
besides, they said, it's just too complex to figure out. Nobody will

understand any of this "for one hundred years or more," they said. "So we're not going to focus on it."

John never forgot these questions. He puzzled over them for years, until one day, in the 1990s, he finally thought of a way he might begin to study them in more detail. If you want to figure out how your brain and your feelings change when you interact with the rest of the world, you could start by looking at what happens in exactly the opposite situation—when you feel lonely and cut off from the world around you. Does that experience, he asked himself, change your brain? Does it change your body?

$\sim$

He began with the simplest study he could think of. John and his colleagues gathered one hundred strangers at the University of Chicago, where he was now based, to take part in a straightforward experiment that nobody had ever tried before.

If you were one of the people taking part, you were told to go out and spend a few days just living your normal everyday life—only with a few little tweaks. You had to wear a cardiovascular monitor to measure your heart rate, and you were given a little beeper and some tubes. You left the lab. On the first day of the experiment, whenever the beeper beeped— which, it turned out, would happen nine times a day—you would have to stop your everyday business and write down two things. First, you had to note how lonely or connected you felt. Second, you had to record your heart rate from the monitor.

On the second day of the experiment you went through the same process, except this time, when you heard the beeper, you'd spit into a tube, seal it, and keep it to hand in to the lab.

John was trying to figure exactly how stressful it is to be lonely. Nobody knew. But when you're stressed, your heartbeat goes up, and your saliva becomes flooded with a hormone called cortisol. So this experiment could—finally—measure how big the effect is.

When John and his colleagues added up the data, they were startled. Feeling lonely, it turned out, caused your cortisol levels to absolutely soar—as much as some of the most disturbing things that can ever happen to you. Becoming acutely lonely, the experiment found, was as stressful as experiencing a physical attack.

It's worth repeating. Being deeply lonely seemed to cause as much stress as being punched by a stranger.

~

John started to dig, to see if any other scientists had studied the effects of loneliness. A professor named Sheldon Cohen, he learned, had carried out a study in which he took a bunch of people and recorded how many friends and healthy social connections each of them had. He then took them into a lab and deliberately exposed them—with their knowledge— to the cold virus. What he wanted to know was—would the isolated people get sicker than the connected people? It turned out that they were *three times* more likely to catch the cold than people who had lots of close connections to other people.

Another scientist, Lisa Berkman, had followed both isolated and highly connected people over nine years, to see whether one group was more likely to die than the other. She discovered that isolated people were two to three times more likely to die during that period. Almost everything became more fatal when you were alone: cancer, heart disease, respiratory problems.

Loneliness itself, John was slowly discovering as he pieced together the evidence, seemed to be deadly. When they added up the figures, John and other scientists found that being disconnected from the people around you had the same effect on your health as being obese—which was, until then, considered the biggest health crisis the developed world faced.

~

So John now knew that loneliness has striking physical effects. But could it, he wanted to investigate next, also be driving the apparent epidemic of depression and anxiety?

At first, this seemed like it would be a tough question to investigate. You can survey people and ask them three things: Are you lonely? Are you depressed? Are you anxious? Then you can match up the answers. If you do that, you always find that lonely people are much more likely to be depressed or anxious. But that doesn't get us very far—because depressed and anxious people often become afraid of the world, and of social interaction, so they tend to retreat from it. It could be that you become depressed first, and that in turn makes you lonely. But John suspected it could possibly be the other way around—that if you become lonely, that might *make* you depressed.

So he started to seek the answer—using two very different kinds of study.

To start with, he took 135 people who had been identified as highly lonely and brought them into his labs at the University of Chicago for a day and a night. They were given personality tests so extensive that John joked they might have been being sent off on a mission to Mars. What these tests found is pretty much what you'd expect—that lonely people are also anxious, have low self-esteem, are pessimistic, and are afraid other people will dislike them. The key now was for John to find a way to make some of them *more lonely* without affecting anything else in their lives—without doing anything that might make them panic, or feel judged, for example. How could that be done?

He split his next experimental group into two—Group A and Group B—and then brought in a psychiatrist named David Spiegel to hypnotize each group in turn. Group A, under hypnosis, was led to remember periods in their lives when they felt really lonely. Group B was led to remember the opposite—a time in their lives when they felt really connected to another person, or to a group. After the subjects had been made to feel super-lonely or super-connected, they were made to do the personality tests all over again.

John figured that if depression is causing loneliness, then making people feel more lonely won't make any difference. But if loneliness can cause depression, then increasing loneliness will increase depression.

What John's experiment found was later regarded as a key turning point in the field. The people who had been triggered to feel lonely became radically more depressed, and the people who had been triggered to feel connected became radically less depressed. "The stunning thing was that loneliness is not merely the result of depression," he told me. "Indeed—it *leads to* depression." It was, he says, like the moment in an episode of *CSI* when the experts finally find the fingerprints that match. "Loneliness," he explains, "definitely had the starring role."

~

But this didn't resolve the question. Lab conditions, John knew, can be artificial in all sorts of ways. So he started to research this question in a different way.

Just beyond Chicago, in a part of Cook County dominated by sprawling suburban concrete and tarmac, he began to follow 229 older Americans who ranged in age from their fifties to their seventies. They were chosen to be a broad cross-section—half men, half women, a third Latino, a third African American, a third white. Crucially, they were not depressed or unusually lonely when the research began. Once a year, they would come in to the lab and go through a whole battery of tests. He would study their health—both physical and mental. Then his team would ask lots of questions about how lonely or isolated they were feeling. How many people were they in contact with every day? How many people were they close to? Who were they sharing moments of joy with in their lives?

What he wanted to know was—when, over time, some of the people in the study developed depression (as inevitably some of them would), what would come first? Would isolation and loneliness come first—or would depression come first?

It turned out that—for the initial five years of data that have been studied so far—in most cases, loneliness *preceded* depressive symptoms. You became lonely, and that was followed by feelings of despair and profound sadness and depression. And the effect was really big. Picture the range of loneliness in our culture as a straight line. At one end, you are 0 percent lonely. At the other end, you are 100 percent lonely. If you moved from being in the middle—50 percent—to being at 65 percent, your chances of developing depressive symptoms increased *eight times.*

The fact he has discovered this through two very different kinds of study—and a great deal more research he has done—led John to a key conclusion, one that has been gathering in scientific support: loneliness, he concluded, is causing a significant amount of the depression and anxiety in our society.

~

As he made this discovery, John began to ask—why? Why would loneliness cause depression and anxiety so much?

He came to suspect there might be a good reason. Human beings first evolved on the savannas of Africa, where we lived in small hunter-gatherer tribes of a few hundred people or less. You and I exist for one reason— because those humans figured out how to cooperate. They shared their food. They looked after the sick. They "were able to take down very large beasts," John points out to me, "but only because they were working together." They only made sense as a group. "Every pre-agricultural society we know about has this same basic structure," he wrote with one of his colleagues. "Against harsh odds they barely survive, but the fact that they survive at all they owe to the dense web of social contacts and the vast number of reciprocal commitments they maintain. In this state of nature, connection and social co-operation did not have to be imposed . . . Nature *is* connection."

Now imagine if—on those savannas—you became separated from the group and were alone for a protracted period of time. It meant you were in terrible danger. You were vulnerable to predators, if you got sick nobody would be there to nurse you, and the rest of the tribe was more vulnerable without you too. You would be right to feel terrible. It was an urgent signal from your body and brain to get back to the group, any damn way you could.

So every human instinct is honed not for life on your own, but for life like this, in a tribe. Humans need tribes as much as bees need a hive.

That sense of dread and alertness triggered by being alone for too long evolved, then, John says, for a really good reason. It pushed people back to the group, and it meant that when they were with the tribe, they had an incentive to treat people well so they didn't get thrown out. "A strong impulse in favor of connection," he explains, "simply produces better outcomes for survival." Or, as he told me later: loneliness is "an aversive state that motivates us to reconnect."

This would help us to understand why loneliness so often comes alongside anxiety. "Evolution fashioned us not only to feel good when connected, but to feel secure," John writes. "The vitally important corollary is that evolution shaped us not only to feel bad in isolation, but to feel insecure."

It's a beautiful theory. But John began to wonder—how could this be tested? It turns out there are still some people who live in the way most humans did at earlier stages in our evolution. For example, John learned that in the Dakotas, there's a very closed, highly religious farming community—a bit like the most fundamentalist wing of the Amish— called the Hutterites. They live off the land, and they work and eat and worship and relax together. Everyone has to cooperate the whole time. (Later in my journey, I went to visit a group like this, as you'll see.)

So John teamed with anthropologists who had been studying the Hutterites for years, to figure out how lonely the Hutterites are. There's one neat way to test it. Anywhere in the world where people describe being lonely, they will also—throughout their sleep—experience more of something called "micro-awakenings." These are small moments you won't recall when you wake up, but in which you rise a little from your slumber. All other social animals do the same thing when they're isolated too. The best theory is that you don't feel safe going to sleep when you're lonely, because early humans literally weren't safe if they were sleeping apart from the tribe. You know nobody's got your back—so your brain won't let you go into full sleep mode. Measuring these "micro-awakenings" is a good way of measuring loneliness. So John's team wired up the Hutterites, to see how many of them they experienced each night.

It turned out they had barely any. "What we found was that the community showed the lowest level of loneliness that I'd seen anywhere in the world," John explained to me. "It really stunned me."

This showed that loneliness isn't just some inevitable human sadness, like death. It's a product of the way we live now.

~

When my mother moved to Edgware and found that there was no community—only polite nods and closed doors—she assumed there was something wrong with Edgware. But it turns out our little suburb was not unusual.

For decades now, a Harvard professor named Robert Putnam has been documenting one of the most important trends of our time. There are all sorts of ways human beings can come together to do something as a group—from a sports team, to a choir, to a volunteer group, to just meeting regularly for dinner. He has been gathering figures for decades about how much we do all these things—and he found they have been in free fall. He gave an example that has become famous: bowling is one of the most popular leisure activities in the United States, and people used to do it in organized leagues—they would be part of a team that competed against other teams, who would mingle and get to know each other. Today, people still bowl, but they do it alone. They're in their own lane, doing their own thing. The collective structure has collapsed.

Think about everything else we do to come together—like supporting your kid's school, say. "In the ten short years between 1985 and 1994" alone, he wrote, "active involvement in community organizations . . . fell by 45 percent." In just a decade—the years of my teens, when I was becoming depressed—across the Western world, we stopped banding together at a massive rate, and found ourselves shut away in our own homes instead.

We dropped out of community and turned inward, Robert explained when I spoke with him. These trends have been happening since the 1930s, but they hugely accelerated during my lifetime.

What this means is that people's sense that they live in a community, or even have friends they can count on, has been plummeting. For example, social scientists have been asking a cross-section of U.S. citizens a simple question for years: "How many confidants do you have?" They wanted to know how many people you could turn to in a crisis, or when something really good happens to you. When they started doing the study several decades ago, the average number of close friends an American had was three. By 2004, the most common answer was none.

It's worth pausing on that: there are now more Americans who have no close friends than any other option.

~

And it's not that we turned inward to our families. The research he gathered showed across the world we've stopped doing stuff with them, too. We eat together as families far less; we watch TV together as families far less; we go on vacation together far less. "Virtually all forms of family togetherness," Putnam shows with a battery of graphs and studies, "became less common over the last quarter of the twentieth century." There are similar figures for Britain and the rest of the Western world.

We do things together less than any humans who came before us. Long before the economic crash of 2008, there was a social crash, in which we found ourselves alone and lonely far more of the time. The structures for looking out for each other—from the family to the neighborhood—fell apart. We disbanded our tribes. We embarked on an experiment—to see if humans can live alone.

∽

One day, while I was doing the research for this book, I found myself low on cash in Lexington, Kentucky, and on my last night in the city, I checked in to a really cheap motel next to the airport. It was a bare concrete hole, with airplanes taking off the whole time, and as I walked to and from my little room, I noticed that in the room next to mine, the door was always open, the TV was always on, and a middle-aged man was perched on the bed, rocking a little, in a strange and awkward position.

The fifth time I walked past, I stopped to ask him what was wrong. He told me in a voice that was hard to understand that he had gotten into a fight with his stepson a few days before—he wouldn't say why—and his stepson had beaten him up and broken his jaw. He'd been to the hospital a few days ago, he said, and they were going to operate on him in forty-eight hours, but in the meantime they'd given him a prescription for pain meds and sent him on his way. The only problem was that he didn't have any money to fill the prescription, so he was sitting there, weeping, alone.

I wanted to say: Don't you have any friends? Isn't there anyone who can help you? But it was clear he had nobody. So he was sitting there, crying softly into his broken jaw.

∽

When I was a child, I was never conscious of missing anything when it came to social connections. But as I spoke to the scientists studying loneliness, I remembered something small. All through my childhood, until my early teens, I had a daydream. It was that my parents' friends—who were scattered across the country, and who we'd see only a few times a year—would all move to live on our street, and I'd be able to go and sit with them when things were hard at home, which was a lot of the time. I would have this daydream every day. But our street consisted only of other people, equally shut away, equally alone.

~

I once heard the comedian Sarah Silverman talk on a radio interview about when her depression first descended on her. She was in her early teens. When her mother and stepfather asked her what was wrong, she couldn't find the vocabulary to explain it. But then, finally, she said she felt homesick, like when she was at summer camp. She said this to the interviewer, Terry Gross of NPR's *Fresh Air*, with puzzlement. She had felt homesick. But she was at home.

I think I understand what was happening to her. When we talk about home today, we mean just our four walls and (if we're lucky) our nuclear family. But that's never been what home has meant to any humans before us. To them, it meant a community—a dense web of people all around us, a tribe. But that is largely gone. Our sense of home has shriveled so far and so fast it no longer meets our need for a sense of belonging. So we are homesick even when we are at home.

~

As John was proving how this effect plays out in humans, other scientists were investigating it in other animals. For example, Professor Martha McClintock separated out lab rats. Some were raised in a cage, alone.

Others were raised in groups. The isolated rats developed eighty-four times the number of breast cancer tumors as the rats who had a community.

~

Many years into his experiments and research, John discovered a cruel twist in this story.

When he put lonely people into brain-scanning machines, he noticed something. They would spot potential threats within 150 milliseconds, while it took socially connected people twice as long, 300 milliseconds, to notice the same threat. What was happening?

Protracted loneliness causes you to shut down socially, and to be more suspicious of any social contact, he found. You become hypervigilant. You start to be more likely to take offense where none was intended, and to be afraid of strangers. You start to be afraid of the very thing you need most. John calls this a "snowball" effect, as disconnection spirals into more disconnection.

Lonely people are scanning for threats because they unconsciously know that nobody is looking out for them, so no one will help them if they are hurt. This snowball effect, he learned, can be reversed—but to help a depressed or severely anxious person out of it, they need more love, and more reassurance, than they would have needed in the first place.

The tragedy, John realized, is that many depressed and anxious people receive *less* love, as they become harder to be around. Indeed, they receive judgment, and criticism, and this accelerates their retreat from the world. They snowball into an ever colder place.

~

After John had spent years investigating people who say they feel lonely, he found himself asking a surprisingly basic question: What *is* loneliness?

This turned out to be unexpectedly difficult to answer. When he asked people "Are you lonely?" they wouldn't find it hard to see what he was talking about, but it's hard to pin down. I assumed, at first, when I hadn't thought about it much, it meant just being physically alone—being deprived of contact with other people. I pictured an elderly woman who's too frail to leave the house and who nobody comes to see.

But John was discovering this wasn't true. In his studies, it turned out that *feeling* lonely was different from simply being alone. Surprisingly, the sensation of loneliness didn't have much to do with how many people you spoke to every day, or every week. Some of the people in his study who felt most lonely actually talked to lots of people every day. "There's a relatively low correlation between the objective connections and perceived connections," he says.

I was puzzled when John first told me this. But then he told me to picture being alone in a big city, where you hardly know anyone. Go to a major public square—the equivalent of Times Square, or the Vegas Strip, or the Place de la République. You won't *be* alone anymore: the place will be crammed with people. But you'll *feel* lonely—probably acutely lonely.

Or picture being in a hospital bed in a busy ward. You're not alone. You're surrounded by patients. You can push a button and have a nurse with you in a few moments. Yet almost everyone feels lonely in that situation. Why?

As he researched this, John discovered that there was a missing ingredient to loneliness, and to recovering from it.

To end loneliness, you need other people—plus something else. You also need, he explained to me, to feel you are sharing something with the other person, or the group, that is meaningful to *both* of you. You have to be in it together—and "it" can be anything that you both think has meaning and value. When you're in Times Square on your first afternoon in New York, you're not alone, but you feel lonely because nobody there cares about you, and you don't care about them. You aren't sharing your joy or your distress. You're nothing to the people around you, and they're nothing to you.

And when you are a patient in a hospital bed, you're not alone—but the help flows only one way. The nurse is there to help you, but you aren't there to help the nurse—and if you try, you'll be told to stop. A one-way relationship can't cure loneliness. Only two-way (or more) relationships can do that.

Loneliness isn't the physical absence of other people, he said—it's the sense that you're not sharing anything that matters with anyone else. If you have lots of people around you—perhaps even a husband or wife, or a family, or a busy workplace—but you don't share anything that matters with them, then you'll still be lonely. To end loneliness, you need to have a sense of "mutual aid and protection," John figured out, with at least one other person, and ideally many more.

~

I thought a lot about this. In the months after my last conversation with John, I kept noticing a self-help cliché that people say to each other all the time, and share on Facebook incessantly. We say to each other: "Nobody can help you except you."

It made me realize: we haven't just started doing things alone more, in every decade since the 1930s. We have started to believe that doing things alone is the natural state of human beings, and the only way to advance. We have begun to think: I will look after myself, and everybody else should look after themselves, as individuals. Nobody can help you but you. Nobody can help me but me. These ideas now run so deep in our culture that we even offer them as feel-good bromides to people who feel down—as if it will lift them up.

But John has proven that this is a denial of human history, and a denial of human nature. It leads us to misunderstand our most basic instincts. And this approach to life makes us feel terrible.

~

Back when John first started asking these questions in the 1970s, his professors had believed social factors were largely irrelevant (or too complex to study) if you wanted to figure out what happened in the brain as your mood and feelings changed. In the years since, John had proved conclusively that they can—on the contrary—be decisive. He pioneered a school of thinking differently about the brain, and it's come to be known as "social neuroscience." Your brain alters, according to how you use it—as I'll discuss later. He told me: "This notion that the brain is static and fixed is not accurate. It changes." Being lonely will change your brain; and coming out of loneliness will change your brain—so if you're not looking at both the brain *and* the social factors that change it, you can't understand what's really going on.

Your brain never was an island. It isn't one now.

~

And yet there is an obvious rebuttal to all this evidence that we are becoming disconnected, one that kept running through my mind. Yes, we have lost one kind of connection—but haven't we gained a whole new kind?

I just opened Facebook. Seventy of my friends, I see, are online now, across several continents. I could talk to them straight away. As I researched this book, I kept coming across this apparent contradiction: I was traveling across the world learning about how we had become profoundly disconnected—and then I would open my laptop, to be shown that we are more connected now than we have ever been at any point in human history.

A huge amount has been written about the way that our mental migration into cyberspace—our spending so much time online—is making us feel. But as I began to dig into this, I realized that we have been missing the most important point. The Internet arrived promising us connection at the very moment when all the wider forces of disconnection were reaching a crescendo.

I only really began to understand what this means when I went to the first rehab center for Internet addicts in the United States. But first of all we have to step back—to see why it was created.

~

One day in the mid-1990s, a twenty-five-year-old walked into Dr. Hilarie Cash's office, near the main Microsoft offices in Washington state. She was a psychotherapist and he was a handsome, smartly dressed young man. After some polite chitchat, he began to tell her about a problem.

James was from a small town, and he had always been the star at his school. He aced his tests and became the captain of one of the sports teams. He cakewalked into the Ivy League and left his community thrumming with pride. But then he arrived at his world-class university, and he felt terrified. For the first time in his life, he wasn't the smartest guy in the room. He looked at how people spoke, the rituals he was meant to take part in, the weird social groups that were forming, and he felt profoundly alone. So when other people were mingling, he went to his room, started up his computer, and launched a game called EverQuest. It was one of the earliest games that you could play simultaneously with many anonymous strangers somewhere out there in cyberspace. This way he could be with people, but in a world where there were clear, neat rules, and where he could be someone again.

James started skipping lectures and tutorials to play EverQuest. As the months passed, it took up more and more of his life. He was vanishing into this electronic world. After a while, the university told him he couldn't go on like this. But he kept returning to the game, as though it were a secret mistress who obsessed him.

When he was expelled, people back home were puzzled. He married his high school girlfriend and promised her he would give up gaming cold turkey. He got a job working with computers, and he seemed to be slowly getting back on track. But when he felt lonely, or confused, he felt intense cravings for the game. One night, he waited until his wife had gone to sleep, sneaked downstairs, and fired up EverQuest. Before long, this became a pattern. He was becoming a compulsive gamer on the down-low. Then one day he waited until his wife left for work, called in sick, and spent all day gaming. This, too, became a pattern. Eventually—just like at the university—his employers said they'd have to let him go. He couldn't bear to tell his wife, so he started to pay their bills on the credit card. The more stressed he became, the more he gamed.

By the time he arrived in Hilarie's therapy office, everything had fallen apart. His wife had realized what he had been doing, and he was suicidal.

When cases like these started to come through her door, Hilarie wasn't a specialist in problematic relationships with the Internet—because nobody was, back then in the mid-1990s. But she was receiving more and more clients like this who were compelled to spend their lives in online worlds. There was a woman who was addicted to online chats: she always had at least six windows open at the same time, imagining she was having a romantic relationship, or cybersex, with all of the people on the other side. There was another young man who couldn't stop playing an online version of Dungeons and Dragons. And on and on they came.

She didn't know what to do when it began. At first, "I was mostly going by instinct," she told me when we sat together in a diner in rural Washington state. There was no rule book for this. Now, when she looks back on those first patients, she said, "I feel like I was seeing the trickle before the flood. And this flood is becoming a tsunami."

~

I stepped out of the car into a clearing in the woods. The maple and cedar trees all around us were swaying a little in the wind. From what looked like a farmhouse, a little dog ran up to me, yapping. Somewhere in the distance, I could hear other animals making noises, but I wasn't sure what or where they were. I was standing in front of the first dedicated rehabilitation center for Internet and gaming addicts in the United States that Hilarie cofounded a decade ago, called reSTART Life.

As a reflex, without thinking, I checked my phone. There was no signal, and—absurdly—I felt a flicker of annoyance.

At first, I was shown around by two of the patients. Matthew was a skinny young Chinese American in his midtwenties, while Mitchell was a white guy, five years older—more of a bro, handsome, balding. This is the exercise room, they explained, where we have been lifting weights. This is the meditation hut, where we have been learning mindfulness. This is the kitchen, where we have been learning to cook.

And then we sat in the woods, just beyond the center, and talked. Matthew told me that when he felt alone, "I'd hide those feelings, and use the computer as a sort of escape," he says. Since his teens, he had become obsessed with the game League of Legends. "It's a five by five game," he told me. "There are five people on a team. You work together toward a common goal, and everyone has specific goals. It's very complex . . . I felt happy—hyperfocused on the game." Before he came to the center, he was playing it fourteen hours a day. He was already skinny, but he had lost thirty pounds because he didn't even want to break away in order to eat. He says: "I would just sit there pretty much the whole time."

Mitchell's story was a little different. For as long as he could remember, he would escape the isolation that came from a difficult home life by gathering information about anything that intrigued him. As a child, he would store huge piles of papers under his bed. Then, at the age of twelve, he discovered dial-up Internet, and he began to print out huge amounts to read, "until I passed out," he says. He could never regulate his ability to seek out information—to say: Okay, I've learned enough now. When he got a job as a software developer and he was given an assignment that made him feel pressured, he found himself endlessly chasing down Internet rabbit holes. He would have three hundred tabs open at any given time.

They felt very familiar to me, Matthew and Mitchell. If you're a typical Westerner in the twenty-first century, you check your phone once every six and a half minutes. If you're a teenager, you send on average a hundred texts a day. And 42 percent of us never turn off our phones. Ever.

When we look for an explanation for how this change happened, we keep being told it's mainly caused by something inside the technology itself. We talk about how each new e-mail that arrives in your in-box gives you a little dopamine hit. We say there's something about smartphones themselves that is addictive. We blame the device. But as I spent time in this Internet rehab center, and as I reflected on my own Internet use, I began to wonder if there was a different and more truthful way of thinking about it.

Of all the people they've treated at this rehab center, Hilarie told me, there are certain things almost everyone has in common. They were all anxious or depressed before the compulsion began. For the patient, the Internet obsession was a way of "escaping his anxiety, through distraction," she said. "That is their exact profile, ninety percent of the time."

Before the Internet addiction, they had felt lost and isolated in the world. Then the online world offered these young people things that they craved but that had vanished from the environment—such as a goal that matters to you, or a status, or a tribe. "The highly popular games," she says, "are the multiplayer games, where you get to be part of a guild—which is a team—and you get to earn your status in that guild. The positive side of that, these guys would say, is—'I'm a team player. I know how to cooperate with my guys.' It's tribalism at its core." Once you have that, Hilarie says, "you can immerse yourself in an alternate reality and completely lose track of where you are. You feel rewarded by the challenges of it, by the opportunity for cooperation, by the community that you're in, and have status in—and [you] have much more control over than the real world."

I thought a lot about this—about how the depression or anxiety *preceded* the compulsive Internet use for everyone here. The compulsive Internet use, she was saying, was a dysfunctional attempt to try to solve the pain they were already in, caused in part by feeling alone in the world. What if that applies not only to the people here, I wondered, but to many more of us?

The Internet was born into a world where many people had already lost their sense of connection to each other. The collapse had already been taking place for decades by then. The web arrived offering them a kind of parody of what they were losing—Facebook friends in place of neighbors, video games in place of meaningful work, status updates in place of status in the world. The comedian Marc Maron once wrote that "every status update is a just a variation on a single request: 'Would someone please acknowledge me?'"

Hilarie told me, "If the culture you are embedded in isn't healthy, you're going to end up with an unhealthy individual. So I've been thinking of that a lot lately. And then"—she ran her fingers through her hair and looked around her—"feeling discouraged." We are living, she has come to believe, in a culture where people are not "getting the connections that they need in order to be healthy human beings," and that is why we can't put down our smartphones, or bear to log off. We tell ourselves that we live so much of our lives in cyberspace because when we are there, we are connected—we are plugged into a swirling party with billions of people. "That is such BS," Hilarie said. She is not opposed to the technology at all—she's on Facebook, and likes it—but "I say it is not what you actually need" at your core. "The kind of connection we need is *this* connection"— she waved her hand between me and her—"which is face-to-face, where we are able to see, and touch, and smell, and hear each other . . . We're social creatures. We're meant to be in connection with one another in a safe, caring way, and when it's mediated by a screen, that's absolutely not there."

The difference between being online and being physically among people, I saw in that moment, is a bit like the difference between pornography and sex: it addresses a basic itch, but it's never satisfying. She looked at me, then glanced at my phone sitting there on the table. "Screen-mediated technology is not giving us what we actually need."

~

After all his years studying loneliness, John Cacioppo told me the evidence is clear: social media can't compensate us psychologically for what we have lost—social life.

But more than that—our obsessive use of social media is an attempt to fill a hole, a great hollowing, that took place before anyone had a smartphone. It is—like much of our depression and anxiety—another symptom of our current crisis.

~

Not long before I left the Internet rehab center, Mitchell—the bro-ish resident—told me he wanted to show me something. "It's just a really neat thing that I noticed happening over here," he said as we walked. "There's a spider's egg that hatched up in the tree. You could tell, because if you've seen [the animated film] *Charlotte's Web*, at the very end, the spiderlings hatch, and then they send out their streamers, and they float off. That's what's been happening! Every time there's a strong breeze, you see some lines shooting off the top of the tree."

He had been standing with the other guys in the rehab center discussing this web for hours, he said. He looked at one of the other residents and smiled.

In another context, I would have found this too hokey—look, the Internet addict is transferring from the World Wide Web to the joys of an actual spider's web, and a web of face-to-face connections with other people! But there was real joy in Mitchell's face, and it stopped me. We both looked at it for a long time. He stared at it, quietly. "It's just," he said, "a really interesting thing that I've never gotten to see before."

I felt moved, and promised myself I would learn from this moment.

And then, when I was ten minutes' drive from the center, I felt a pang of loneliness, and I noticed my phone reception had come back. I checked my e-mails right away.

~

These days, when my parents go back to the places where they grew up—which had been so rich with community when they were kids—they find that those places, too, have turned into another Edgware. People nod to each other and close their doors. This disconnection has spread over the entire Western world. There's a quote from the biologist E. O. Wilson that John Cacioppo—who has taught us so much about loneliness—likes: "People must belong to a tribe." Just like a bee goes haywire if it loses its hive, a human will go haywire if she loses her connection to the group.

John had discovered that we—without ever quite intending to—have become the first humans to ever dismantle our tribes. As a result, we have been left alone on a savanna we do not understand, puzzled by our own sadness.

CHAPTER 8

Cause Three: Disconnection from Meaningful Values

When I was in my late twenties, I got really fat. It was partly a side effect of antidepressants, and partly a side effect of fried chicken. I could still, from memory, talk you through the relative merits of all the fried chicken shops in East London that were the staples of my diet, from Chicken Cottage to Tennessee Fried Chicken (with its logo of a smiling cartoon chicken holding a bucket of fried chicken legs: who knew cannibalism could be an effective marketing tool?). My own favorite was the brilliantly named Chicken Chicken Chicken. Their hot wings were, to me, the Mona Lisa of grease.

One Christmas Eve, I went to my local branch of Kentucky Fried Chicken, and one of the staff behind the counter saw me approaching and beamed. "Johann!" he said. "We have something for you!" The other staff turned and looked at me expectantly. From somewhere behind the grill and the grizzle, he took out a Christmas card. I was forced, by their expectant smiles, to open it in front of them. "To our best customer," it said, next to personal messages from every member of the staff.

I never ate at KFC again.

Most of us know there is something wrong with our physical diets. We aren't all gold medalists in the consumption of lard like I was, but more and more of us are eating the wrong things, and it is making us physically sick. As I investigated depression and anxiety, I began to learn something similar is happening to our values—and it is making many of us emotionally sick.

This was discovered by an American psychologist named Tim Kasser—so I went to see him, to learn his story.

~

As a little boy, Tim arrived in the middle of a long stretch of swampland and open beaches. His dad worked as a manager at an insurance company, and in the early 1970s, he was posted to a place called Pinellas County, on the west coast of Florida. The area was mostly undeveloped and had plenty of big, broad outdoor spaces for a kid to play—but this county soon became the fastest-growing in the entire United States, and it was about to be transformed in front of Tim's eyes. "By the time I left Florida," he told me, "it was a completely different physical environment. You couldn't drive along the beach roads anymore and see the water, because it was all condos and high-rises. Areas that had been open land with alligators and rattlesnakes . . . [became] subdivision after subdivision after shopping mall."

Tim was drawn to the shopping malls that replaced the beaches and marshes, like all the other kids he knew. There, he would play Asteroids and Space Invaders for hours. He soon found himself longing for stuff—the toys he saw in ads.

It sounds like Edgware, where I am from. I was eight or nine when its shopping mall—the Broadwalk Centre—opened, and I remember wandering around its bright storefronts and gazing at the things I wanted to buy in a thrilled trance. I obsessively coveted the green plastic toy of Castle Grayskull, the fortress where the cartoon character He-Man lived, and Care-a-Lot, the home in the clouds of some animated creatures called the Care Bears. One Christmas, my mother missed my hints and failed to buy me Care-a-Lot, and I was crestfallen for months. I ached and pined for that lump of plastic.

Like most kids at the time, I spent at least three hours a day watching TV—usually more—and whole days would pass in the summer when my only break from television would be to go to the Broadwalk Centre and back again. I don't remember anyone ever telling me this explicitly, but it seemed to me then that happiness meant being able to buy lots of the things on display there. I think my nine-year-old self, if you had asked him what it meant to be happy, would have said: somebody who could walk through the Broadwalk Centre and buy whatever he wanted. I would ask my dad how much each famous person I saw on television earned, and he would guess, and we would both marvel at what we would do with the money. It was a little bonding ritual, over a fantasy of spending.

I asked Tim if, in Pinellas County where he grew up, he ever heard anyone talking about a different way of valuing things, beyond the idea that happiness came from getting and possessing stuff. "Well—I think—not growing up. No," he said. In Edgware, there must have been people who acted on different values, but I don't think I ever saw them.

When Tim was a teenager, his swim coach moved away one summer and gave him a small record collection, and it included albums by John Lennon and Bob Dylan. As he listened to them, he realized they seemed to be expressing something he didn't really hear anywhere else. He began to wonder if there were hints of a different way to live lying in their lyrics, but he couldn't find anyone to discuss it with.

It was only when Tim went to study at Vanderbilt University, a very conservative college in the South, at the height of the Reagan years, that it occurred to him—slowly—to think more deeply about this. In 1984, he voted for Ronald Reagan, but he was starting to think a lot about the question of authenticity. "I was stumbling around," he told me. "I think I was questioning just about everything. I wasn't just questioning these values. I was questioning lots about myself, I was questioning lots about the nature of reality and the values of society." He feels like there were piñatas all around him and he was hitting chaotically at them all. He added: "I think I went through that phase for a long time, to be honest."

When he went to graduate school, he started to read a lot about psychology. It was around this time that Tim realized something odd.

For thousands of years, philosophers had been suggesting that if you overvalue money and possessions, or if you think about life mainly in terms of how you look to other people, you will be unhappy—that the values of Pinellas County and Edgware were, in some deep sense, mistaken. It had been talked about a lot, by some of the finest minds who ever lived, and Tim thought it might be true. But nobody had ever conducted a scientific investigation to see whether all these philosophers were right.

This realization is what launched him on a project that he was going to pursue for the next twenty-five years. It led him to discover subtle evidence about why we feel the way we do—and why it is getting worse.

~

It all started in grad school, with a simple survey.

Tim came up with a way of measuring how much a person really values getting things and having money compared to other values, like spending time with their family or trying to make the world a better place. He called it the Aspiration Index, and it is pretty straightforward. You ask people how much they agree with statements such as "It is important to have expensive possessions" and how much they agree with very different statements such as "It is important to make the world a better place for others." You can then calculate their values.

At the same time, you can ask people lots of other questions—and one of them is whether they are unhappy or if they are suffering (or have suffered) from depression or anxiety. Then—as a first step—you see if they match.

Tim's first tentative piece of research was to give this survey to 316 students. When the results came back and were all calculated out, Tim was struck by the results: materialistic people, who think happiness comes from accumulating stuff and a superior status, had much higher levels of depression and anxiety.

This was, he knew, just a primitive first shot in the dark. So Tim's next step was—as part of a larger study—to get a clinical psychologist to assess 140 eighteen-year-olds in depth, calculating where they were on the Aspiration Index and if they were depressed or anxious. When the results were added up, they were the same: the more the kids valued getting things and being seen to have things, the more likely they were to be suffering from depression and anxiety.

Was this something that happened only with young people? To find out, Tim measured one hundred citizens of Rochester in upstate New York, who came from a range of age groups and economic backgrounds. The result was the same.

But how could he figure out what was really happening—and why?

Tim's next step was to conduct a more detailed study, to track how these values affect you over time. He got 192 students to keep a detailed mood diary in which, twice a day, they had to record how much they were feeling nine different emotions, such as happiness or anger, and how much they were experiencing any of nine physical symptoms, such as backache. When he calculated out the results, he found—again—higher depression among the materialistic students; but there was a result more important than that. It really did seem that materialistic people were having a worse time, day by day, on all sorts of fronts. They felt sicker, and they were angrier. "Something about a strong desire for materialistic pursuits," he was starting to believe, "actually affected the participants' day-to-day lives, and decreased the quality of their daily experience." They experienced less joy, and more despair.

~

Why would this be? What could be happening here? Ever since the 1960s, psychologists have known that there are two different ways you can motivate yourself to get out of bed in the morning. The first are called *intrinsic* motives—they are the things you do purely because you value them in and of themselves, not because of anything you get out of them. When a kid plays, she's acting totally on intrinsic motives—she's doing it because it gives her joy. The other day, I asked my friend's five-year-old son why he was playing. "Because I love it," he said. Then he scrunched up his face and said "You're silly!" and ran off, pretending to be Batman. These intrinsic motivations persist all through our lives, long after childhood.

At the same time, there's a rival set of values, which are called *extrinsic* motives. They're the things you do not because you actually want to do them, but because you'll get something in return—whether it's money, or admiration, or sex, or superior status. Joe, who you met two chapters ago, went to work every day in the paint shop for purely extrinsic reasons— he hated the job, but he needed to be able to pay the rent, buy the Oxy that would numb his way through the day, and have the car and clothes that he thought made people respect him. We all have some motives like that.

Imagine you play the piano. If you play it for yourself because you love it, then you are being driven to do it by intrinsic values. If you play in a dive bar you hate, just to make enough cash to ensure you don't get thrown out of your apartment, then you are being driven to do it by extrinsic values.

These rival sets of values exist in all of us. Nobody is driven totally by one or the other.

Tim began to wonder if looking into this conflict more deeply could reveal something important. So he started to study a group of two hundred people in detail over time. He got them to lay out their goals for the future. He then figured out with them if these were extrinsic goals— like getting a promotion, or a bigger apartment—or intrinsic goals, like being a better friend or a more loving son or a better piano player. And then he got them to keep a detailed mood diary.

What he wanted to know was—Does achieving extrinsic goals make you happy? And how does that compare to achieving intrinsic goals?

The results, when he calculated them out, were quite startling. People who achieved their extrinsic goals didn't experience *any* increase in day-to-day happiness—none. They spent a huge amount of energy chasing these goals, but when they fulfilled them, they felt the same as they had at the start. Your promotion? Your fancy car? The new iPhone? The expensive necklace? They won't improve your happiness even one inch.

But people who achieved their intrinsic goals *did* become significantly happier, and less depressed and anxious. You could track the movement. As they worked at it and felt they became (for example) a better friend— not because they wanted anything out of it but because they felt it was a good thing to do—they became more satisfied with life. Being a better dad? Dancing for the sheer joy of it? Helping another person, just because it's the right thing to do? They do significantly boost your happiness.

Yet most of us, most of the time, spend our time chasing extrinsic goals—the very thing that will give us nothing. Our whole culture is set up to get us to think this way. Get the right grades. Get the best-paying job. Rise through the ranks. Display your earnings through clothes and cars. That's how to make yourself feel good.

What Tim had discovered is that the message our culture is telling us about how to have a decent and satisfying life, virtually all the time, is not true. The more this was studied, the clearer it became. Twenty-two different studies have, in the years since, found that the more materialistic and extrinsically motivated you become, the more depressed you will be. Twelve different studies found that the more materialistic and extrinsically motivated you become, the more anxious you will be. Similar studies, inspired by Tim's work and using similar techniques, have now been carried out in Britain, Denmark, Germany, India, South Korea, Russia, Romania, Australia, and Canada—and the results, all over the world, keep coming back the same.

~

Just as we have shifted en masse from eating food to eating junk food, Tim has discovered—in effect—that we have shifted from having meaningful values to having junk values. All this mass-produced fried chicken looks like food, and it appeals to the part of us that evolved to need food; yet it doesn't give us what we need from food—nutrition. Instead, it fills us with toxins.

In the same way, all these materialistic values, telling us to spend our way to happiness, look like real values; they appeal to the part of us that has evolved to need some basic principles to guide us through life; yet they don't give us what we need from values—a path to a satisfying life. Instead, they fill us with psychological toxins. Junk food is distorting our bodies. Junk values are distorting our minds.

Materialism is KFC for the soul.

~

When Tim studied this in greater depth, he was able to identify at least four key reasons why junk values are making us feel so bad.

The first is that thinking extrinsically poisons your relationships with other people. He teamed up again with another professor, Richard Ryan—who had been an ally from the start—to study two hundred people in depth, and they found that the more materialistic you become, the shorter your relationships will be, and the worse their quality will be. If you value people for how they look, or how they impress other people, it's easy to see that you'll be happy to dump them if someone hotter or more impressive comes along. And at the same time, if all you're interested in is the surface of another person, it's easy to see why you'll be less rewarding to be around, and they'll be more likely to dump you, too. You will have fewer friends and connections, and they won't last as long.

~

Their second finding relates to another change that happens as you become more driven by junk values. Let's go back to the example of playing the piano. Every day, Tim spends at least half an hour playing the piano and singing, often with his kids. He does it for no reason except that he loves it—it makes him, on a good day, feel satisfied, and joyful. He feels his ego dissolve, and he is purely present in the moment. There's strong scientific evidence that we all get most pleasure from what are called "flow states" like this—moments when we simply lose ourselves doing something we love and are carried along in the moment. They're proof we can maintain the pure intrinsic motivation that a child feels when she is playing.

But when Tim studied highly materialistic people, he discovered they experience significantly fewer flow states than the rest of us. Why would that be?

He seems to have found an explanation. Imagine if, when Tim was playing the piano every day, he kept thinking: Am I the best piano player in Illinois? Are people going to applaud this performance? Am I going to get paid for this? How much? Suddenly his joy would shrivel up like a salted snail. Instead of his ego dissolving, his ego would be aggravated and jabbed and poked.

That is what your head starts to look like when you become more materialistic. If you are doing something not for itself but to achieve an effect, you can't relax into the pleasure of a moment. You are constantly monitoring yourself. Your ego will shriek like an alarm you can't shut off.

~

This leads to a third reason why junk values make you feel so bad. When you are extremely materialistic, Tim said to me, "you've always kind of got to be wondering about yourself—how are people judging you?" It forces you to "focus on other people's opinions of you, and their praise of you—and then you're kind of locked into having to worry what other people think about you, and if other people are going to give you those rewards that you want. That's a heavy load to bear, instead of walking around doing what it is you're interested in doing, or being around people who love you just for who you are."

If "your self-esteem, your sense of self-worth, is contingent upon how much money you've got, or what your clothes are like, or how big your house is," you are forced into constant external comparisons, Tim says. "There's always somebody who's got a nicer house or better clothes or more money." Even if you're the richest person in the world, how long will that last? Materialism leaves you constantly vulnerable to a world beyond your control.

~

And then, he says, there is a crucial fourth reason. It's worth pausing on this one, because I think it's the most important.

All of us have certain innate needs—to feel connected, to feel valued, to feel secure, to feel we make a difference in the world, to have autonomy, to feel we're good at something. Materialistic people, he believes, are less happy—because they are chasing a way of life that does a bad job of meeting these needs.

What you really need are connections. But what you are *told* you need, in our culture, is stuff and a superior status, and in the gap between those two signals—from yourself and from society—depression and anxiety will grow as your real needs go unmet.

You have to picture all the values that guide why you do things in your life, Tim said, as being like a pie. "Each value" you have, he explained, "is like a slice of that pie. So you've got your spirituality slice, and your family slice, and your money slice, and your hedonism slice. We've all got all the slices." When you become obsessed with materialism and status, that slice gets bigger. And "the bigger one slice gets, the smaller other slices have to get." So if you become fixated on getting stuff and a superior status, the parts of the pie that care about tending to your relationships, or finding meaning, or making the world better have to shrink, to make way.

"On Friday at four, I can stay [in my office] and work more—or I can go home and play with my kids," he told me. "I can't do both. It's one or the other. If my materialistic values are bigger, I'm going to stay and work. If my family values are bigger, I'm going to go home and play with my kids." It's not that materialistic people don't care about their kids—but "as the materialistic values get bigger, other values are necessarily going to be crowded out," he says, even if you tell yourself they won't.

And the pressure, in our culture, runs overwhelmingly one way—spend more; work more. We live under a system, Tim says, that constantly "distracts us from what's really good about life." We are being propagandized to live in a way that doesn't meet our basic psychological needs—so we are left with a permanent, puzzling sense of dissatisfaction.

~

For millennia, humans have talked about something called the Golden Rule. It's the idea that you should do unto others as you would have them do unto you. Tim, I think, has discovered something we should call the I-Want-Golden-Things Rule. The more you think life is about having stuff and superiority and showing it off, the more unhappy, and the more depressed and anxious, you will be.

~

But why would human beings turn, so dramatically, to something that made us less happy and more depressed? Isn't it implausible that we would do something so irrational? In the later phase of his research, Tim began to dig into the question.

Nobody's values are totally fixed. Your level of junk values, Tim discovered by following people in his studies, can change over your lifetime. You can become more materialistic, and more unhappy; or you can become less materialistic, and less unhappy. So we shouldn't be asking, Tim believes, "Who is materialistic?" We should be asking: "*When* are people materialistic?" Tim wanted to know: What causes the variation?

There's an experiment, by a different group of social scientists, that gives us one early clue. In 1978, two Canadian social scientists got a bunch of four- and five-year-old kids and divided them into two groups. The first group was shown no commercials. The second group was shown two commercials for a particular toy. Then they offered these four- or five-year-old kids a choice. They told them: You have to choose, now, to play with one of these two boys here. You can play with this little boy who has the toy from the commercials—but we have to warn you, he's not a nice boy. He's mean. Or you can play with a boy who doesn't have the toy, but who is really nice.

If they had seen the commercial for the toy, the kids mostly chose to play with the mean boy with the toy. If they hadn't seen the commercial, they mostly chose to play with the nice boy who had no toys.

In other words, the advertisements led them to choose an inferior human connection over a superior human connection—because they'd been primed to think that a lump of plastic is what really matters.

Two commercials—just two—did that. Today, every person sees way more advertising messages than that in an average morning. More eighteen-month-olds can recognize the McDonald's *M* than know their own surname. By the time an average child is thirty-six months old, she already knows a hundred brand logos.

Tim suspected that advertising plays a key role in why we are, every day, choosing a value system that makes us feel worse. So with another social scientist named Jean Twenge, he tracked the percentage of total U.S. national wealth that's spent on advertising, from 1976 to 2003—and he discovered that the more money is spent on ads, the more materialistic teenagers become.

A few years ago, an advertising agency head named Nancy Shalek explained approvingly: "Advertising at its best is making people feel that without their product, you're a loser. Kids are very sensitive to that . . . You open up emotional vulnerabilities, and it's very easy to do with kids because they're the most emotionally vulnerable."

This sounds harsh, until you think through the logic. Imagine if I watched an ad and it told me—Johann, you're fine how you are. You look good. You smell good. You're likable. People want to be around you. You've got enough stuff now. You don't need any more. Enjoy life.

That would—from the perspective of the advertising industry—be the worst ad in human history, because I wouldn't want to go out shopping, or lunge at my laptop to spend, or do any of the other things that feed my junk values. It would make me want to pursue my intrinsic values—which involve a whole lot less spending, and a whole lot more happiness.

When they talk among themselves, advertising people have been admitting since the 1920s that their job is to make people feel inadequate— and then offer their product as the solution to the sense of inadequacy they have created. Ads are the ultimate frenemy—they're always saying: Oh babe, *I* want you to look/smell/feel great; it makes me so sad that that at the moment you're ugly/stinking/miserable; here's this thing that will make you into the person you and I really want you to be. Oh, did I mention you have to pay a few bucks? I just want you to be the person you deserve to be. Isn't that worth a few dollars? You're worth it.

This logic radiates out through the culture, and we start to impose it on each other, even when ads aren't there. Why did I, as a child, crave Nike air-pumps, even though I was as likely to play basketball as I was to go to the moon? It was partly because of the ads—but mostly because the ads created a group dynamic among everyone I knew. It created a marker of status, that we then policed. As adults, we do the same, only in slightly more subtle ways.

This system trains us, Tim says, to feel "there's never enough. When you're focused on money and status and possessions, consumer society is always telling you more, more, more, more. Capitalism is always telling you more, more, more. Your boss is telling you work more, work more, work more. You internalize that and you think: Oh, I've got to work more, because my self depends on my status and my achievement. You internalize that. It's a kind of form of internalized oppression."

He believes it also explains why junk values lead to such an increase in anxiety. "You're always thinking—Are they going to reward me? Does the person love me for who I am, or for my handbag? Am I going to be able to climb the ladder of success?" he said. You are hollow, and exist only in other people's reflections. "That's going to be anxiety-provoking."

We are all vulnerable to this, he believes. "The way I understand the intrinsic values," Tim told me, is that they "are a fundamental part of what we are as humans, but they're fragile. It's easy to distract us from them . . . You give people social models of consumerism . . . and they move in an extrinsic way." The desire to find meaningful intrinsic values is "there, it's a powerful part of who we are, but it's not hard to distract us." And we have an economic system built around doing precisely that.

~

As I sat with Tim, discussing all this for hours, I kept thinking of a middle-class married couple who live in a nice semidetached house in the suburbs in Edgware, where we grew up. They are close to me; I have known them all my life; I love them.

If you peeked through their window, you'd think they have everything you need for happiness—each other, two kids, a good home, all the consumer goods we're told to buy. Both of them work really hard at jobs they have little interest in, so that they can earn money, and with the money they earn, they buy the things that we have learned from television will make us happy—clothes and cars, gadgets and status symbols. They display these things to people they know on social media, and they get lots of likes and comments like "OMG—so jealous!" After the brief buzz that comes from displaying their goods, they usually find they become dissatisfied and down again. They are puzzled by this, and they often assume it's because they didn't buy the right thing. So they work harder, and they buy more goods, display them through their devices, feel the buzz, and then slump back to where they started.

They both seem to me to be depressed. They alternate between being blank, or angry, or engaging in compulsive behaviors. She had a drug problem for a long time, although not anymore; he gambles online at least two hours a day. They are furious a lot of the time, at each other, at their children, at their colleagues, and, diffusely, at the world— at anyone else on the road when they are driving, for example, who they scream and swear at. They have a sense of anxiety they can't shake off, and they often attach it to things outside them—she obsessively monitors where her teenage son is at any moment, and is afraid all the time that he will be a victim of crime or terrorism.

This couple has no vocabulary to understand why they feel so bad. They are doing what the culture has been priming them to do since we were infants—they are working hard and buying the right things, the expensive things. They are every advertising slogan made flesh.

Like the kids in the sandbox, they have been primed to lunge for objects and ignore the prospect of interaction with the people around them.

I saw now they aren't just suffering from the absence of something, such as meaningful work, or community. They are also suffering from the *presence* of something—an incorrect set of values telling them to seek happiness in all the wrong places, and to ignore the potential human connections that are right in front of them.

When Tim discovered all these facts, it didn't just guide his scientific work. He began to move toward a life that made it possible for him to live consistent with his own findings—to go back, in a sense, to something more like the beach he had discovered joyfully in Florida as a kid. "You've got to pull yourself out of the materialistic environments—the environments that are reinforcing the materialistic values," he says, because they cripple your internal satisfactions. And then, he says, to make that sustainable, you have to "replace them with actions that are going to provide those intrinsic satisfactions, [and] encourage those intrinsic goals."

So, with his wife and his two sons, he moved to a farmhouse on ten acres of land in Illinois, where they live with a donkey and a herd of goats. They have a small TV in the basement, but it isn't connected to any stations or to cable—it's just to watch old movies on sometimes. They only recently got the Internet (against his protestations), and they don't use it much. He works part time, and so does his wife, "so we could spend more time with our kids, and be in the garden more and do volunteer work and do activism work and I could write more"—all the things that give them intrinsic satisfaction. "We play a lot of games. We play a lot of music. We have a lot of family conversations." They sing together.

Where they live in western Illinois is "not the most exciting place in the world," Tim says, "but I have ten acres of land, I have a twelve-minute commute with one flashing light and three stop signs on my way to my office, and we afford that on one [combined full-time] salary."

I ask him if he had withdrawal symptoms from the materialistic world we were both immersed in for so long. "Never," he says right away. "People ask me that: "Don't you miss this? Don't you wish you had that?" No, I don't, because [I am] never exposed to the messages telling me that I should want it . . . I don't expose myself to those things, so—no, I don't have that."

One of his proudest moments was when one of his sons came home one day and said: "Dad, some kids at school are making fun of my sneakers." They were not a brand name, or shiny-new. "Oh, what'd you say to them?" Tim asked. His son explained he looked at them and said: "Why do you care?" He was nonplussed—he could see that what they valued was empty, and absurd.

By living without these polluting values, Tim has, he says, discovered a secret. This way of life is more pleasurable than materialism. "It's more fun to play these games with your kids," he told me. "It's more fun to do the intrinsically motivated stuff than to go to work and do stuff you don't necessarily want to do. It's more fun to feel like people love you for who you are—instead of lov[ing] you because you gave them a big diamond ring."

Most people know all this in their hearts, he believes. "At some level I really believe that most people know that intrinsic values are what's going to give them a good life," he told me. When you do surveys and ask people what's most important in life, they almost always name personal growth and relationships as the top two. "But I think part of why people are depressed is that our society is not set up in order to help people live lifestyles, have jobs, participate in the economy, [or] participate in their neighborhoods" in ways that support their intrinsic values. The change Tim saw happening in Florida as a kid—when the beachfronts were transformed into shopping malls and people shifted their attention there—has happened to the whole culture.

Tim told me people can apply these insights to their own life, on their own, to some extent. "The first thing is for people to ask themselves—Am I setting up my life so I can have a chance of succeeding at my intrinsic values? Am I hanging out with the right people, who are going to make me feel loved, as opposed to making me feel like I made it? . . . Those are hard choices sometimes." But often, he says, you will hit up against a limit in our culture. You can make improvements, but often "the solutions to the problems that I'm interested in can't be easily solved at the individual person level, or in the therapeutic consulting room, or by a pill." They require something more—as I was going to explore later.

When I interviewed Tim, I felt he solved a mystery for me. I had been puzzled back in Philadelphia about why Joe didn't leave the job he hated at the paint company and go become a fisherman in Florida, when he knew life in the Sunshine State would make him so much happier. It seemed like a metaphor for why so many of us stay in situations we know make us miserable.

I think I see why now. Joe is constantly bombarded with messages that he shouldn't do the thing that his heart is telling him would make him feel calm and satisfied. The whole logic of our culture tells him to stay on the consumerist treadmill, to go shopping when he feels lousy, to chase junk values. He has been immersed in those messages since the day he was born. So he has been trained to distrust his own wisest instincts.

When I yelled after him "Go to Florida!" I was yelling into a hurricane of messages, and a whole value system, that is saying the exact opposite.

CHAPTER 9

Cause Four: Disconnection from Childhood Trauma

When the women first came into Dr. Vincent Felitti's office, some of them found it hard to fit through the door. These patients weren't just a bit overweight: they were eating so much that they were rendering themselves diabetic and destroying their own internal organs. They didn't seem to be able to stop themselves. They were assigned here, to his clinic, as their last chance.

It was the mid-1980s, and in the California city of San Diego, Vincent had been commissioned by the not-for-profit medical provider Kaiser Permanente to look into the fastest-growing driver of their costs—obesity. Nothing they were trying was working, so he was given a blank sheet of paper. Start from scratch, they said. Total blue-sky thinking. Figure out what we can do to deal with this. And so the patients began to come. But what he was going to learn from them led—in fact—to a major breakthrough in a very different area: how we think about depression and anxiety.

~

As he tried to scrape away all the assumptions that surround obesity, Vincent learned about a new diet plan based on a maddeningly simple thought. It asked: What if these severely overweight people simply stopped eating, and lived off the fat stores they'd built up in their bodies until they were down to a normal weight? What would happen?

In the news, curiously, there had recently been an experiment in which this was tried, eight thousand miles away, for somewhat strange reasons. For years in Northern Ireland, if you were put in jail for being part of the Irish Republican Army's violent campaign to drive the British out of Northern Ireland, you were classed as a political prisoner. That meant you were treated differently from people who committed (say) bank robberies. You were allowed to wear your own clothes, and you didn't have to perform the same work as other inmates.

The British government decided to shut down that distinction, and they argued that the prisoners were simply common criminals and shouldn't get this different treatment anymore. So the prisoners decided to protest by going on a hunger strike. They began, slowly, to waste away.

So the designers of this new diet proposal looked into the medical evidence about these Northern Ireland hunger strikers to find out what killed them. It turns out that the first problem they faced was a lack of potassium and magnesium. Without them, your heart stops beating properly. Okay, the radical dieters thought—what if you give people supplements of potassium and magnesium? Then that doesn't happen. If you have enough fat on you, you get a few more months more to live—until a protein deficiency kills you.

Okay—what if you also give people the supplements that will prevent that? Then, it turns out, you get a year to live—provided there's enough fat. Then you'll die from a lack of vitamin C—scurvy—or other deficiencies.

Okay—what if you give people supplements for that, too? Then it looks as though you'll stay alive, Vincent discovered in the medical literature, and healthy, and you'll lose three hundred pounds a year. Then you can start eating again, at a healthy level.

All this suggested that in theory, even the most obese person would be down to a normal weight within a manageable time. The patients coming to him had been through everything—every fad diet, every shaming, every prodding and pulling. Nothing had worked. They were ready to try anything. So—under careful monitoring, and with lots of supervision—they began this program. And as the months passed, Vincent noticed something. It worked. The patients were shedding weight. They were not getting sick—in fact, they were returning to health. People who had been rendered disabled by constant eating started to see their bodies transform in front of them.

Their friends and relatives applauded. People who knew them were amazed. Vincent believed he might have found the solution to extreme overweight. "I thought—my god, we've got this problem licked," he said.

And then something happened that Vincent never expected.

~

In the program, there were some stars—people who shed remarkable amounts of weight, remarkably quickly. The medical team—and all their friends—expected these people who had been restored to health to react with joy. Except they didn't react that way.

The people who did best, and lost the most weight, were often thrown into a brutal depression, or panic, or rage. Some of them became suicidal. Without their bulk, they felt they couldn't cope. They felt unbelievably vulnerable. They often fled the program, gorged on fast food, and put their weight back on very fast.

Vincent was baffled. They were fleeing from a healthy body they now knew they could achieve, toward an unhealthy body they knew would kill them. Why? He didn't want to be an arrogant, moralistic doctor, standing over his patients, wagging his finger and telling them they were ruining their lives—that's not his character. He genuinely wanted to help them save themselves. So he felt desperate. That's why he did something no scientist in this field had done with really obese people before. He stopped telling them what to do—and started listening to them instead. He called in the people who had panicked when they started to shed the pounds, and asked them: What happened when you lost weight? How did you feel?

There was one twenty-eight-year-old woman, who I'll call Susan to protect her medical confidentiality. In fifty-one weeks, Vincent had taken Susan down from 408 pounds to 132 pounds. It looked like he had saved her life. Then—quite suddenly, for no reason anyone could see—she put on 37 pounds in the space of three weeks. Before long, she was back above 400 pounds. So Vincent asked her gently what had changed when she started to lose weight. It seemed mysterious to both of them. They talked for a long time. There was, she said eventually, one thing. When she was very obese, men never hit on her—but when she got down to a healthy weight, one day she was propositioned by a man, a colleague who she happened to know was married. She fled, and right away began to eat compulsively, and she couldn't stop.

This was when Vincent thought to ask a question he hadn't asked his patients before. When did you start to put on weight? If it was (say) when you were thirteen, or when you went to college—why then, and not a year before, or a year after?

Susan thought about the question. She had started to put on weight when she was eleven years old, she said. So he asked: Was there anything else that happened in your life when you were eleven? Well, Susan replied—that was when my grandfather began to rape me.

Vincent began to ask all his patients these three simple questions. How did you feel when you lost weight? When in your life did you start to put on weight? What else happened around that time? As he spoke to the 183 people on the program, he started to notice some patterns. One woman started to rapidly put on weight when she was twenty-three. What happened then? She was raped. She looked at the ground after she confessed this, and said softly: "Overweight is overlooked, and that's the way I need to be."

"I was incredulous," he told me when I sat with him in San Diego. "It seemed every other person I was asking was acknowledging such a history. I kept thinking—it can't be. People would know if this was true. Somebody would've told me. Isn't that what medical school is for?" When five of his colleagues came in to conduct further interviews, it turned out some 55 percent of the patients in the program had been sexually abused— far more than people in the wider population. And even more, including most of the men, had had severely traumatic childhoods.

Many of these women had been making themselves obese for an unconscious reason: to protect themselves from the attention of men, who they believed would hurt them. Being very fat stops most men from looking at you that way. It works. It was when he was listening to another grueling account of sexual abuse that it hit Vincent. He told me later: "What we had perceived as the problem—major obesity—was in fact, very frequently, the solution to problems that the rest of us knew nothing about."

Vincent began to wonder if the anti-obesity programs—including his own—had been doing it all wrong, by (for example) giving out nutritional advice. Obese people didn't need to be told what to eat; they knew the nutritional advice better than he did. They needed someone to understand why they ate. After meeting a person who had been raped, he told me, "I thought with a tremendously clear insight that sending this woman to see a dietitian to learn how to eat right would be grotesque."

Far from teaching the obese people, he realized they were the people who could teach him what was really going on. So he gathered the patients in groups of around fifteen, and asked them: "Why do you think people get fat? Not how. How is obvious. I'm asking why . . . What are the benefits?" Encouraged to think about it for the first time, they told him. The answers came in three different categories. The first was that it is sexually protective: men are less interested in you, so you are safer. The second was that it is physically protective: for example, in the program there were two prison guards, who lost between 100 and 150 pounds each. Suddenly, as they shed their bulk, they felt much more vulnerable among the prisoners—they could be more easily beaten up. To walk through those cell blocks with confidence, they explained, they needed to be the size of a refrigerator.

And the third category was that it reduced people's expectations of them. "You apply for a job weighing four hundred pounds, people assume you're stupid, lazy," Vincent said. If you've been badly hurt by the world—and sexual abuse is not the only way this can happen—you often want to retreat. Putting on a lot of weight is—paradoxically—a way of becoming invisible to a lot of humanity.

"When you look at a house burning down, the most obvious manifestation is the huge smoke billowing out," he told me. It would be easy, then, to think that the smoke is the problem, and if you deal with the smoke, you've solved it. But "thank God that fire departments understand that the piece that you treat is the piece you don't see—the flames inside, not the smoke billowing out. Otherwise, house fires would be treated by bringing big fans to blow the smoke away. [And that would] make the house burn down faster."

Obesity, he realized, isn't the fire. It's the smoke.

∼

One day, Vincent went to a medical conference dedicated to obesity to present his findings. After he had spoken, a doctor stood up in the audience and explained: "People who are more familiar with these matters recognize that these statements by patients"—describing their sexual abuse—"are basically fabrications, to provide a cover for their failed lives."

It turned out people treating obesity had noticed before that a disproportionate number of obese people described being abused. They just assumed that they were making excuses.

Vincent was horrified. He had in fact verified the abuse claims of many of his patients—by talking to their relatives, or to law enforcement officials who had investigated them. But he knew he didn't have hard scientific proof yet to rebut people like this. His impressions from talking to individual patients—even gathering the figures from within his group— didn't prove much. He wanted to gather proper scientific data. So he teamed up with a scientist named Dr. Robert Anda, who had specialized for years in the study of why people do self-destructive things like smoking. Together, funded by the Centers for Disease Control—a major U.S. agency funding medical research—they drew up a way of testing all this, to see if it was true beyond the small sample of people in Vincent's program.

They called it the Adverse Childhood Experiences (ACE) Study— and it's quite simple. It's a questionnaire. You are asked about ten different categories of terrible things that can happen to you when you're a kid— from being sexually abused, to being emotionally abused, to being neglected. And then there's a detailed medical questionnaire, to test for all sorts of things that could be going wrong with you, like obesity, or addiction. One of the things they added to the list—almost as an afterthought—was the question: Are you suffering from depression?

This survey was then given to seventeen thousand people who were seeking health care—for a whole range of reasons—from Kaiser Permanente in San Diego. The people who filled in the form were somewhat wealthier and a little older than the general population, but otherwise fairly representative of the city's population.

When the results came in, they added them up—at first, to see if there were any correlations.

It turned out that for every category of traumatic experience you went through as a kid, you were radically more likely to become depressed as an adult. If you had six categories of traumatic events in your childhood, you were *five times* more likely to become depressed as an adult than somebody who didn't have any. If you had seven categories of traumatic events as a child, you were 3,100 percent more likely to attempt to commit suicide as an adult.

"When the results came out, I was in a state of disbelief," Dr. Anda told me. "I looked at it and I said—really? This can't be true." You just don't get figures like this in medicine very often. Crucially, they hadn't just stumbled on proof that there is a correlation—that these two things happen at the same time. They seemed to have found evidence that these traumas help cause these problems. How do we know? The greater the trauma, the greater your risk of depression, anxiety, or suicide. The technical term for this is "dose-response effect." The more cigarettes you smoke, the more your risk of lung cancer goes up—that's one reason we know smoking causes cancer. In the same way, the more you were traumatized as a child, the more your risk of depression rises.

Curiously, it turned out emotional abuse was more likely to cause depression than any other kind of trauma—even sexual molestation. Being treated cruelly by your parents was the biggest driver of depression, out of all these categories.

When they showed the results to other scientists—including the Centers for Disease Control (CDC), who cofunded the research—they too were incredulous. "The study shocked people," Dr. Anda told me. "People didn't want to believe it. People at the CDC didn't want to believe it. There was resistance within the CDC when I brought the data around, and the medical journals [initially] didn't want to believe it, because it was so astonishing that they had to doubt it. Because it made them challenge the way they thought about childhood ... It challenged so many things, all at one time." In the years that followed, the study has been replicated many times—and it always finds similar results. But we have barely begun, Vincent told me, to think through its implications.

~

So Vincent—as he absorbed all this—came to believe that we have been making the same mistake with depression that he had been making before with obesity. We have failed to see it as a symptom of something deeper that needs to be dealt with. There's a house fire inside many of us, Vincent had come to believe, and we've been concentrating on the smoke.

Many scientists and psychologists had been presenting depression as an irrational malfunction in your brain or in your genes, but he learned that Allen Barbour, an internist at Stanford University, had said that depression isn't a disease; depression is a normal response to abnormal life experiences. "I think that's a very important idea," Vincent told me. "It takes you beyond the comforting, limited idea that the reason I'm depressed is I have a serotonin imbalance, or a dopamine imbalance, or what have you." It is true that something is happening in your brain when you become depressed, he says, but that "is not a causal explanation"; it is "a necessary intermediary mechanism."

Some people don't want to see this because, at least at first, "it's more comforting," Vincent said, to think it's all happening simply because of changes in the brain. "It takes away an experiential process and substitutes a mechanistic process." It turns your pain into a trick of the light that can be banished with drugs. But they don't ultimately solve the problem, he says, any more than just getting the obese patients to stop eating solved their problems. "Medications have a role," he told me. "Are they the ultimate and end-all? No. Do they sometimes short-change people? Absolutely."

To solve the problem for his obese patients, Vincent said, they had all realized—together—that they had to solve the problems that were leading them to eat obsessively in the first place. So he set up support groups where they could discuss the real reasons why they ate and talk about what they had been through. Once that was in place, far more people became able to keep going through the fasting program and stay at a safe weight. He was going to start exploring a way to do this with depression, with startling results—as I'll discuss later.

~

More than anyone else I spoke to about the hidden causes of depression, Vincent made me angry. After I met with him, I went to the beach in San Diego and raged against what he had said. I was looking hard for reasons to dismiss it. Then I asked myself—Why are you so angry about this? It seemed peculiar, and I didn't really understand it. Then, as I discussed it with some people I trust, I began to understand.

If you believe that your depression is due solely to a broken brain, you don't have to think about your life, or about what anyone might have done to you. The belief that it all comes down to biology protects you, in a way, for a while. If you absorb this different story, though, you have to think about those things. And that hurts.

I asked Vincent why he thinks traumatic childhoods so often produce depressed and anxious adults, and he said that he honestly doesn't know. He's a good scientist. He didn't want to speculate. But I think I might know, although it goes beyond anything I can prove scientifically.

When you are a child and you experience something really traumatic, you almost always think it is your fault. There's a reason for this, and it's not irrational; like obesity, it is, in fact, a solution to a problem most people can't see. When I was young, my mother was ill a lot, and my father was mostly gone, usually in a different country. In the chaos of that, I experienced some extreme acts of violence from an adult in my life. For example, I was strangled with an electrical cord on one occasion. By the time I was sixteen, I left to go and live in another city, away from any adults I knew, and when I was there, I found myself—like many people who have been treated this way at a formative age—seeking out dangerous situations where I was again treated in ways I should not have been treated.

Even now—as a thirty-seven-year-old adult—I feel like writing this down, and saying it to you, is an act of betrayal of the adult who carried out these acts of violence, and the other adults who behaved in ways they shouldn't have.

I know you can't figure out who these people are from what I've written. I know that if I saw an adult strangling a child with an electrical cord, it would not even occur to me to blame the child, and that if I heard somebody try to suggest such a thing, I would assume they were insane. I know rationally where the real betrayal lies in this situation. But still, I feel it. It's there, and that feeling almost stopped me from saying this.

Why do so many people who experience violence in childhood feel the same way? Why does it lead many of them to self-destructive behavior, like obesity, or hardcore addiction, or suicide? I have spent a lot of time thinking about this. When you're a child, you have very little power to change your environment. You can't move away, or force somebody to stop hurting you. So you have two choices. You can admit to yourself that you are powerless—that at any moment, you could be badly hurt, and there's simply nothing you can do about it. Or you can tell yourself it's your fault. If you do that, you actually gain some power—at least in your own mind. If it's your fault, then there's something you can do that might make it different. You aren't a pinball being smacked around a pinball machine. You're the person controlling the machine. You have your hands on the dangerous levers. In this way, just like obesity protected those women from the men they feared would rape them, blaming yourself for your childhood traumas protects you from seeing how vulnerable you were and are. You can become the powerful one. If it's your fault, it's under your control.

But that comes at a cost. If you were responsible for being hurt, then at some level, you have to think you deserved it. A person who thinks they deserved to be injured as a child isn't going to think they deserve much as an adult, either.

This is no way to live. But it's a misfiring of the thing that made it possible for you to survive at an earlier point in your life.

~

You might have noticed that this cause of depression and anxiety is a little different from the ones I have discussed up to now, and it's different from the ones I'm going to discuss next.

As I mentioned before, most people who have studied the scientific evidence accept that there are three different kinds of causes of depression and anxiety—biological, psychological, and social. The causes I've discussed up to now—and will come back to in a moment—are environmental. I'll come to biological factors soon.

But childhood trauma belongs in a different category. It's a psychological cause. By discussing it here, I'm hoping childhood trauma can indicate toward the many other psychological causes of depression that are too specific to be discussed in a big, broad way. The ways our psyches can be damaged are almost infinite. I know somebody whose wife cheated on him for years with his best friend and who became deeply depressed when he found out. I know somebody who survived a terror attack and was almost constantly anxious for a decade after. I know someone whose mother was perfectly competent and never cruel to her but was relentlessly negative and taught her always to see the worst in people and to keep them at a distance. You can't squeeze these experiences into neat categories—it wouldn't make sense to list "adultery," "terror attacks," or "cold parents" as causes of depression and anxiety.

But here's what we know. Psychological damage doesn't have to be as extreme as childhood violence to affect you profoundly. Your wife cheating on you with your best friend isn't a malfunction in your brain. But it is a cause of deep psychological distress—and it can cause depression and anxiety. If you are ever told a story about these problems that doesn't talk about your personal psychology, don't take it seriously.

~

Dr. Anda—one of the pioneers of this research—told me it had forced him to turn his thinking about depression and other problems inside out.

"When people have these kind of problems, it's time to stop asking what's wrong with them," he said, "and time to start asking what happened to them."

CHAPTER 10

Cause Five: Disconnection from Status and Respect

It's hard to describe what depression and acute anxiety feel like. They are such disorientating states that they seem to escape language, but we have a few clichés that we return to. We often say, for example, that we feel "down." It sounds like a metaphor—but I don't think it quite is. When I feel depressed, I feel as if I have been almost physically pushed down. I want to keep my head down, my body slumped and low. Other people who've experienced depression have said the same.

Many years ago, a scientist noticed something about this—and it led him to a discovery.

~

One afternoon in the late 1960s, in the Museum of Natural History in New York City, an eleven-year-old Jewish boy named Robert Sapolsky was staring into a glass cage at a vast stuffed silverback gorilla. He kept nagging his mother to bring him back there. He was fascinated, entranced by the animal, although he didn't quite know why. When he was younger, he had dreamed of being a zebra, running across the savannas of Africa;

then he dreamed of being an insect; but now he was pining for a community of primates he could call his own. It looked, to him, as he stared into those cages, like a refuge—a place where he would belong.

Just over a decade later, Robert made it. He was standing alone on those savannas, trying to figure out how to act like a baboon. They live in troops of between 50 and 150, on long open stretches of grassland across Kenya. He would listen as they called to each other across the landscape, and he spent hours trying to imitate their calls.

As he watched them, he kept being reminded that they are—in evolutionary terms—our cousins. One day, "a female with a young kid was climbing around in a tree: this was her first kid, she wasn't hugely competent, and basically—she dropped the kid," Robert told me. All five of the female baboons who were watching gasped—and so did he. They all peered closely, to see if the baby had survived. She got to her feet and rejoined her mother. All five women clucked with relief. So did he.

He had come here not for a vacation, but to try to solve a mystery of his own. Back in New York, Robert had the first of his depressions, and he suspected that a key to understanding depression might lie out here, with our cousins.

~

It wasn't long after Robert arrived that he first saw the alpha baboon. At the top of the troop of baboons he was going to follow for the next twenty years, there was a king of the swingers, a jungle VIP—who he quickly named Solomon, after the wisest king in the Old Testament. Baboons live in a strict hierarchy, and everybody knows their place in the rankings, from top to bottom. He saw that Solomon, at the top, could do whatever he wanted. If he saw anyone else in the troop chewing something, he could snatch it from their hands and take it for himself. He could have sex with any female he wanted—half of all the sexual activity in the whole troop cut Solomon in on the action. When it was hot, he could just shove anyone who was sitting in the shade out of the way and claim the cool places for himself. He had climbed to this position by terrorizing the old alpha male, and driving him into submission.

It didn't take long for Solomon to start to assert his dominance over Robert, too. One day, he walked up to the young primatologist while he was sitting on a rock and pushed him so hard that he fell off and smashed his binoculars.

If you're a female baboon, you inherit your place in the hierarchy from your mother, as if you were a posh Englishman in the Middle Ages, but if you're a male baboon, your place is established through a brutal conflict to see who can clamber to the top.

And you really want to avoid being at the bottom. There, in this troop, Robert saw a scrawny, feeble creature who he named Job, after the unluck-iest man in the Torah and the Bible. Job would tremble a lot of the time and have what looked like seizures. Sometimes his hair would just fall out. Anyone in the troop who was having a bad day could take it out on Job. His food was snatched, he was shoved into the heat, and he was beaten up a lot. Like all low-status baboons, he was covered with bite marks.

In between Solomon and Job, there was a chain of male control and command. Number 4 stood above Number 5 and could take from him. Number 5 stood over Number 6 and could take from him. And on and on. Your place in the hierarchy determined what you ate, whether you got to have sex, and every moment of your life.

~

Robert would wake up in his tent every morning at five thirty to the sounds of an awakening savanna all around him and prepare a medical kit and a tranquilizer dart. It was his job to go out and fire a tranquilizer at one of the baboons so he could take a blood sample. They became quite skilled at avoiding him, and he had to figure out how to fire when they weren't looking—to dart them in the back. This blood sample would then be tested for several key factors—and one was how much of the stress hormone cortisol they were carrying. He wanted to know which baboons were experiencing the most stress—because he believed it could reveal something crucial.

It turned out—when his blood samples were tested—that when there is a war on for the position of alpha male, the most stressed baboons are the ones at the top. But the vast majority of the time, the lower you are in the hierarchy, the more stressed you are; and the baboons at the very bottom of the pile, like Job, are stressed constantly.

~

To avoid getting savaged, the baboons with the lowest status would have to compulsively show that they knew they were defeated. They would do this by making what are called subordinance gestures—they lowered their heads, crawled on their bellies. It was how they signaled: Stop attacking me. I'm beaten. I'm no threat to you. I give up.

And here's the striking thing. When a baboon is behaving this way—when nobody around him shows him any respect, and he's been pushed to the bottom of the pile—he looks an awful lot like a depressed human being. He keeps his head down and his body low; he doesn't want to move; he loses his appetite; he loses all his energy; when somebody comes near him, he backs away.

~

One day, after Solomon had been at the top of the hierarchy for a year, a younger baboon, Uriah, did something shocking. When Solomon was lying on a rock with one of the hottest babes of the troop, Uriah walked up in between them and started trying to have sex with her—right in front of the boss-man. Incensed, Solomon attacked him and ripped Uriah's upper lip. Uriah ran away.

But the next day, Uriah came back. And the next. And the next. He kept getting beaten up—but every time, Solomon got a little more exhausted, and more wary.

And then one day, when Uriah struck, Solomon backed off a little. Only for a moment. Within a year, Uriah was king, and Solomon had sunk to Number 9 in the hierarchy—and everyone he had smited or spited was seeking revenge. The whole troop began to torment him, and his stress levels went through the roof.

One day, Solomon was so despairing he simply walked away into the savanna and never came back.

~

Robert had discovered that our closest cousins are most stressed in two situations—when their status is threatened (like Soloman, when Uriah struck), and when their status is low (like poor Job all the time).

When he first published his research, it began to stir further scientific probing into these questions, and he rose to become a leading professor of biology and neurology at Stanford.

A few years after Robert's initial breakthrough, it was discovered that depressed humans are flooded with the very same stress hormone that you find in low-ranking male baboons. As Robert investigated these questions further, he discovered even more: you get, he explains, "the same constellation of changes in the brain and pituitary and adrenal glands . . . [as in] depressed humans," too.

So some other scientists began to suspect that depression might be, in part, something deep in our animal nature.

The psychologist Paul Gilbert started to make the case that depression is, for humans, in part a "submission response"—the evolutionary equivalent of Job, the baboon at the bottom of the hierarchy, saying—No, no more. Please, leave me alone. You don't have to fight me. I'm no threat to you.

After I learned about this, I began to wonder—especially as I inter-viewed many depressed people—if depression is, in part, a response to the sense of humiliation the modern world inflicts on many of us. Watch TV and you'll be told the only people who count in the world are celebrities and the rich—and you already know your chances of joining either group are vanishingly small. Flick through an Instagram feed or a glossy magazine, and your normal-shaped body will feel disgusting to you. Go to work and you'll have to obey the whims of a distant boss earning hundreds of times more than you.

Even when we are not being actively humiliated, even more of us feel like our status could be taken away at any moment. Even the middle class—even the rich—are being made to feel pervasively insecure. Robert had discovered that having an insecure status was the one thing even more distressing than having a low status.

So it seemed like there might be something in the theory that depres-sion and anxiety are a response to the constant status anxiety many of us live with today. But how could this theory be tested?

~

I went to see a married couple who had taught me about this science and found an intriguing way of investigating it. Kate Pickett and Richard Wilkinson's research into these questions—distilled in their book *The Spirit Level*—has made them two of the most influential social scientists in the world.

When they looked at Robert's work, they knew that with baboons, the hierarchies are fairly fixed: they are always going to live that way, with only minor variations. But Kate and Richard knew that for humans, it doesn't quite work like that. As a species, we have found lots of different ways to live together. Some human cultures (like the United States) have very large gaps between the people at the top and the people at the bottom. In those places, there is a small number of Solomons at the top, and most people are left like Job at the bottom. But other human cultures (like Norway) are quite different—with highly equal ways of living, where the top and bottom are close together. In those cultures, there are hardly any Solomons and hardly any Jobs—most people live in a middle zone, like Numbers 10 to 13 in the baboon hierarchy.

If Robert's insights apply to humans, then Richard and Kate knew that in highly unequal societies like the United States they would find higher levels of mental distress, and in highly equal societies like Norway they'd find less. So they embarked on a massive research program to find out, sifting enormous amounts of data.

When they were finally able to plot the data on a graph, they were startled by how close the relationship was. The more unequal your society, the more prevalent all forms of mental illness are. Other social scientists then broke this down to look at depression specifically—and found the higher the inequality, the higher the depression. This is true if you compare different countries, and if you compare different states within the United States. It strongly suggested that something about inequality seems to be driving up depression and anxiety.

When you have a society with huge gaps in income and status, Richard told me, it creates the sense that "some people seem supremely important, and others seem of no importance at all." This doesn't affect only people at the bottom. In a highly unequal society, everyone has to think about their status a lot. Am I maintaining my position? Who's threatening me? How far can I fall? Just asking these questions—as you have to when inequality grows—loads more and more stress into our lives.

This means that more people will unconsciously respond to this stress by offering a response from deep in our evolutionary history—we put our head down. We feel defeated.

"We're extraordinarily sensitive to these things," Richard said. When the status gap is too big, it creates "a sense of defeat that you can't escape from."

~

Today, we are living with status gaps that are bigger than any in human history. If you work for a company, in living memory it used to be that your boss would likely earn twenty times more than the average employee. It's now three hundred times more. The six heirs to the Walmart fortune own more than the bottom 100 million Americans. Eight billionaires own more wealth than the bottom half of the human race.

Once you understand all this, Richard explained to me, you can see why the distress so many of us feel isn't due to some spontaneous misfiring of your brain chemistry. No—it is "something," he told me, "that you share with so many other people. This is a common human response to the circumstances in which we all live. This is not something that separates you from the world. It's something, actually, you share with countless others." We need to see "this is not just my personal problem," he said, but "a shared problem—and attributable to the kind of society we live in."

~

After he had returned from living with his troop of wild baboons on the savannas of Kenya, Robert Sapolsky had a recurring dream. He was on the New York subway, and a menacing gang approached him, determined to beat him up. Robert looked at the gang, terrified. There's a hierarchy here in this dream—and he's at the bottom of it. He's going to become prey, like Job, the weak baboon covered in bite marks because anybody could take a swing at him.

But in the dream, Robert does something unexpected. He talks to the violent gang. He explains to the people who are poised to attack him that this is a crazy situation, and it doesn't have to be this way. On some nights, he speaks to the thugs about the source of their pain—why they want to beat somebody up—and he empathizes with them and their distress, and offers them a little impromptu therapy. Other times, he makes jokes, and they laugh with him. Every time, they decide not to hurt him.

I think this is a dream about how we can be. Baboons are locked in their hierarchy. They need somebody at the bottom to beat up and humiliate. Job couldn't persuade Solomon to treat him well by offering jokes and therapy, and he couldn't persuade the other baboons to choose to live in a more egalitarian way.

But humans do have a choice. We can—as I learned later—find practical ways to dismantle hierarchies and create a more equal place, where everybody feels they have a measure of respect and status. Or we can build up hierarchies and ramp up the humiliation—as we are doing today.

When we do that, many of us will feel we are being pushed down, almost physically, and many of us will show signs of submission. We'll lower our heads and our bodies and silently say: Leave me alone. You beat me. I can't take this any more.

CHAPTER 11

Cause Six: Disconnection from the Natural World

Isabel Behncke stood in the shadow of a mountain and looked at me. I will only explain to you how being cut off from the natural world can cause depression, she said, if you agree to climb it with me, now. She waved her arms upward at Tunnel Mountain, which towers over the Canadian town of Banff. I followed her wave warily with my eyes. I couldn't see its peak anywhere, but I knew from the postcards it was somewhere above me, covered in snow, with lakes behind it in the distance.

I coughed and explained to Isabel as politely as possible that I don't do nature. I like nice concrete walls, covered with bookshelves. I like skyscrapers. I like subway stations opening out onto taco trucks. I regard Central Park as excessively rural, and walk up Tenth Avenue to avoid it. I go out into the natural world only when I'm forced to because I'm chasing a story.

So Isabel explained—no mountain trek, no interview. "Come on," she said. "Let's see where we can avoid dying and take a danger selfie!" And so, reluctantly—for journalistic reasons only—I began to trudge. As we started to walk, it occurred to me that of all the people I know, Isabel is the one most likely to survive an apocalypse. She grew up on a farm in rural Chile, so "I was always strangely comfortable with the wild," she told me as we walked. "I was riding horses when I was ten on my own, and falling. My dad had eagles. We had three eagles living free inside the house." Eagles? In the house? I asked—didn't they attack you? "I come from a very unusual background," she replied, and we walked some more. Her family had been like a band of nomads, roaming through nature. They would go sailing for days out into the ocean, and at the age of eight, Isabel would sketch the killer whales she had seen with her own eyes. Not long after, she started venturing into the rainforest for the first time.

When she was in her early twenties, she started training to be an evolutionary biologist—which means, she says, that she studies "the nature of human nature." Her job, operating out of Oxford University, is to figure out how we became the way we are, in part by studying our evolutionary ancestors and cousins. Her first major piece of research was at Twycross Zoo, in Southern England, where her project was to study the differences between chimpanzees and bonobos in captivity. Bonobos look like slimmer chimpanzees, and they have funny hair—it's parted in the middle and flips up, resembling an airplane that's about to take off. They grow to be large: an adult is about the size of a twelve-year-old human child. As Isabel watched them, she quickly observed the most famous thing about bonobos—they bond by having very frequent group sex, most of which is lesbian.

Isabel loved to watch as the British mothers unwittingly brought their young children to witness this orgy. "Mummy! Mummy! What are they doing?" they would ask. The mothers would quickly shepherd their kids away, to the Galapagos tortoises in a pen opposite. But then breeding season came for the tortoises, "and you have no idea how pornographic" tortoises can be, she says, "because the male mounts the female, and the male makes *that* sound."

From her observation spot in the zoo, Isabel would cackle as pale English mothers staggered from the bonobo orgies to the orgasming tortoises, muttering "Oh my god, oh my god."

There, she fell in love with the bonobos, and with their whole way of looking at the world. She was especially impressed when she saw one of the female bonobos make a dildo. "She was given food one day in a bucket that was kind of cut in half—a blue bucket," and she rolled it up, and "she took it wherever she went and she would just use it to masturbate. Amazing! And then I understood it—because, of course, plastic is smooth. Are you going to use branches? It's not so smooth. It was like a kind of genius solution."

But there was something wrong with these bonobos—something she wasn't going to understand until later.

She realized that if she really wanted to understand this species, she had to follow them out into their natural habitat, in the center of Africa—but nobody had done that for years. A horrific war had been destroying the Democratic Republic of the Congo, although it now seemed to be drawing to a close. When she told people what she wanted to do, they looked at her as if she were mad. But Isabel is not a woman many people can say no to. That's how she ended up—after a lot of lobbying—in the heart of the Congolese rainforest for three years, living in a house made of mud and stalking a troop of bonobos all day, every day. She walked, on average, seventeen kilometers a day. She got charged by a wild boar. In this time, she learned to understand bonobos better than almost anyone else alive. And there, she realized something with implications for us.

~

Out in the Congo, she noticed that many of the things she had seen the bonobos do when they were taken out of their natural habitat and put in the zoo—things she took to be normal—were actually highly unusual.

In the rain forest—the landscape they evolved to live in—bonobos will sometimes be bullied by their social group, and when this happens, they start behaving differently. They might scratch themselves a lot, compulsively. They'll sit at the edge of the group and stare out. They'll groom themselves a lot less, and they'll refuse to be groomed by other bonobos. When Isabel saw this behavior, she recognized it right away. It was, she believed, clearly the bonobo equivalent of depression—for the same reasons as I described in the last chapter. They were being treated badly—and they were reacting with sadness and a loss of hope.

But here's the strange thing. In the wild, for bonobos, there's a limit to how far this depression goes. It's there—especially for the low-status ones—but there is a floor below which the animals won't sink. Yet in zoos, it seemed the bonobos would slip further and further down, in a way they never would in the wild. They would scratch until they bled. They would howl. They would develop tics, or start rocking obsessively. In their natural habitat, she never saw the bonobos develop this "full-blown, chronic depression," she says, but in zoos, it was quite common.

This isn't limited to bonobos, it turns out. We know now from over a century of observing animals in captivity that when they are deprived of their natural habitat, they will often develop symptoms that look like extreme forms of despair. Parrots will rip their own feathers out. Horses will start unstoppably swaying. Elephants will start to grind their tusks—their source of strength and pride in the wild—against the walls of their cells until they are gnarled stumps. Some elephants in captivity are so traumatized they sleep upright for years, moving their bodies neurotically the whole time. None of these species ever behave this way in the wild. Many animals in captivity lose the desire to have sex—that's why it's so hard to get animals to mate in zoos.

So Isabel began to ask—Why would animals become far more depressed outside their natural habitat?

~

This became a quite personal question for her when she was writing up some of her research at an Oxford college. Shut inside all day, trying to work, she found herself depressed for the first time in her life. She couldn't sleep, couldn't bring her mind to focus on how to get out of her terrible sense of pain. She took antidepressants, but like most people who take them, she was still depressed. She started to ask herself: Could her own depression be linked to the depression she'd seen in the caged bonobos? What if, she wondered, humans become more depressed when we are deprived of access to the kind of landscape we evolved in, too? Was that why she felt so bad?

~

It's been known for a long time that all sorts of mental health problems— including ones as severe as psychosis and schizophrenia—are considerably worse in cities than in the countryside, but the psychological effects of being cut off from the natural world have only begun to be studied properly in the past fifteen years.

A group of scientists at the University of Essex in Britain have conducted the most detailed research into this question so far. They tracked the mental health of more than five thousand households over three years. They wanted to look at two types of households in particular— people who moved from a leafy green rural area to a city, and people who moved from a city to a leafy green rural area. They wanted to know— Would there be any changes in how depressed they got?

What they found was clear: the people who moved to green areas saw a big reduction in depression, and the people who moved away from green areas saw a big increase in depression. This was just one of many studies with similar findings, it turns out. Of course, the scientists looking at this knew there are all sorts of things that could be playing a role here: maybe rural areas have stronger communities and less crime and less pollution, and maybe that—rather than the green space—is why people feel better. So another British study decided to screen out that effect. They compared deprived inner-city areas that had some green space to very similar deprived inner-city areas without green space. Everything else—like levels of social connections—was the same. But it turned out there was less stress and despair in the greener neighborhood.

As I read through all this evidence, one of the studies that was most striking to me was perhaps the most simple. They got people who lived in cities to take a walk in nature, and then tested their mood and concentration. Everyone, predictably, felt better and was able to concentrate more—but the effect was dramatically bigger for people who had been depressed. Their improvement was *five times* greater than the improvement for other people.

Why would this be? What was going on?

~

We were halfway up the mountain, and Isabel was staring off toward the lakes in the distance, when I confessed something to her. I could see this scene was beautiful in some abstract way. But I am so cut off from enjoying this sort of thing that, to me, what it looked like, if I'm honest, was a screensaver. A lovely screensaver. I felt an unconscious itch when I looked at it: I felt as if I had waited too long before pushing a key on my laptop.

Isabel laughed, but it was a sad laugh. "Now I feel *personally* responsible if you feel this is a screensaver! I feel it is my mission. I cannot feel [there's any] integrity in talking about this and [then saying]—let's go back to sit in front of a screen." She made me promise we'd make it to the top of the mountain. So we started to trudge upward again, and as we talked more, I learned that Isabel has essentially distilled her thoughts on this subject—which draw on a broad range of science—down to three theories. She says candidly that we need a lot more research into all of them, and they overlap to some degree.

To understand why we feel better in landscapes like this, she said, you have to start with something really basic: "The thing is that we are animals. We keep forgetting that," and as animals—she indicated toward her body—"this thing is made to move." When we look for solutions to our bad feelings, she says, we try to find it in language, and in the symbols we have created as a species. But these symbols are—in the long sweep of things—very recent. "We have been vertebrate for nearly five hundred million years now. We've been mammals for two hundred fifty, three hundred million years. We've been primates for sixty-five [million years]." All those years she spent in the Congolese rain forest, living and sleeping and eating with the bonobos, she explained, she was being educated in how close we are to them. "We have been animals that move for a lot longer than we have been animals that talk and convey concepts," she said to me. "But we still think that depression can be cured by this conceptual layer. I think [the first answer is more] simple. Let's fix the physiology first. Get out. Move."

It's hard for a hungry animal moving through its natural habitat and with a decent status in its group to be depressed, she says—there are almost no records of such a thing. The scientific evidence is clear that exercise significantly reduces depression and anxiety. She thinks this is because it returns us to our more natural state—one where we are embodied, we are animal, we are moving, our endorphins are rushing. "I do not think that kids or adults who are not moving, and are not in nature for a certain amount of time, can be considered fully healthy animals," she says.

But there must be, she says, something deeper going on than that. When scientists have compared people who run on treadmills in the gym with people who run in nature, they found that both see a reduction in depression—but it's higher for the people who run in nature. So what are the other factors?

As we reached this part of our conversation, I realized we were at the top of the mountain. On either side, I could see sweeping vistas. "Now," Isabel said, "you have screen[savers] on both sides. We're surrounded."

~

A chipmunk was tentatively approaching us, and it walked up to a point just a few inches from my feet. On the ground, I laid down a piece of jerky I had bought in town earlier that day.

There is another theory put forward by scientists about why being in the natural world seems to lift depression for many people, Isabel said to me. The biologist E. O. Wilson—one of the most important people in his field in the twentieth century—argued that all humans have a natural sense of something called "biophilia." It's an innate love for the land-scapes in which humans have lived for most of our existence, and for the natural web of life that surrounds us and makes our existence possible. Almost all animals get distressed if they are deprived of the kinds of landscape that they evolved to live in. A frog *can* live on land—it'll just be miserable as hell and give up. Why, Isabel wonders, would humans be the one exception to this rule? Looking around us, Isabel says: "Fucking hell—it's our habitat."

This is a hard concept to test scientifically, but there has been one attempt to do it. The social scientists Gordon Orians and Judith Heer-wagen worked with teams all over the world, in radically different cultures, and showed them a range of pictures of very different land-scapes, from the desert to the city to the savanna. What they found is that everywhere, no matter how different their culture, people had a preference—for landscapes that look like the savannas of Africa. There's something about it, they conclude, that seems to be innate.

~

This leads to another reason Isabel thinks depressed or anxious people feel better when they get out into natural landscapes. When you are depressed—as Isabel knows from her own experience—you feel that "now everything is about you." You become trapped in your own story and your own thoughts, and they rattle around in your head with a dull, bitter insistence. Becoming depressed or anxious is a process of becoming a prisoner of your ego, where no air from the outside can get in. But a range of scientists have shown that a common reaction to being out in the natural world is the precise opposite of this sensation—a feeling of awe.

Faced with a natural landscape, you have a sense that you and your concerns are very small, and the world is very big—and that sensation can shrink the ego down to a manageable size. "It's something larger than yourself," Isabel said, looking around her. "There's something very deeply, animally healthy in that sensation. People love it when it occurs—its brief, fleeting moments." And this helps you see the deeper and wider ways in which you are connected to everything around you. "It's almost like a metaphor for belonging in a grander system," she says. "You're always embedded in a network," even when you don't realize it; you are "just one more node" in this enormous tapestry.

In Oxford, she found it easy to become depressed when she was sealed away from all this. In Congo, living with the bonobos, she found she couldn't get depressed. She would sometimes have a bleak thought, and "nature goes—I don't think so . . . You are camping in the savanna and you hear lions roar and you think—Oh fuck, I am protein." That release from self-enclosure in her own ego, she says, released her from despair.

The chipmunk sniffed the jerky I had laid down on the ground, looked disgusted, and scampered away. It's only when I looked at the packaging that I realized what I had offered him was something called salmon jerky—which apparently Canadians voluntarily choose to eat. "The chipmunk has excellent taste," Isabel said, looking at the packaging in horror, and started to lead me back down the mountain.

In the State Prison of Southern Michigan in the 1970s, there was—quite by accident—an experiment exploring some of these ideas. Because of the way the prison was built, half the prisoners' cells looked out over rolling farmland and trees, and half looked out onto bare brick walls. An architect named Ernest Moore studied the medical records for these different groups of prisoners (who didn't differ in any other way), and he found that if you were in the group who could see the natural world, you were 24 percent less likely to get physically or mentally sick.

"I have to say," Professor Howard Frumkin—one of the leading experts on this subject in the world—told me later, "that if we had a medication for which preliminary results showed such efficacy, we would be all over researching that medication . . . Here is a treatment that has very few side effects, is not expensive, doesn't require a trained or licensed professional to prescribe it, and has pretty good evidence of efficacy so far." But the research is very hard to find funding for, he said, because "a lot of the shape of modern biomedical research has been defined by the pharmaceutical industry," and they're not interested because "it's very hard to commercialize nature contact." You can't sell it, so they don't want to know.

But I kept wondering, as I absorbed all this—So why have I been so resistant to the natural world all my life? It was only when I thought about this for months, and listened again and again to the audio of my mountain trek with Isabel, that I realized something. In nature, I do feel my ego shrinking, and I do feel a sensation that I am very small and the world is very big, just as she predicted—yet for most of my life, that has caused me a sensation not of relief, but of anxiety.

I *want* my ego. I want to cling to it.

It was only later in this journey that I understood this properly—as you'll see.

~

Isabel had seen captivity reduce bonobos to depression-like symptoms they could not have experienced in the wild. As humans, "I think we have many modern forms of captivity," she told me. The lesson the depressed bonobos had taught her, she said, is: "Don't be in captivity. Fuck captivity."

Right at the top of that mountain in Banff, there is a ledge where if you walk along it, you have a view in every direction over the Canadian landscape, stretching out before you. I looked on it with terror. Isabel insisted on taking my hand and leading me out there. The cruelest thing about depression, she said, is that it drains you of the desire to be as fully alive as this—to swallow experience whole. "We want to feel alive," she said. We want it, and need it, so badly. Later, she said: "Obviously, we were facing death, but you felt alive, right? You might have been horrified—but you were not depressed."

No. I was not depressed.

CHAPTER 12

Cause Seven: Disconnection from a Hopeful or Secure Future

I had noticed something else about my depression and anxiety over the years. It often made me feel, in some peculiar way, radically shortsighted. When it came, I would only be able to think about the next few hours: how long they would seem, and how painful they would be. It was as if the future vanished.

As I talked with many depressed or severely anxious people, I noticed that they often described a similar sensation. One friend told me that she always knew her depression was lifting when she felt her sense of time expanding again—she would find herself able to think about where she would be a month from then or a year from then.

I wanted to understand this apparent quirk, and once I began to dig into it, it led me to some remarkable scientific research. Of all the causes of depression and anxiety I learned about, this was the one it took me longest to absorb—but once I did, it helped me to clear up several mysteries.

～

Not long before he died, a Native American named Chief Plenty Coups sat in his home on the flatlands of Montana and looked out across a landscape where once his people had roamed alongside the buffalo, and now there was nothing. He had been born in the last days when his people—the Crow—had lived as a nomadic hunting tribe.

One day, a white cowboy arrived and said he wanted to tell the chief's story—to faithfully record it, in the chief's own words, for the ages. Many white men had stolen Native American stories and warped them, so it took a long time to build trust between these two men. But once it was there, Chief Plenty Coup began to tell this man a story. It was about the end of the world.

When he was young, he explained, his people had ranged across the Great Plains on horseback, and their lives had always been organized around two crucial activities. They hunted, and they prepared for the wars they fought against rival Native American tribal groups in their area. Everything they did was designed to prepare them for one of these two organizing poles of life. If you cooked a meal, it was in preparation for the hunt, or for the fight. If you conducted the ceremonial Sun Dance, it was to ask for strength in the hunt, or in the fight. Even your name—and the name of everyone you knew—was based on your role in the hunt, or in the fight.

This was the world.

He described its many rules. For example, at the heart of the Crow worldview was the idea of planting something called a coupstick—a carved wooden spike. As you traveled across the plains, you would mark out your own tribe's territory by planting a coupstick in the ground. The stick meant: anybody who passes beyond this point is an enemy and will be attacked. The most admirable thing you could do, in the Crow culture, was to plant and defend the coupsticks. These were at the core of their moral vision.

Chief Plenty Coups continued to describe the rules of his lost world in great detail. He conjured his life, the spiritual values of his people, their relationship with the buffalo and with their rival tribes. It was a world as complex as the civilizations of Europe or China or India, and as structured with rules and meaning and metaphor.

But the cowboy noticed there was something strange about this story. The chief was just a teenager when the white Europeans came, and the wild buffalo were all killed, and the Crow were killed, and the survivors were penned into reservations. But the chief's story always ended there. As for the rest of his life, the majority of it—he had no stories. He had nothing to say.

He would get to the point where the Crow were shut into reservations, and say: "After this, nothing happened."

Of course the cowboy knew—everyone knew—that the chief had done many more things in his life. A lot had happened. But in a very real sense, the world had ended, for him, and for his people.

Sure, on the reservation, they could still plant coupsticks in the ground, but it made no sense. Who was going to cross them? How could they be defended? Sure, they could talk about courage, the value they most cherished—but how could they show courage in any way that made sense to them when there was no more hunting, no more fighting? Sure, they could still perform the Sun Dance, but why bother, when there were no hunts and no battles to ask for success in? How could you show ambition, or spirit, or bravery?

Even everyday activities seemed pointless. Before, meals had been preparation for the hunt or the fight. "Obviously, the Crows continued to cook meals," the philosopher Jonathan Lear explained when he wrote about this. "And if asked, they could say what they were doing. And if asked further about it, they could say that they were trying to survive, trying to hold their family together from one day to the next." But "there was no larger framework of significance into which it could fit."

~

A century later, a psychology professor named Michael Chandler made a discovery. He had been watching on the news—like so many of his fellow Canadians—as a horrifying story was reported, year after year.

Scattered across his country, there were 196 First Nations groups, the Canadian term for the Native American groups who were able to survive this European invasion—albeit on reservations, disoriented like Chief Plenty Coups and his Crow people. Like in the United States, successive Canadian governments had for many years resolved to destroy their culture by taking their children away from them and raising them in orphanages, banning them from speaking their own languages, and preventing them from having any say over how they lived. This continued until a few decades ago. The result was that the people who had gone through all this—and their children—had the highest levels of suicide in the country. By 2016, this became a front-page issue in Canada when in a single reservation on a single night, eleven First Nations people attempted to kill themselves.

Michael had wanted to understand why. So in the 1990s he started to look at the statistics about suicides among First Nations peoples, to see where they were happening. He noticed something intriguing. Half of the indigenous nations (or "tribes" as they would be called in the United States) had no suicides at all, while others had extraordinarily high rates. Why would this be? What could explain the difference? What was happening in the no-suicide indigenous nations that wasn't happening in the high-suicide indigenous nations?

He had a hunch. "Governments historically have treated indigenous people as children, and assumed some kind of loco parentis [acting as parents] control over their lives," Michael explained to me. But "in the last decades, indigenous groups have fought against this kind of approach, and tried to reassemble control of their own lives." Some have been able to reclaim control of their traditional lands, revive their own languages, and get control of their own schools, health services, and police so they can elect and run them for themselves. In some places, the authorities have given in to organizing by First Nations peoples and conceded some freedoms, and in others they haven't.

That means there's a big gap between those First Nations groups that are still totally controlled and at the mercy of whatever decisions are made by the Canadian government about them, and other indigenous nations who have been able to achieve some freedom to rebuild a culture that makes sense to them—to try to build a world where, in their terms, something happens.

So Michael and his colleagues spent years carefully gathering and studying the statistics. They developed nine ways to measure the control a tribal group had, and slowly, over time, they plotted this against the suicide statistics. What they wanted to know was: Is there any relationship?

Then they compiled the results. It turned out the communities with the highest control had the lowest suicide; and the communities with the lowest control had the highest suicide. If you plotted these two factors on a graph, across these 196 tribal groups, it was a remarkably straight line— you could very often predict the rate of suicide just by looking at the rate of community control. This is certainly not the only factor causing agony to First Nations peoples. To name just one of many: the fact that their families were deliberately destroyed and broken up by the Canadian state, and that they were sent to horribly abusive "boarding schools," has caused a cascade of trauma down the generations. But Michael had proven that lack of community control was a massive and major factor.

This discovery was explosive in itself. But it then led Michael to think more deeply still.

∼

As he looked at the results from the First Nations study, Michael found himself thinking back to a study he had carried out several years before.

It's a little more complex than the studies I've discussed up to now, but stick with me.

Ever since he graduated from the University of California, Berkeley, as a young psychologist in 1966, Michael had been curious about one of the oldest and most fundamental questions humans have—How do you develop your sense of identity? How do you know who you are? It seems like an impossibly big question. But ask yourself this: What is the connecting thread that runs from your baby self, vomiting out teething biscuits, to the person who is reading this book now? Will you be the same person twenty years from now? If you met her, would you recognize her? What is the relationship between you in the past and you in the future? Are you the same person all along?

Almost everyone finds these questions hard to answer. We instinctively feel we are the same person all through our lives—but we find it hard to explain why. There is one group of people, however, who seem to find it impossible.

Michael went into a psychiatric unit in Vancouver for teenagers, and he spent months interviewing the kids there. They were living in bunk beds, receiving treatment, and—often—covering up the scars on their arms in shame. He asked them many kinds of questions about their lives. Some of his questions went to the heart of this debate—how do you form your identity? He raised this topic with them in different ways—and one was quite simple. In Canada, they have a series of comic books that are adaptations of classic novels. One of them is an adaptation of the Charles Dickens story *A Christmas Carol*. You probably know the plot: it is the story of an old miser named Scrooge, who is visited by three ghosts and is transformed by the experience and becomes super-generous. Another comic book is an adaptation of the Victor Hugo classic *Les Misérables*. You probably know this one too: a poor man named Jean Valjean commits a crime and runs away. He changes his name and identity and rises to become the mayor of his town—until Inspector Javert comes to hunt him down (and sing some terrible musical numbers).

Michael got two different groups of institutionalized teenagers to read these comic books. One group consisted of teenagers who had anorexia that was bad enough for them to be hospitalized; the other group consisted of teenagers who had been suicidally depressed. He asked both groups of kids to think about these characters. Will Scrooge be the same person in the future, after he meets the ghosts and goes through a change of heart? If he is, why? Will Jean Valjean be the same man after he runs away and changes his name? Tell me how.

Both groups of kids were equally sick, and their distress levels were similar. Yet the anorexic kids could answer these questions normally, while the depressed kids couldn't. "Almost unique to the suicidal group was a kind of across-the-board failure to be able to understand how a person could go on being the same individual," Michael told me. The very depressed kids could answer all sorts of other questions normally—but when it came to these questions about what they or anyone else would be in the future, they would look puzzled. They knew they should be able to give an answer. But then they would say, sadly: "I don't have the foggiest idea."

And here's the interesting thing. Just as they couldn't see who Jean Valjean would be in the future, it turned out they couldn't see who they, as individuals, would be in the future, either. For them, the future had disappeared. Asked to describe themselves five or ten or twenty years from now, they were at a loss. It was like a muscle they couldn't work.

At some profound level, Michael had discovered, extremely depressed people have become disconnected from a sense of the future, in a way that other really distressed people have not. From this early research, though, it was hard to tell if these kids' symptoms were a cause or an effect. It could go either way. Maybe losing a sense of the future makes you suicidal—or maybe being extremely depressed makes it hard to think about the future. How, he wondered, could he figure this out?

The research into First Nations Canadians, he came to believe, gives you an answer. If you live in a First Nations community with no control over its own destiny, it's hard to construct a picture of a hopeful or stable future in your mind. You're at the mercy of alien forces that have destroyed your people many times before. But if you live in a First Nations community that *does* have control over its destiny, you can easily construct a vision of a hopeful future—because, together, you'll be deciding it.

It was, he concluded, the loss of the future that was driving the suicide rates up. A sense of a positive future protects you. If life is bad today, you can think—this hurts, but it won't hurt forever. But when it is taken away, it can feel like your pain will never go away.

~

After conducting this research, Michael told me he is now highly skeptical about the way we talk about depression and anxiety as if they are mainly caused by defects in our brain or genes. "It's a kind of holdover from a highly Westernized, medicalized vision of health and well-being," he told me, and it lacks "any serious appreciation of the cultural context in which these things are happening." If you act this way, you ignore "the legitimacy of being depressed" for many people who have been stripped of hope. Instead of thinking about these causes of depression, though, we have been simply putting people on drugs, and "that's become an industry."

~

When I was back in London for a while, I arranged to meet up with an old friend I had known at university twelve years before but had somehow lost touch with over the years. I'll call her Angela. When we studied together, she was one of those people who seemed to be doing everything at once—starring in a play, reading Tolstoy, being everyone's best friend, going out with the hottest boys. She was like a firework of adrenaline, cocktails, and old books. But I had heard from some of our mutual friends that—in the years since—she had developed a serious problem with anxiety and depression, and this seemed so incongruous that I wanted to talk with her.

I took her for a long lunch, and she started to tell me the story of her life since we last met, in a hurried gabble punctuated by her apologizing a lot, although it was never quite clear what for.

After we graduated, Angela explained, she earned a master's degree, and when she started to apply for jobs, she kept getting a consistent piece of feedback: they said she was overqualified and that if they offered her a place, she would only leave. This dragged on for months. And then a year had passed, and she was still hearing the same thing. Angela was a hard worker, and being out of work was weird for her. In the end, she couldn't pay her bills, so she applied for shifts at a call center at £8 (around $10) an hour, a little above Britain's minimum wage at that time.

On her first day, she arrived at an old paint-mixing factory in East London. There was a row of plastic-topped desks with skinny legs—the kind you find in British elementary schools—with computers on them, and in the center, at a bigger desk, sat a supervisor. He could be listening in to your calls at any time, she was told, and he will give you feedback. The center made calls on behalf of three of Britain's leading charities, and Angela's job was to cold-call people and get through what they called "three asks." First you ask for a big sum: Could you afford £50 a month? If they say no, you ask for a smaller sum: How about £20? If they say no, they ask: How about £2 a month? Your call only counts as a success if you manage to get in all three asks.

At this center, there were no "jobs," in the old sense that Angela's grandparents—who had been a servant girl and a factory worker—would have known. If we keep you on, the supervisor explained, you'll get an e-mail once a week, listing your shifts for the following week. You might get four, you might get none. It's up to me, and how well you perform, day by day.

At the end of her first day, the supervisor told her she was doing the calls all wrong, and if she didn't improve, she wouldn't get another shift. She had to be more assertive. You had to maintain a high rate of people letting you hit them with your three asks, and then you needed a high rate of people saying yes. She learned over the next few weeks that if your rate dropped even 2 percent from your previous shift, the supervisor would scream at you and it might well be your last shift.

Sometimes, Angela would cold-call people and they would tell her, crying, that they could no longer afford to donate. "I know the blind children need me," one old woman sobbed; "maybe I can buy a different brand of dog food," she said, so she could give the pennies she saved to the blind. Angela was instructed to go in for the kill.

For the first month, Angela thought she would get better at it and the work would become tolerable until finally she got a proper job. "I'd be like—I don't really like it, but it'll be okay. It'll be okay," she told me. In the weeks when she got four shifts, she was finally able to take the bus to work, and to buy a whole chicken that she would strip to make several meals throughout the week. In the weeks when she got two shifts or fewer, she ate beans and walked to work. Her boyfriend was forced into doing similar chronically insecure work, and one day he got sick. She found herself feeling furious at him for not forcing himself to go in: Don't you know we need that £60?

It was at the start of the second month that Angela realized she was shaking on the bus every day on the way to work. She couldn't tell why. After work, she would sometimes let herself buy a half-pint of Guinness in the pub across the street, and for the first time in her life, she found herself crying in public. Around the same time, she also found herself becoming angry in a way she had never been before. Sometimes there would be a batch of new applicants for shifts and so her own shifts would be cut back. "You start to really hate the new people," she said. She and her boyfriend were starting to scream at each other over little things.

When I asked her to describe how she felt doing this work, she paused. "It's like being squeezed—like trying to fit down a very tight tube all the time. You know—like trying to go down a slide, and just realizing everything about you is not right, and not being able to breathe, and feeling quite sick, and like you'll never get out. And feeling stupid—incompetent, like a child, like a child who can't manage their own life, so you've been relegated to the shitty world where people can tell you you're not good enough and fire you like that"—and she snapped her fingers.

Angela's grandmother had a job as a maid, and she'd get her contract renewed once a year, on Lady's Day. Angela's mother had a middle-class job with a permanent contract. Angela felt she had regressed back beyond even what her grandmother had in the 1930s. She was auditioning for her job every hour, every call, she said. It made her feel "frightened of going in to work," she says, "because of how horrible the day would be, and the fear that this would be the day I really fucked up and got fired, and then we would be in trouble."

She realized one day that she could never shake off "that sense of having no future." She couldn't plan even a few days ahead. When she heard friends talking about mortgages and pensions, it sounded to her almost utopian—dispatches from a country she could only visit. "It completely takes away any sense of identity that you might have, and replaces it with shame and worry and fear . . . What are you? I'm nothing. What are you?" She couldn't conjure any sense of herself in the future that looked any different from the way it did today: "I'm terrified of being as poor when we're in our sixties and seventies as we were in our twenties," she said. It felt like "an eternal traffic jam," where she would never move an inch. She started drinking cheap alcohol at night, because she was too anxious to close her eyes.

For the past thirty years, across almost all of the Western world, this kind of insecurity has been characterizing work for more and more people. Around 20 percent of people in the United States and Germany have no job contract, but instead have to work from shift to shift. The Italian philosopher Paolo Virno says we have moved from having a "proletariat"—a solid block of manual workers with jobs—to a "precariat," a shifting mass of chronically insecure people who don't know whether they will have any work next week and may never have a stable job.

When Angela had a sense of a positive future, back when we were students, she had been a whirl of positivity. Now, sitting opposite me, talking about being choked off from a sense of a hopeful future, she was drained, almost affectless.

There was a window when people on middle-class and working-class incomes had some sense of security and could plan for the future. That window has been closing, as a direct result of political decisions to free businesses from regulation and to make it very hard for workers to organize to protect their rights, and what we are losing is a predictable sense of the future. Angela didn't know what was waiting for her. Working this way meant she couldn't create a picture of herself in a few months, never mind in a few years, or a few decades.

First, this sense of precariousness started with people in the lowest-paying jobs. But ever since, it has been rising further and further up the chain. By now, many middle-class people are working from task to task, without any contract or security. We give it a fancy name: we call it being "self-employed," or the "gig economy"—as if we're all Kanye playing Madison Square Garden. For most of us, a stable sense of the future is dissolving, and we are told to see it as a form of liberation.

∼

It would be grotesque to compare what has happened to workers in the West to what has happened to the Native peoples of the Americas, who have survived a genocide and more than a century of persecution. But while I researched this book, I spent some time in the Rust Belt. A few weeks before the U.S. presidential election in 2016, I went to Cleveland to try to get the vote out to stop Donald Trump from being elected. One afternoon I walked down a street in the southwest of the city where a third of the houses had been demolished by the authorities, a third were abandoned, and a third still had people living in them, cowering, with steel guards on their windows. I knocked on a door, and a woman answered who, from looking at her, I would have guessed was fifty-five. She began to rage—how terrified she was of her neighbors, how the kids in the area "have got to go," how she was desperate for anyone who would make things better, how there wasn't even a grocery store anywhere nearby any more and she had to take three buses just to get food. She mentioned in passing that she was thirty-seven years old, which took me aback.

And then she said something that stayed with me long after the election. She described what the area was like when her grandparents lived there, and you could work in a factory and have a middle-class life—and she made a verbal slip. She meant to say "when I was young." What she actually said was "when I was alive."

$$\sim$$

After she said that, I remembered what that Crow member told an anthropologist in the 1890s: "I am trying to live a life I do not understand."

Angela—and my other friends who have been swallowed into the precariat—can't make sense of their lives, either: the future is constantly fragmenting. All the expectations they were raised with for what comes next seem to have vanished.

When I told Angela about Michael Chandler's studies, she smiled sadly. It made intuitive sense to her, she said. When you have a stable picture of yourself in the future, she explained, what it gives you is "perspective—doesn't it? You are able to say—'Okay, I'm having a shitty day. But I'm not having a shitty life.'" She never expected, she says, to be partying with Jay-Z, or to own a yacht. But she did expect to be able to plan on an annual vacation. She did expect—by the time she got into her late thirties—to know who her employer would be next week, and the week after that. But instead, she got trapped in the precariat.

And after that, nothing happened.

CHAPTER 13

Causes Eight and Nine: The Real Role of Genes and Brain Changes

The story we have been told about our brains—that we are depressed and anxious because they are simply and spontaneously low in serotonin—is not, I knew by now, true. Yet I saw that some people conclude from this that *none* of the biological stories on this subject we have been told are right—that they are entirely caused by social and psychological factors. But when I interviewed them, even the strongest advocates for the environmental and social causes of depression stressed to me that biological causes do exist, and are very real.

So I wanted to investigate—What role do they play? How do they work? And how do they relate to everything else I had learned?

~

Marc Lewis's friends thought he was dead.

It was the summer of 1969, and this young student in California was desperate to block out his despair any way he could. He had swallowed, snorted, or injected any stimulant he could find for a week now. After he had been awake for thirty-six hours straight, he got a friend to inject him with heroin, so he could finally crash. When Marc regained consciousness, he realized his friends were trying to figure out where they could find a bag big enough to dump his body in.

When Marc suddenly began to talk, they were freaked out. His heart, they explained to him, had stopped beating for several minutes.

Finally, about ten years after that night, Marc left drugs behind, and he started to study neuroscience. By the time I first met him—initially in Sydney, Australia—he was a leading figure in the field, and a professor in the Netherlands. He wanted to know—How does your brain change when you are deeply distressed? Do those changes make it harder to recover?

If you look at a brain scan of a depressed or highly anxious person, Marc explained to me, it will look different from the brain scan of somebody without these problems. The areas that relate to feeling unhappy, or to being aware of risk, will be lit up like Christmas tree lights. They will be bigger, and more active. He showed me diagrams and traced these parts of the brain for me.

This fits, I told him, with what my doctor told me back in my teens— that I was depressed because my brain was physically broken, and it would have to be fixed with drugs. Was that story right all along?

When I said that, he looked sad and said no, it doesn't mean that at all.

To understand why, he said, you have to grasp a crucial concept called neuroplasticity. Fifteen years ago, if you had shown me a diagram of my brain and described what it was like, I—and most people—would have thought: that's me, then. If the parts of the brain that relate to being unhappy, or being frightened, are more active, then I'm fixed as a person who is always going to be more unhappy, or more frightened. You might have short legs, or long arms; I have a brain with more active parts related to fear and anxiety; that's how it is.

But we now know that this is not the case. Think of it, he explained, in a different way. If I showed you an X-ray of a man's arms, they might look spindly and weak. Now imagine he did a weight training course for six months and then came back for another X-ray. His arms would look different. They aren't fixed. They would change, according to how he used them. Your brain, he said, is like that: it changes according to how you use it. "Neuroplasticity is the tendency for the brain to continue to restructure itself based on experience," he said. So, for example, to get their license, London taxi drivers have to memorize the entire map of London for a fiercely difficult test called the Knowledge. If you do a brain scan of a London taxi driver, the part of the brain related to spatial awareness is much bigger in him than it would be in me or you. It doesn't mean he was born different. It means he uses his brain differently in his life.

Your brain is constantly changing to meet your needs. It does this mainly in two ways: by pruning the synapses you don't use, and by growing the synapses you do use. So, for example, if you raise a baby in total darkness, the baby will shed the synapses that relate to eyesight—the brain has figured out he won't need them and that it's better to deploy that brainpower somewhere else.

For as long as you live, this neuroplasticity never stops, and the brain "is always changing," Marc explained to me. This is why, he says, what I was told as a teenager about my brain was badly wrong: he told me that a doctor saying to a depressed person " 'now you've got a fucked-up brain, because it's different from a normal brain,' makes no sense in the current context—because we know that brains are changing their wiring all the time. Physiology is always paralleling psychology. It just does." A brain scan is "a snapshot of a moving picture," he says. "You can take a snapshot of any moment in a football game—it doesn't tell you what's going to happen next, or where the brain is going." The brain changes as you become depressed and anxious, and it changes again when you stop being depressed and anxious. It's always changing in response to signals from the world.

When Marc was addicted, his brain would have looked very different from the way it does today. That just tells you that he is using it differently.

When I told Marc that I had been given antidepressants for thirteen years and had always been told that all my distress had been caused by a problem inside my brain, he said: "It's crazy. It's *always* related to your life and your personal circumstances." The seven social and psychological factors I had been investigating, Marc believes, have the capacity to physically change the brains of millions of people. If learning the map of London changes your brain, then being lonely, or isolated, or grossly materialistic—these things change your brain, too. And, crucially, reconnection can change it back. We have been thinking too simplistically, he says. You couldn't figure out the plot of *Breaking Bad* by dismantling your TV set. In the same way, you can't figure out the root of your pain by dismantling your brain. You have to look at the signals the TV, or your brain, is receiving to do that.

Depression and anxiety are "not like a tumor, where something is growing in the brain because there is a real fuck-up in the tissue which precedes the psychological problems," he says. "It's not like that. They"— the distress caused by the outside world, and the changes inside the brain—"come together."

~

But, Marc says, there's a crucial caveat to this—a way in which what happens in the brain *does* change the story for depressed or anxious people.

Imagine you are subjected to some of the seven causes of depression or anxiety I have been discussing up to now. Once this process begins, it—like everything else that happens to us—causes real changes in the brain, and they can then acquire a momentum of their own that deepens the effects from the outside world.

Imagine, he told me, that "your marriage just broke up, and you lost your job, and you know what? Your mother just had a stroke. It's pretty overwhelming." Because you are feeling intense pain for a long period, your brain will assume this is the state in which you are going to have to survive from now on—so it might start to shed the synapses that relate to the things that give you joy and pleasure, and strengthen the synapses that relate to fear and despair. That's one reason why you can often start to feel you have become somehow fixed in a state of depression or anxiety even if the original causes of the pain seem to have passed. John Cacioppo—the scientist I spoke with who had discovered how this works with loneliness—called this, I remembered, a "snowballing" effect.

So, Marc says, while it's wrong to say the origin of these problems is solely within the brain, it would be equally wrong to say that the responses within the brain can't make it worse. They can. The pain caused by life going wrong can trigger a response that is "so powerful that [the brain] tends to stay there [in a pained response] for a while, until something pushes it out of that corner, into a more flexible place." And if the world keeps causing you deep pain, of course you'll stay trapped there for a long time, with the snowball growing.

But telling depressed people that it was simply caused by their brains all along is to hand them a false map, he believes—one that won't be of any use in trying to figure out why they really feel this way, or how to find their way back. It might, in fact, trap them.

~

In his first and only inaugural address as president, John F. Kennedy famously said: "Ask not what your country can do for you. Ask what you can do for your country." Marc told me that if you want to understand how to think about the origins of depression, and how they relate to the brain, in a more truthful way than we've been taught to for the last few decades, it helps to know something the psychologist W. M. Mace said years ago, riffing on JFK:

"Ask not what's inside your head," he said. "Ask what your head's inside of."

~

There is one other physical cause of depression and anxiety that most people have heard about.

My mother had periods of being seriously depressed before I was born (and after). Both my grandmothers had periods of being depressed— although nobody used that word back then. So all those years I was taking antidepressants, insofar as I had thought about depression as related to anything other than a brain malfunction, I had assumed I inherited it in my genes. I sometimes thought of depression as a lost twin, born in the womb alongside me. As the years passed, I would often hear other people say this, too—"I was born with depression," one friend, who had gone through long bouts of being suicidal, told me once, on a long night when we sat up and I tried to talk to him about reasons to live.

So I wanted to know—how much of depression is carried in your genes? As I researched this, I learned that scientists haven't identified a specific gene or set of genes that can, on their own, cause depression and anxiety. But we do know there is a big genetic factor—and there's a quite simple way to test it.

You take large groups of identical twins, and large groups of nonidentical twins, and you compare them. All twins are genetically similar, but identical twins are much more genetically similar: they come from the same egg, which split in two. So if you find a higher rate of (say) red hair, or addiction, or obesity, in identical twins than in nonidentical twins, you know there's a larger genetic component. By looking at the degree of difference, scientists reckon you can figure out roughly how much it can be put down to genes.

This has been done with depression and anxiety. What the leading scientists found—according to the National Institutes of Health overview of the best twin research—is that for depression, 37 percent of it is inherited, while for severe anxiety, it is between 30 and 40 percent. To give you a comparison, how tall you are is 90 percent inherited; whether you can speak English is zero percent inherited. So the people who study the genetic basis for depression and anxiety have concluded that it's real, but it doesn't account for *most* of what is going on. There is, however, a twist here.

A group of scientists led by a geneticist named Avshalom Caspi did one of the most detailed studies of the genetics of depression ever conducted. For twenty-five years, his team followed a thousand kids in New Zealand from being babies to adulthood. One of the things they were trying to figure out was which genes make you more vulnerable to depression.

Years into their work, they found something striking. They discovered that having a variant of a gene called 5-HTT *does* relate to becoming depressed.

Yet there was a catch. We are all born with a genetic inheritance—but your genes are activated by the environment. They can be switched on, or off, by what happens to you. And Avshalom discovered—as Professor Robert Sapolsky explains—"that if you have a particular flavor of 5-HTT, you have a greatly increased risk of depression, but *only in a certain environment.*" If you carried this gene, the study showed, you *were* more likely to become depressed—but only if you had experienced a terribly stressful event, or a great deal of childhood trauma. (They didn't test for most of the other causes of depression I've been talking about here, such as loneliness, so we don't know if they also interact with genes in this way.)

If those bad things *hadn't* happened to you, even if you had the gene that related to depression, you were no more likely to become depressed than anyone else. So genes increase your sensitivity, sometimes significantly. But they aren't—in themselves—the cause.

This means that if other genes work like 5-HTT—and it looks as if they do—then nobody is condemned to be depressed or anxious by their genes. Your genes can certainly make you more vulnerable, but they don't write your destiny. We all know how this works when it comes to weight. Some people find it really hard to put on weight: they can guzzle Big Macs and remain bone-thin. But some other people (cough, cough) have only to eat one fun-size Snickers for us to start to look like whales on Boxing Day. We all hate those skinny Big Mac munchers—but we also know that even if you are genetically more prone to put on weight, you still have to have lots of food in your environment for your genetic propensity to put on weight to kick in. Stranded in the rain forest or the desert with nothing to eat, you'll lose weight whatever your genetic inheritance is.

Depression and anxiety, the current evidence suggests, are a little like that. The genetic factors that contribute to depression and anxiety are very real, but they also need a trigger in your environment or your psychology. Your genes can then supercharge those factors, but they can't create them alone.

∼

But as I dug further, I realized I couldn't leave the questions of the role played by brains and genes there.

It used to be thought—as I explained earlier—that some depressions are caused by what happened to us in our lives, and then there is another, purer kind of depression that is caused by something going badly wrong in your brain. The first kind of depression was called "reactive," and the second, purely internal kind was called "endogenous."

So, I wanted to know, is there some group of depressed people whose pain really is caused in just the way my doctor explained to me—by their brain wiring going wrong, or some other innate flaw? If it exists, how common is it?

The only proper scientific study of this I could track down was—as I mentioned earlier—by George Brown and Tirril Harris, the scientists who did that very first study into the social causes of depression with women in South London. They looked at people who had been hospitalized for reactive depressions and compared them to people who had been classed as having endogenous depressions. It turned out that their circumstances were exactly the same: they had had an equal amount of things happen to them to trigger their despair. The distinction seemed, to them at that time, based on their evidence, to be meaningless.

But that doesn't necessarily mean that endogenous depression doesn't exist. It might just mean that doctors weren't good at spotting the difference back then. There hasn't—so far as I can see—been any definitive research on this. So I asked many people involved in treating depressed patients if they believe endogenous depression—the kind caused just by a malfunctioning brain or body—is real. They disagreed with one another. Professor Joanna Moncrieff told me she thinks it doesn't exist at all. Dr. David Healy told me it's "a vanishingly small number of people—no more than one in a hundred [of] the people who get labeled as depressed, maybe less." Dr. Saul Marmot told me it could be as many as one in twenty of the people who come to him with depression.

But everyone agreed that if it exists at all, it's a tiny minority of depressed people. This means that telling all depressed people a story that focuses only on these physical causes is a bad idea—for reasons I'll come to in a moment.

Yet what about, I wanted to know, things like bipolar or manic depression? It seems like there is more of a physical component with them. Professor Joanna Moncrieff said that this does seem to be correct—but it shouldn't be overstated. They are a very small proportion of depressed people, but with them, she says, "I think the depression does have some biological component." A manic episode, she says, is a bit like taking lots of amphetamines, which leaves you with a low that's a bit like "an amphetamine comedown." But that shouldn't mislead us, she says. Even when there is a real biological component, as in these cases, it's certainly not the whole picture—and several studies have found that the social causes of depression and anxiety will still affect the depth and frequency of their depression.

There are other situations where we know that a biological change can make you more vulnerable. People with glandular fever, or underactive thyroids, are significantly more likely to become depressed.

It is foolish to deny there is a real biological component to depression and anxiety (and there may be other biological contributions we haven't identified yet)—but it is equally foolish to say they are the only causes.

~

So why do we cling so stubbornly to a story that focuses only on the brain or genes? As I interviewed many people about this, I could find four main reasons. Two are very understandable; and two are unforgivable.

Everyone reading this will know somebody who became depressed, or anxious, yet seemingly had nothing to be unhappy about. It can be totally baffling: someone who looks to you like they have every reason to be happy is suddenly in total despair. I have known lots of people like this. For example—I had an elderly friend who had a loving partner, and a nice apartment, and plenty of money, and a bright red sports car. One day he started to feel profoundly sad, and within a few months he was begging his partner to kill him. It was so sudden, and seemingly so unrelated to his life. It seemed that the cause must be physical. What else could explain it?

I began to think about him—and the many people like him—differently only when I started, by coincidence, to read some of the early feminist classics from the 1960s, and I realized something.

Picture a 1950s housewife living before modern feminism. She goes to her doctor to say there is something terribly wrong with her. She says something like: "I have everything a woman could possibly want. I have a good husband who provides for me. I have a nice house with a picket fence. I have two healthy children. I have a car. I have nothing to be unhappy about. But look at me—I feel terrible. I must be broken inside. Please—can I have some Valium?"

The feminist classics talk a lot about women like this. There were millions of women saying things just like it. And the women meant what they said. They were sincere. Yet now, if we could go back in a time machine and talk to these women, what we'd say is: You had everything a woman could possibly want *by the standards of the culture.* You had nothing to be unhappy about *by the standards of the culture.* But we now know that the standards of the culture were wrong. Women need more than a house and a car and a husband and kids. They need equality, and meaningful work, and autonomy.

You aren't broken, we'd tell them. The culture is.

And if the standards of the culture were wrong then, I realized, they can be wrong now. You can have everything a person could possibly need by the standards of our culture—but those standards can badly misjudge what a human actually needs in order to have a good or even a tolerable life. The culture can create a picture of what you "need" to be happy—through all the junk values I had been taught about—that doesn't fit with what you *actually* need.

I thought again about my elderly friend who was suddenly plunged into despair. He said he felt that nobody needed him, or had any interest in an old man. He said his life from now on was going to be all about being ignored, and it was humiliating, and he couldn't bear it. I wanted to see it as a brain malfunction, I realized now—because I didn't want to see what our culture was doing to him. I was like a doctor telling a 1950s housewife that the only reason a woman could be unhappy—without work, without creativity, and without control over her own life—was a defect in her brain or nerves.

~

The second reason we cling to the idea these problems are caused only by our brains runs even deeper. For a long time, depressed and anxious people have been told their distress is not real—that it is just laziness, or weakness, or self-indulgence. I have been told this various times in my life. The right-wing British pundit Katie Hopkins recently said depression is "the ultimate passport to self-obsession. Get a grip, people," and added that they should just go out for a run and get over their moaning.

The way we have resisted this form of nastiness is to say that depression is a disease. You wouldn't hector a person with cancer to pull themselves together, so it's equally cruel to do it to somebody with the disease of depression or severe anxiety. The path away from stigma has been to explain patiently that this is a physical illness like diabetes or cancer.

So I was worried that if I told people the evidence that depression is not primarily caused by a problem in the brain or the body, I'd be reopening the door to this jeering. See! Even you admit it's not a disease like cancer. So pull yourself together!

We have come to believe that the only route out of stigma is to explain to people that this is a biological disease with purely biological causes. So—based on this positive motive—we have scrambled to find the biological effects, and held them up as evidence to rebut the sneerers.

This question troubled me for months. One day I was discussing it with the neuroscientist Marc Lewis, and he asked me why I assumed that telling people something is a disease would reduce the stigma surrounding it. Everybody knew, right from the start, that AIDS was a disease, he said. It didn't stop people with AIDS from being horribly stigmatized. "People with AIDS are *still* stigmatized, greatly stigmatized," he said. Nobody ever doubted leprosy was a disease, and lepers were persecuted for millennia.

I had never thought about that before, and it threw me. Does saying something is a disease really reduce stigma? Then I discovered that in 1997, a research team at Auburn University in Alabama had investigated this very question. The professor in charge—Sheila Mehta, who I later interviewed—set up an experiment to figure out whether saying that something is a disease makes people kinder to the sufferer, or crueler.

If you took part in her experiment, you were taken into a room where they explained that this was a test designed to look at how people learn new information, and they asked you to wait a little, while they got it ready. As you waited, the person next to you started chatting with you.

You didn't know this, but the person talking to you was in fact an actor. He would mention in passing that he had a mental illness, and he then said one of two things about it. He either said that it was "a disease like any other," the result of his "biochemistry" not working properly; or he said it was because of things that had happened to him in his life, such as a disturbed childhood.

You then went into a different room, and you were told the test was beginning.

You were taught how to push buttons in a complex pattern, and your job was then to teach that pattern to the other person in the experiment— the guy you don't realize is an actor. We want to figure out, the experimenters told you, how well people learn these things. And here's the catch. When the other person fails to get the button-pushing pattern right, you should hit this big red button here—and that will give him an electric zap. It won't maim or kill him, but it will hurt.

As the actor got the patterns wrong, you would give him a succession of little zaps. In reality, he was only pretending to be zapped—but you didn't know that. So far as you knew, you were hurting him.

What Sheila and the other experimenters wanted to know was: Would there be a difference between how many times and how hard the actor was zapped, depending on which reason he had given for his depression?

It turns out that you were more likely to hurt somebody if you believed their mental illness was the result of their biochemistry than if you believed it was the result of what had happened to them in life. Believing depression was a disease didn't reduce hostility. In fact, it increased it.

This experiment—like so much of what I had learned—hints at something. For a long time, we have been told there are only two ways of thinking about depression. Either it's a moral failing—a sign of weakness—or it's a brain disease. Neither has worked well in ending depression, or in ending its stigma. But everything I had learned suggests that there's a third option—to regard depression as largely a reaction to the way we are living.

This way is better, Marc said, because if it's an innate biological disease, the most you can hope for from other people is sympathy—a sense that you, with your difference, deserve their big-hearted kindness. But if it's a response to how we live, you can get something richer: empathy—because it could happen to any of us. It's not some alien thing. It's a universal human source of vulnerability.

The evidence suggests Marc is right—looking at it this way makes people less cruel, to themselves and to other people.

~

The weird thing is that most of what I was learning should not, in one sense, have been controversial, or new to anyone. As I described before, for decades, psychiatrists have—in their training—been taught something called the bio-psycho-social model. They are shown that depression and anxiety have three kinds of causes: biological, psychological, and social. And yet almost nobody I know who has become depressed or severely anxious was told this story by their doctor—and most were not offered help for anything except their brain chemistry.

I wanted to understand why, so I went to Montreal to meet with Laurence Kirmayer, the head of the Department of Social Psychiatry at McGill University, who is one of the most thoughtful people about these questions that I had read anywhere.

"Things have changed in psychiatry," he said—and he then explained to me two more crucial reasons why we are being told stories only about our brains and our genes. "Psychiatry has undergone a real constriction from this bio-psycho-social approach. While some people still pay lip service to it, mainstream psychiatry has become very biological." He furrowed his brow. "It's very problematic." We have ended up with "a grossly oversimplified picture" of depression that he said "doesn't look at social factors . . . But at a deeper level for me, it doesn't look at basic human processes."

One reason why is that it is "much more politically challenging" to say that so many people are feeling terrible because of how our societies now work. It fits much more with our system of "neoliberal capitalism," he told me, to say, "Okay, we'll get you functioning more efficiently, but please don't start questioning . . . because that's going to destabilize all sorts of things."

This observation fits, he believes, with the other big key reason. "The pharmaceutical [companies] are major forces shaping a lot of psychiatry, because it's this big, big business—billions of dollars," he said. They pay the bills, so they largely set the agenda, and they obviously want our pain to be seen as a chemical problem with a chemical solution. The result is that we have ended up, as a culture, with a distorted sense of our own distress. He looked at me. The fact that "the entire program of psychiatric research should look like [this]," he said, "is really disturbing."

～

Some months later, Dr. Rufus May, a British psychologist, told me that telling people their distress is due mostly or entirely to a biological malfunction has several dangerous effects on them.

The first thing that happens when you're told this is "you leave the person disempowered, feeling they're not good enough—because their brain's not good enough." The second thing is, he said, that "it pitches us against parts of ourselves." It says there is a war taking place in your head. On one side there are your feelings of distress, caused by the malfunctions in your brain or genes. On the other side there's the sane part of you. You can only hope to drug the enemy within into submission—forever.

But it does something even more profound than that. It tells you that your distress has no meaning—it's just defective tissue. But "I think we're distressed for good reasons," Rufus said.

This, I realized, was the biggest division between the old story about depression and anxiety and the new story. The old story says our distress is fundamentally irrational, caused by faulty apparatus in our head. The new story says our distress is—however painful—in fact rational, and sane.

Rufus tells his patients when they come to him feeling deeply depressed or anxious: You're not crazy to feel so distressed. You're not broken. You're not defective. He sometimes quotes the Eastern philosopher Jiddu Krishnamurti, who explained: "It is no measure of health to be well-adjusted to a sick society."

I thought a lot about this, over the course of a year. It was hard to absorb, and I had to hear it from many directions and in many places before I truly understood. My job now was to give meaning to my pain. And, perhaps, to our pain.

PART III

Reconnection. Or, a Different Kind of Antidepressant

CHAPTER 14

The Cow

Early in the twenty-first century, a South African psychiatrist named Dr. Derek Summerfield landed in Cambodia, in a stretch of countryside that looked like all the clichés of South Asia you've ever seen—peaceful rice paddies rippling to the far horizon. Most people there were subsistence rice farmers, living as people had for centuries—but they had a problem. Every now and then, one of them would stand on a covered mound of earth, and an explosion would echo out across the paddies. Old land mines left behind by the U.S. war in the 1960s and 1970s were still lying there, all around them.

Derek was there to learn about how this danger affects the mental health of the local Cambodians. (In the course of researching this book, I went there too.) By coincidence, not long before he arrived, antidepressants had begun to be marketed in Cambodia for the very first time—but there was a problem for the companies trying to sell them. It turned out there was no obvious translation for the word "antidepressant" into the Khmer language. It was an idea that seemed to puzzle them.

Derek tried to explain it. Depression is, he said, a profound sense of sadness that you can't shake off. The Cambodians thought about this carefully and said, yes, we do have some people like that. They gave an example: a farmer whose left leg was blown off by a land mine, who came to the doctors for medical help and got fitted with a new limb but didn't recover. He felt constantly anxious about the future and was filled with despair.

They then explained that they didn't need these new-fangled antidepressants, because they already had antidepressants for people like this in Cambodia. Derek was intrigued, so he asked them to explain more.

When they realized this man was despondent, the doctors and his neighbors sat with him, and talked through his life and his troubles. They realized that even with his new artificial limb, his old job—working in the rice paddies—was just too difficult, and he was constantly stressed and in physical pain, and that was making him want to just stop living, and give up.

So they had an idea. They believed that he would be perfectly capable of being a dairy farmer, and that would involve less painful walking on his false leg and fewer disturbing memories. So they bought him a cow.

In the months and years that followed, his life changed. His depression—which had been profound—went away. "You see, doctor, the cow was an analgesic, and antidepressant," they told Derek. To them, an antidepressant wasn't about changing your brain chemistry, an idea that seemed bizarre to their culture. It was about the community, together, empowering the depressed person to change his life.

When he reflected on it, Derek realized this was true in his own psychiatric practice, back in a leading London hospital. He thought about the people he worked with there, and it hit him: "When I make a difference, it's when I'm addressing their social situation, not what's between their ears," he told me later over a beer.

This seems strange to most of us in the Western world in the age of chemical antidepressants. We have been told depression is caused by a chemical imbalance, so the idea of a cow as an antidepressant seems almost like a joke. But here's the thing. That Cambodian farmer *did* cease to be depressed when his social circumstances were changed. This wasn't an individualistic solution—they weren't telling him the problem was all in his head and to pull his socks up or swallow a pill. It was a collective solution. He could never have gotten that cow on his own; the solution couldn't have come from him alone, because he was too distressed, and anyway he didn't have the cash. Yet it did solve his problem, and that solved his despair.

As I traveled in Southeast Asia meeting people in similar situations, and after I walked away from my long conversation with Derek, I began to ask myself for the first time—What if we have just been defining antidepressants in the wrong way? We have thought of antidepressants solely as the pills we swallow once (or more) a day. But what if we started to think of antidepressants as something very different? What if changing the way we live—in specific, targeted, evidence-based ways—could be seen as an antidepressant, too?

What if what we need to do now is expand our idea of what an antidepressant is?

Soon after, I discussed everything I had learned with the clinical psychologist Dr. Lucy Johnstone, who said she found a lot of it persuasive. Now, though, I had to answer a different question, she told me. "How different would it be," she said, "if when you went to your doctor, she 'diagnosed' us with 'disconnection'?" What would happen then?

∼

Because we have been framing the problem incorrectly, we have been finding flawed solutions. If this is primarily a brain problem, it makes sense to look for answers primarily in the brain. But if this is to a more significant degree a problem with how we live, we need to look primarily for answers out here, in our lives. Where, I wanted to know, could I begin?

It seemed clear that if disconnection is the main driver of our depression and anxiety, we need to find ways to reconnect. So I traveled thousands of miles, interviewing anyone who might understand this.

I quickly discovered that this question has been studied even less than the causes of depression and anxiety. You could fill aircraft hangars with studies of what happens in the brain of a depressed person. You could fill an aircraft with the research that's been conducted into the social causes of depression and anxiety. And you could fill a toy airplane with the research into reconnection.

But in time, I was able to discover seven kinds of reconnection that early evidence suggests can begin to heal depression and anxiety. I started to think of them as social or psychological antidepressants, in contrast to the chemical antidepressants we have been offered up to now. As I look back today at the seven solutions I have learned about, I'm conscious of two things—that they might seem too small, and that at the same time they might seem impossibly large.

In one sense, these seven forms of reconnection are only tentative first steps, because they are built on provisional early research. I want to stress that we are at the early stages of understanding them, and while there is evidence that they would start to deal with a great amount of the depression and anxiety we are experiencing, it is also true that they would only be a start—there would still be much more to do even if we implemented all of them. But I think that if we look at them in detail, we might start to see an alternative direction of travel. They don't represent a program. They represent points on a compass.

Yet in another sense, they will seem audacious, because they require big changes—in our personal lives and in our wider societies—at a time when we have lost faith in our ability to make collective changes. I wondered at times—am I asking too much? But when I reflected on it, I realized that the audacity of the changes we need now doesn't tell you anything about me. It reveals only how deep this problem runs. If those changes seem big, that tells you only that the problem is big.

But a big problem is not necessarily an insoluble problem.

~

I want to be candid with you about how I felt while I was investigating this. When I put on my journalist's hat and quizzed people, I found it fascinating; but when I would get back to my hotel room, there was often a jarring moment when I had to think about how it related to my own life. What these scientists were telling me—in their different ways—is that for all of my adult life, I had been looking for explanations for my depression and anxiety in the wrong places. I found this hurtful. Adjusting my mind so I could start to see the sources of pain they were telling me about was not easy.

It was in this state of mind that I found myself in Berlin as winter began. I don't know quite why I went there. I sometimes wonder whether we are all drawn, in some unspoken way, to the places where our parents were happiest. My parents lived in West Berlin, in the shadow of the wall, when it was a divided city, and my brother was born there. Or maybe it was because several of my friends had moved to the German capital in the previous few years, to escape London or New York, in their attempt to find a sane way to live. A friend of mine, the writer Kate McNaughton, kept telling me on the phone that Berlin was a place where people like us—nudging beyond our midthirties—worked less and lived more. Nobody she knew worked nine to five. It was a place where people could breathe, in a way that they couldn't in the pressure-cooker cities where I lived. Berlin seemed to her like a long party, with no bouncers and no entry fee. Come and stay, she said.

So I was awoken every morning by her flatmate's cat in an anonymous apartment in the anonymous Berlin district of Mitte. For weeks

I wandered the city, talking to people aimlessly. I spent hours talking with elderly Berliners who had survived a near-century in the city. To be an elderly Berliner is to have seen the world remade and ruined and remade again. An elderly woman named Regina Schwenke took me down to the bunker where she hid, as a girl, with her family, and prayed to live. Another walked the route of the wall with me.

And then, one day, somebody told me a story about a place in Berlin and how it had changed his life. I went there the next day. I ended up staying there for a long time, interviewing dozens of people, and I kept coming back, again and again, over the next three years.

It was, I think, the place that taught me how to begin to reconnect.

CHAPTER 15

We Built This City

In the summer of 2011, in a concrete housing project in Berlin, a sixty-three-year-old woman in a headscarf forced herself to climb up from her wheelchair to stick a notice in her window. It explained that she was being evicted from her home for being behind on her rent, and so, before the bailiffs came, in exactly one week's time, she was going to kill herself. She wasn't asking for help, because she knew it wouldn't come. She just didn't want her death to happen without people knowing why. She told me later: "I could feel I was at the end—that the end was coming."

Nuriye Cengiz barely knew her neighbors, and they barely knew her. The housing project where she lived was in a neighborhood named Kotti, which is Berlin's Bronx—the place middle-class parents told their kids never to go at night. This housing project was like ones I've seen across the world, from East London to West Baltimore—a big, anonymous place where people hurried to their doors and triple-locked them. Nuriye's despair was just one signal, out of many, that this was no place to live. The project was awash in anxiety and antidepressants.

Before long, some of the other residents started to knock on Nuriye's door. They approached tentatively. Was she okay? Did she need any help?

She was wary. "I thought it was just fleeting interest. I thought they saw me as a stupid woman in a headscarf," she said.

In the hallways and on the street outside Nuriye's apartment, people who had scuttled past each other for years stopped and looked at each other. They had a good reason to understand where Nuriye was coming from. All over Berlin, rents were rising—but people in this neighborhood were facing especially steep increases because of a historical accident. When the Berlin Wall was built in a rush in 1961, cutting the city in half, the route of the wall was drawn pretty arbitrarily, with some strange zigzags—and this area, Kotti, ended up as the part of West Berlin that jutted into East Berlin like a tooth. That meant it was the front line: if the Soviets invaded, it would be taken first. So the neighborhood was semi-demolished, and the only people who wanted to live in the wreckage were the people who were shunned by other Berliners—Turkish manual workers like Nuriye, left-wing squatters and rebels, and gay people.

As they moved in to this half-abandoned place, the Turkish workers physically rebuilt Kotti, and the left-wing squatters and gay people prevented the Berlin authorities from knocking the whole place down and turning it into a highway. They saved the neighborhood.

But these groups had been glaring at each other with suspicion for years. They may have been united in their poverty, but they were divided in every other way. Then the wall came down—and suddenly Kotti wasn't the danger zone; it was prime real estate. It was as though one morning New Yorkers woke up and the South Bronx was in midtown Manhattan. In the space of two years, apartments being rented for 600 euros were going for 800 euros. Most people living on this housing project were spending more than half of their income on rent. As a result, there were some families left to survive on 200 euros a month between them. Many people were being forced to move out, leaving the only neighborhood they'd ever known.

So Nuriye's sign stopped people on the housing project in their tracks, not just out of sympathy, but because they identified with her.

In the months leading up to her decision to post the sign in her window, different people in the neighborhood had been trying to find a way to express their own rage. This was the year of the Tahrir Square revolution (and, soon, the Occupy movement), and after watching the events flicker across the news, one of the neighbors had an idea. There is a big main street that runs past their housing project into the center of the city. Some of the neighbors had been gathering there, on and off, to protest about the rising rents already.

What if, they wondered, we blocked the street with some chairs and some wood, and the residents who were being pushed out of the neighborhood—including Nuriye—came out of their apartments and went there? What if Nuriye sat in the middle of it, in her big electric wheelchair, and we stood with her and said we're not leaving until she gets to stay in her home?

We'd get attention, the media would probably come, and maybe Nuriye wouldn't kill herself.

Most people were skeptical, but a small group of neighbors went to Nuriye and proposed she come and sit with them in their little makeshift protest camp blocking the street. She thought they were a little bit crazy. But one Berlin morning, she went out, and sat there, right by the main intersection. The sight of an elderly headscarfed woman in a wheelchair in the middle of the street, next to some impromptu barricades, seemed peculiar. But the local media turned up on cue, to find out what was happening. Very different neighbors started to tell their stories to the cameras. People talked about living on almost nothing, and of being afraid of being forced to move out to the suburbs where there was a lot more prejudice against Turks, or left-wing rebels, or gay people. One of the Turkish women who had been forced by poverty to leave her country thirty years before explained to me later: "We lost the place we are from once. We cannot lose it twice."

There's a Turkish saying—if the baby doesn't cry, it doesn't get the nipple. They said they had begun the protest because they thought it was the only thing that would make anyone listen.

But soon after, the police came and said—okay, you've had your fun; it's time to take this down and go home. The neighbors explained that they hadn't been given an assurance that Nuriye could stay in her home, and even more crucially, they now wanted an assurance that everyone's rent would be frozen. Sandy Kaltenborn, whose parents were construction workers from Afghanistan, explains: "We built this city. We are not the scumbags of society. We have a right to the city, because we built this neighborhood." It wasn't the investors demanding higher rents who made this city livable, "it's everybody."

The neighbors suspected that in the night, the police would physically take away the chairs and the wood they had erected—so they developed, spontaneously, a plan. Another person who lived in Kotti—a woman named Taina Gartner—happened to have a loud klaxon in her apartment. She went to fetch it. She explained that they should draw up a timetable to man the protest site, and if the police came, whoever was there could make a huge noise with the klaxon. Then everyone could come down from their apartments and stop them.

In a scramble, people started to write down their names on a timetable to do shifts, through the day and night, to man the protest site in the street. You had no idea who you would be paired with—only that it was a random neighbor you had never met.

"I didn't think we would make [it for] more [than] three days," remembers Uli Hamann, one of the neighbors who were there that night.

Almost everyone suspected the same.

~

It was the middle of a freezing Berlin night, and Nuriye was in the street, in her wheelchair. People were afraid to be outside in the dark in Kotti, but, she says, "I thought—I have nothing to do, I have no money; if people want to kill me then I'm dead, so it's nothing to worry about."

It looked as if the whole protest camp would fall apart right there—because people were being paired, through the randomness of where they wrote their name, with people they had been suspicious of for a long time. Nuriye was paired first with Taina, a forty-six-year-old single mother with peroxided hair, a chest and arms covered with tattoos, and a miniskirt she wears even in a German winter. Standing next to each other, they looked like a comedy duo, the polar opposites of Berlin life—the religious Turkish immigrant and the German hipster.

They sat together, manning the barricades. Taina thought she knew everything about this neighborhood, but watching it in the darkness, she started to see it differently—how silent it was at night, how the streetlamps glowed dimly.

At first, Taina would tap away at her laptop, awkwardly. But then, as the nights went on, they began to talk haltingly about their lives. And they discovered something. They had both come to Kotti as very young women—and they were both on the run.

Nuriye had grown up cooking her food on an open fire, because in the poor neighborhood where she grew up, she had no electricity and no running water. When she was seventeen, she got married and started to have children. She was determined that her children would have a better life—so at the age of seventeen, she pretended to be several years older so she could come to Kotti and work on a factory floor assembling parts. In the factory, she was raising money so she could send for her husband. But when she did send for him, she received a message from back home: he had died unexpectedly. Suddenly, Nuriye realized she was alone in Germany, in her late teens, far from home, with two children to raise.

She had to work relentlessly. When she left her shift at the factory, she went to clean; and then she would go home to sleep for just a few hours before waking at dawn to deliver newspapers.

Taina first came to Kotti when she was fourteen years old, she explained, after her mother threw her out. She didn't want to end up in a children's home, and, she tells me, "I was always curious to go to Kreutzberg 36 [Kotti]," because her mother told her that if you go there "you'll get a knife in your back." This seemed to her impossibly exciting. When she arrived, she found "all the houses were looking more or less like after the Second World War—it was all empty and destroyed . . . So we started to occupy the houses in the shadow of the wall. It was only some people like me and some Turkish people who lived here before, in the rubbish houses they had been given."

When she went into the wrecked houses, "sometimes it was really spooky, [because there was] all the furniture, the place fully equipped, and the people were gone. So we thought—What happened here?" With a few of her friends, Taina set up a commune, and they lived together collectively in the remains. "We had been punks at that time. We were political punks—in a lot of houses, we had our clubs and our bands there. It didn't cost anything—only one, two, three marks, so the band had a little bit, and the price for beer and other drinks was very cheap."

After a few years, she realized she was pregnant, and living in a squat. "For me, it was a very bad situation. Suddenly I was alone with my son. I had nobody around to help me. It was a really strange situation."

Taina and Nuriye had both been alone, and single mothers, in a place they didn't know.

On the day the wall came down, Taina was pushing her baby son in a buggy when she saw a couple of East German punks crawling through a hole in the wall. "Where's the nearest record shop?" they asked her. "We want to buy punk records." She replied: "There's one very near, but I don't think you have the money." They asked her the price, and when she told them, their faces fell. Taina had almost no money at that time, but she opened her purse and gave them everything she had. "Hey, people," she said. "Go. Go buy a punk record."

When Nuriye heard Taina speak like this, she thought to herself: "It's another crazy one like me!" She had never told anyone before, but she confided to Taina that her husband didn't die in Turkey because he had heart trouble, as she had always said. He died of tuberculosis. "I was always ashamed to say it," she said. "It's a disease of poverty. He didn't have enough food, he didn't have medical care. That's one reason I came here—I thought he would get medical treatment and maybe I could bring him. But it was too late already."

After Nuriye and Taina's hours on the night shift, next up was Mehmet Kavlak, a seventeen-year-old Turkish German kid in baggy jeans. He listened to a lot of hip-hop and he was on the brink of being thrown out of school. Mehmet was paired with a retired white teacher named Detlev, who was an old-fashioned Communist, and he told Mehmet grumpily: "This is against all my beliefs." He regarded this kind of "reformist" politics—trying to bring about gradual change—as nonsense. But still, he was there. As the nights passed, Mehmet started to talk about his problems at school. After a while, Detlev suggested that he bring his schoolwork along so they could talk about it. As the weeks and then months passed, "he became like a grandfather to me," Mehmet told me. His schoolwork started to improve, and the school stopped threatening to expel him.

~

The umbrella that covered this little makeshift camp was donated by Sudblock, a gay café and club that had opened a few years before, directly opposite the housing project. When it opened, some of the Turkish residents were outraged, and its windows were smashed in the night. "I thought they shouldn't fucking open a gay café in my neighborhood," Mehmet told me.

Richard Stein—a former nurse who opened the club—has a little pointed beard. He came here to Kotti, he told me, in his early twenties from a little village next to Cologne, and he, too, like Nuriye and Taina, saw himself as a runaway. "When you grow up in a little village in West Germany," he says, "when you are a gay person, you have to leave. There was no other choice." When he first came here, to get to West Berlin you had to travel along a narrow little highway surrounded by armed guards, because, he says, "West Berlin was this island in the Communist sea," and Kotti "was surrounded by the wall," so he saw it as a wrecked island within the wrecked island. The truest Berliner, he told me, is always from somewhere else. And this was his true Berlin.

The first bar Richard opened, in the early 1990s, was called Café Anal. (The other name he considered was Gay Pig.) They had transvestite nights, and in the years after the fall of the wall, when the world headed to Berlin to party in the new Wild West, their parties were regarded as some of the most hardcore in the city. So when Richard came here to open Sudblock, he invited the neighbors to come to the café for coffee and cake, but they were wary—or worse. Some people would scowl at him.

When Nuriye's protest began, Richard and everyone else at Sudblock provided the chairs and the umbrella, the drinks and the food—all for free. When Richard proposed that the residents could meet whenever they wanted to in Sudblock—they could hold all the planning meetings there—"some of us were skeptical about it," Matthias Clausen, one of the residents, told me, "because there are a lot of conservative people here." Sandy Kaltenborn adds: "A lot of them were actually homophobic." So they were worried people wouldn't come.

But at the first meeting, there they were, albeit tentatively—all these old women in headscarves, these religious men, sitting with people in miniskirts, in a gay club. There was nervousness on all sides: some gay people were anxious about it, too, thinking this would ruin the unity of the residents by pushing the Turkish protesters too far. But the need to fight the rent rises overcame even this concern, it seemed. "Everybody made so many steps," Uli Kaltnhorn remembers.

Some of the more consciously left-wing residents, who had been involved in protests before, discovered something right away at those early meetings. "We spoke literally different languages," Matthias Clausen told me. If they used the stock phrases of left-wing activism—the usual language that leftists speak among themselves—these ordinary people literally didn't know what they were talking about. They would look back, puzzled. So, Matthias says, "We had to find a way to speak . . . that everyone could understand. That forced us—me—to think about what I wanted to say, not to take refuge in some well-formulated phrases that in the end don't say anything at all." And it involved listening to people he'd never listened to before.

Everyone agreed on a goal—the rents are too high, and they need to fall. "It was a moment when people were like—we can't take it any more," one of the residents told me. "We are here. We built this neighborhood. And we don't want to move."

Some of the construction workers who lived in Kotti suspected this was going to be a long fight, and so they felt they should turn a protest camp consisting of some chairs and umbrellas into a more permanent structure. They gave it walls and a roof. Somebody took a beautiful old samovar—a way to boil water for tea and other hot drinks that's popular in Turkey—from their apartment and gave it to the protesters. They named the camp Kotti and Co. Before, a handful of the residents—on their own—had contacted Berlin politicians to complain about the rent rises, but they had been snubbed, or shrugged off. Now people from all over the city were coming to see the protest, and the protesters were appearing on the front page of newspapers. Nuriye was becoming a symbol. So politicians started to turn up, and they pledged to look into the question.

People living in Kotti who had been totally cut off before—scuttling from home to work, avoiding people's gaze—started making eye contact. "Suddenly, you enter a space you wouldn't have entered before, day by day," one of the residents, Sandy, told me. "You have to listen more . . . We have met people we would never have met before." He found himself listening one night to two older men as they described what it was like to do military service in Turkey. He'd never thought about his neighbors' lives in this way.

Nuriye was amazed that people had responded to the sign in her window. "They seemed to like me, I don't really know why," she told me. "They always came and spent time with me."

They decided—after a few months—that they had to step up their protests, and so they resolved to organize a march. Nuriye had never been to a physical protest before, and she wanted to stay at the back. Taina—in her miniskirt—told her this was nonsense: they were going to be at the very front, leading the march. And so there they were, leading the protest. People banged pots and pans, and as they walked through Kotti, people cheered them on the streets. From a window, a family had hung a banner: WE WILL ALL STAY HERE, it said.

The residents started to investigate why the rents were rising. They discovered that years before, back in the 1970s, a series of strange property deals had been made. At that time, people were abandoning West Berlin as a place to live, and the West German government knew it would be a deep embarrassment for the West if this showroom for freedom in the middle of communism emptied out—so property developers were offered remarkably generous rents, guaranteed by the state, for generations, in return for building on the front line. So once you factored in the rents that had been paid over the years, the protesters calculated that the costs of the building had already been paid off five times over. But here the residents were, having to pay more and more.

Their protests continued as the months passed. Sometimes lots of people came; sometimes not many people came.

One day, one of the most engaged residents, Uli Kaltnhorn, burst into tears at one of the meetings. She was exhausted. There had been so many night shifts, and so much action, and nothing much seemed to be changing with their rents. "You look so exhausted. You look so down," another one of the residents said. "We should stop it—we should stop the protests and go home. It's not worth it when you are so down." She concluded: "We have to stop this, if this is the cost."

"We looked at each other," Uli remembers, "to see—what can we bear?"

~

About three months after the protest began, a man in his early fifties appeared one day at the Kotti and Co. protest site. His name was Tuncai; he had only a few teeth, and a malformed palate that made it hard for him to speak. He had clearly been homeless for a while. He started—without anyone's asking—to tidy up the site. He asked if there was anything else he could volunteer to do.

Tuncai hung around for a few days, fixing a few small things and carrying water from the gay club across the street to the protest camp, until Mehmet—the young hip-hop fan who was one of the people on the night shift—told him he was welcome to sleep overnight there. Over the next few weeks, Tuncai got talking to some of the most conservative Turkish residents, who had been staying away from the protest. They brought him clothes, and food, and they started to stick around.

Before long, the camp was being run during the day by local Turkish women—who had often been confined to their homes, alone, for most of the time. They adored Tuncai.

"We need you permanently," Mehmet told Tuncai one day, and they made him a bed, and everyone started to chip in to provide for Tuncai, until the gay bar across the street, Sudblock, gave him a paid job. He became a key part of the camp: whenever people were down, he would hug them. When they led marches, he would be out in front, blowing a whistle.

Then one day, the police came to one of the protests. Tuncai hated people arguing, so when he thought there was a dispute brewing, he walked up to one of the police officers and tried to hug him. They arrested him.

That's when it was discovered that many months before Tuncai arrived at Kotti and Co., he had escaped from a psychiatric institution where he had been detained for almost his entire adult life. The police took him back there. Psychiatric patients are distributed throughout Berlin's secure units according to the first letter of their surname, so he was sent to the opposite side of the city. He was locked in a room with no furniture that was empty except for a bed, and a closed window. "It is always closed because just outside is the guard," he told me. "It is always closed." He added: "The worst thing was the isolation. You are isolated from everything."

Back at Kotti and Co., people demanded to know where Tuncai was. The elderly Turkish women walked into Sudblock and said to Richard Stein, the manager: "They took Tuncai! We have to bring him back. He belongs with us."

The residents went to the police, and at first they weren't told anything. Eventually they tracked Tuncai down at the psychiatric unit where he was being held. Thirty of the people from Kotti and Co. descended on it to explain they wanted Tuncai back. When they were told he had to be detained, they said: "That cannot be. Tuncai is not a person who should be [put away]. He needs to be out with us here."

The camp turned itself into a Free Tuncai movement—they put together a petition to get him out, and they kept showing up at the facility, in big groups, to demand to see him, and for him to come home with them. The place was surrounded with barbed wire, and the security to get in was like an airport. They said to the psychiatrists: "We all know him as he is, and we love him."

The psychiatric authorities were baffled. They'd never had a mass protest for a release. "They never heard a story where somebody would be interested in one of their so-called clients," Sandy told me. Uli added: "Our stubbornness, our refusal to believe this fucking system would take so long, made us push them." They learned that Tuncai had escaped five times before, and every time, he was brought back and imprisoned. "Nobody gave him any kind of chance," Sandy realized. "It is a typical example of how a lot of people don't get any chance."

Finally—after eight weeks of protest—the psychiatric authorities agreed to release Tuncai if certain conditions could be met. He needed to have an apartment, and a permanent paid position. "Anybody who knows Tuncai knows those are the last things he would think of," Uli says. "What he needed was a sense of community he was attached to and he was useful for. He needed *sense*—a social sense, an aim he liked and he shared. They never saw that." But—fine. Sudblock comfirmed he had a permanent job working with them. And an elderly man decided to move out of his apartment after his TV caught fire, so Tuncai was given his apartment, and the community moved in to renovate and decorate it to welcome him home.

When I sat with Tuncai in the protest camp, he told me: "They gave me so much—they gave me clothes and warm food and a place to stay. When I was in the hospital they made a petition—I don't know how to give all that back. It was incredible." Later, he said: "I am incredibly happy. With my family—Uli and Mehmet and all the people who stand behind me—just incredibly happy . . . To be here and to be over there at Café Sudblock—that's the thing."

"He was fifty-three years old," Uli told me, "and it was the first time he found his home."

Lots of the people who were drawn to the protests at Kotti felt like that. Matthias Clausen, a student who lived in the housing project, told me: "Since I was a little kid, I moved once every four or six years—and I never felt at home like I do here. I never knew so many neighbors—it's very special . . . I never had [something like] this with any neighbor in my life—and few other people have."

In the fight for lower rents, in the fight for Tuncai, the protesters were changing one another. The fact that the gay club had rallied to rescue this Turkish guy in need impressed all the Turkish neighbors. Mehmet—who had been appalled by the gay club when it opened—told me: "When I got to know them I realized—everyone can do what they want to do. We get great support from Sudblock . . . It has definitely changed me." And when it comes to the wider protests, he says: "The one person that surprised me most was myself. I realized what I could do—my own competence."

When people remarked on how strange it was—this coalition of Muslims and gays, squatters and hijab wearers—the people at Kotti would scoff. "That's not my problem! That's the problem of people who think like that!" Nuriye told me. "That's not my issue. If somebody worries about Taina's short skirts and my headscarf, that's not my issue. We think they match." She laughed. "If this isn't normal to you—see a psychologist! We are friends. I learned in my family and through my whole life—don't care for appearances. What matters is the inside."

It wasn't a straight line toward greater tolerance. It had zigs and zags. "Everybody should do what they want, so long as they don't try to convert me," Nuriye told me. "I'm not sure how I'd react if my children said they were gay—I don't know." Sudblock offered to sponsor the Turkish teenage girls' soccer team. Their parents said it was a step too far—to put the name of this gay club on their daughters' jerseys.

One day, long into the protest, Richard Stein was in his bar when one of the most conservative Turkish residents—a woman who wears the full niqab—gave him some cakes. He opened the box. Out of icing, on top of one of them, she had made a little rainbow flag.

~

But while Kotti and Co. were coming together, the evictions were continuing. One day, Nuriye met a woman rather like herself. Rosemary was in her sixties, mostly confined to a wheelchair, and she was being evicted from her home in another part of Berlin because she couldn't pay the rent anymore. "She had suffered a lot in East Germany, under the [communist] regime—she was tortured, and she wasn't healthy—she was mentally ill, she was physically ill," Nuriye remembers. "It moved me, that this woman was being kicked out." So Nuriye decided to take more direct action. When she heard an eviction was happening, she would go there— often with Taina—and she would use her large electric wheelchair to physically block the entrance, so the bailiffs couldn't get in.

"I got so angry I decided to block the door any way possible," she says. When the police came and tried to physically remove her, she said she had just had an operation to remove her gall bladder—which was true. "I said if you touch me, if anything happens to me, I have all these witnesses around me—it's going to be very bad for you . . . I'm not going to resist, I'm not going to curse you, but what you are doing is wrong. Don't touch me."

"You could see in their faces that is not what they had been expecting," Taina told me. "A protest like that, having a Muslim woman in a wheel-chair not moving and not being afraid of them. They had all their stuff on looking like Darth Vader, and she just sits there in her wheelchair and smiles and says 'I will not move.'"

But Rosemary was thrown out of her home. Two days later, in a cold homeless shelter, she died of a heart attack.

Nuriye herself was, not long after this, forced to leave her home, too— although, after a long and frenetic hunt, the community found her another apartment only a short journey away.

So Kotti and Co. stepped up their organizing. They protested more. They argued more. They marched more. They attracted more media. They dug more into the financials of the companies that owned their homes—and found that even the city's politicians didn't understand the ludicrous contracts that had been drawn up so long ago.

And then—one day, a year after their protest began—the news came through. Thanks to Kotti's political pressure, their rents would be frozen. There was a guarantee they would remain at the same rate. This didn't happen at any other housing projects in Berlin, but it happened here. It was the direct result of their activism.

Everyone was thrilled—and yet when I spoke to people, they told me they no longer thought of the protest as being only about the rents. One of the Turkish German women at Kotti, Neriman Tuncer, told me she had gained something so much more important than a lower rent—it led her "to realize how many beautiful people are living around you, as your neighbors." They had been there all along, but they had never seen one another. And now—here they all were. When they lived in Turkey, the women there had referred to their entire village as "home." And when they came to Germany, they learned that what you are supposed to think of as home is your own four walls and the space within them—a pinched, shriveled sense of home. But as these protests erupted, their sense of home expanded once again—to cover the whole housing project, and the dense network of people who live there.

As Neriman said that to me, I wondered how many of us—in our culture—are, by the standards of Kotti and Co., homeless. How many of us—if we were thrown out of our homes, or were carted off to a psychiatric institution—would have dozens and dozens of people standing by our side, protecting us? "That is the heart of this protest—we all going over the limit by caring for each other," one of the protesters told me. "By caring for each other, we grew."

Over the samovar, Mehmet told me that if this protest hadn't happened, he would have dropped out of high school. He said he learned: "Here is something you can lean on, and together, we can become strong . . . I am so happy I got to know so many beautiful people." Taina told me: "We all learned a lot—I can see something through the eyes of another person and that's a new [source of] meaning . . . We are like a family."

Another of the protesters, Sandy, told me the protests showed how weird it is—the idea that we should all sit apart from one another, pursuing our own little story, watching our own little TV, and ignoring everyone around us. "It's normal," he said, "that you care."

~

I sometimes think the people at Kotti and Co. think I am crazy, because I would turn up every now and then, sit with them, listen to their stories, and at some point, I would start to cry.

Before the protests, Sandy noticed that "a lot of people are depressed. They pull back . . . Highly depressed. On medication . . . They were sick, ill, because of these issues." Nuriye had been so depressed she was going to kill herself. But then, "because of these protests, they became very political people again." Sandy said gently: "It's like therapy for us."

One of the protesters, Uli, told me that at Kotti, they "made themselves public." At first, when she said this, I thought it was a slightly clunky translation, in her otherwise perfect English. But then I thought about it more, and I realized she had actually found the ideal words for what they did. They had stopped being solely private. They had stopped sitting alone. They had made themselves public. And it was only by doing that—by being released into something bigger than themselves—that they had found a release from their pain.

~

Two years after Nuriye first posted her plea for help in her window, when I arrived there for another visit, I found that the people from Kotti had teamed up with other activists across Berlin to step up their struggle. In the German capital, you—as an ordinary citizen—can trigger a referendum for everyone in the city to vote on, if you gather enough signatures on the street from people who say they want it. So the people I had met at Kotti fanned out across the city, approaching other Berliners to get them to sign up for a referendum that would keep rents low for everyone. It was a package of lots of reforms—more subsidies, elected boards to control the housing system, a commitment that any money made from the system would go toward paying for more low-cost social housing, an end to the evictions of poor people.

They gathered the largest number of signatures for a referendum in the long history of the city of Berlin. The members of the Berlin Assembly—panicked by the radicalism of the proposals—approached the people at Kotti and the others who had organized the referendum and offered to cut a deal. If you withdraw the referendum proposal, they said, we'll agree to most of what you want. If you don't, when you win, we'll challenge the result in the European courts for breaching European competition law, which would hold up the reforms for years and years.

They offered a smorgasbord of changes. If you were poor and couldn't afford the rent, you'd get an extra subsidy of 150 euros a month—a large amount for a poor family. Eviction would be reduced to the absolute last resort and become rare. And the management of the housing companies would from now on have elected members of the residents on the boards. "It wasn't what we wanted," Matti told me, but it's "a lot. That's a lot, definitely."

～

On my last day in Kotti, I sat outside Café Sudblock and many of the characters from this story wandered around me as I sat with Taina, who was chain-smoking happily in the cold sunshine. The protest site across the street is now a permanent structure. It will never be taken down. Some

Turkish women were drinking coffee, and some kids were kicking a ball around them.

As she inhaled, Taina told me that in modern society, if you are down, you are made to "feel it's only in your house. It's only you. Because you didn't succeed—you didn't get a job where you earn much more money. It's your fault. You are a bad father. And then suddenly, when we went on the street, a lot of people realized—hey, I'm the same! I thought I was the only one . . . It was what a lot of people told me too—I was feeling so lost and depressed, but now, okay . . . I am a fighter. I feel good. You come out of your corner crying, and you start to fight."

She blew her smoke away from me, into the air. "It changes you," she said. "You feel strong then."

CHAPTER 16

Reconnection One:
To Other People

In most parts of the Western world, Nuriye would have been told there was something wrong with her brain chemistry. So would everyone else in Kotti. They would have taken their pills and stayed alone in their little apartments until they were thrown out and scattered. I never felt more keenly that this story was wrong than at Kotti. They taught me that when people rediscover each other, problems that previously seemed insoluble start to look soluble. Nuriye was suicidal. Tuncai was shut away in a psychiatric hospital. Mehmet was going to be thrown out of school. What solved their problems? It seemed to me it was other people standing by their side, committed to walking on the path with them, finding collective solutions to their problems. They didn't need to be drugged. They needed to be together.

But all this was just an impression. So I was left with two questions. Is there any scientific evidence that changes like this reduce anxiety and depression, beyond the anecdotal stories of the people I met there? And is there any way we could we replicate it, beyond the unusual circumstances of Kotti?

After I read about one important area of research into this, I went to Berkeley, California, to talk with one of the social scientists who carried it out—a brilliant woman named Brett Ford. We met in a coffee shop in downtown Berkeley, which is seen by the outside world as a font of left-wing radicalism, but on my way to meet her, I passed lots of young homeless people, all begging, all being ignored. Brett was tapping away frantically on her laptop when I arrived. She was, she explained, in the middle of applying for jobs. With her colleagues Maya Tamir and Iris Mauss—both professors—she had begun, several years before, conducting some research into a pretty basic question.

They wanted to know: Does trying consciously to make yourself happier actually work? If you decided—today, now—to dedicate more of your life to deliberately seeking out happiness, would you actually be happier a week from now, or a year from now? The team studied this question in four countries: the United States, Russia (at two different locations), Japan, and Taiwan. They tracked thousands of people, some of whom had decided to deliberately pursue happiness and some of whom hadn't.

When they compared the results, they found something they had not expected. If you deliberately try to become happy, you will *not* become happier—if you live in the United States. But if you live in Russia, Japan, or Taiwan, you *will* become happier. Why, they next wanted to know, would that be?

Social scientists have known for a long time that—to put it crudely—there is a significant difference between how we think of ourselves in Western societies and how people in most of Asia conceive of themselves. There are lots of little experiments you can carry out to see this. For example—take a group of Western friends, and show them a picture of a man addressing a crowd. Ask them to describe what they see. Then approach the next group of Chinese tourists you see, show them the same picture, and ask them to describe it. The Westerners will almost always

describe the individual at the front of the crowd first, in a lot of detail—
then they describe the crowd. For Asians, it's the other way around: they'll
usually describe the crowd, and then, afterward, almost as an afterthought,
they'll describe the guy at the front.

Or take a picture of a little girl who is smiling broadly, in the middle
of a group of other little girls who look sad. Show it to some kids and ask
them—does this girl in the middle seem happy or sad to you? Western
kids think she is happy. Asian kids think she is sad. Why? Because the
Western kids have no problem isolating an individual from the group,
whereas Asian kids take it for granted that if a kid is surrounded by
distress, she'll be distressed, too.

In other words: in the West, we mostly have an individualistic way of
looking at life. In Asia, they mostly have a collective way of looking at life.

When Brett and her colleagues looked deeper, this seemed to offer the
best explanation for the difference they had discovered. If you decide to
pursue happiness in the United States or Britain, you pursue it for yourself—because you think that's how it works. You do what I did most of
the time: you get stuff for yourself, you rack up achievement for yourself,
you build up your own ego. But if you consciously pursue happiness in
Russia or Japan or China, you do something quite different. You try to
make things better for your group—for the people around you. That's
what you think happiness means, so it seems obvious to you. These are
fundamentally conflicting visions of what it means to become happier.
And it turns out—for all the reasons I described earlier—that our
Western version of happiness doesn't actually work—whereas the collectivist vision of happiness does.

"The more you think happiness is a social thing, the better off you are,"
Brett explained to me, summarizing her findings and reams of other social
science.

As Brett talked me through this research, I realized what I had been
seeing at Kotti all along. They had shifted from an individualistic vision

of how to live—shut yourself in your home, accumulate stuff for yourself there—to a collectivist vision of how to live: we're a group; we belong together; we are connected. In the West, we have shrunk our sense of self to just our ego (or, at most, our family), and this has made our pain swell, and our happiness shrivel.

This evidence suggests if we return to seeing our distress and our joy as something we share with a network of people all around us, we will feel different.

~

And yet this bumped up against something I am a little embarrassed to confess. When I started work on this book, I wanted quick solutions to my depression and anxiety—ones that I could pursue on my own, fast. I wanted something I could do now, for myself, to make *me* feel better. I wanted a pill, and if the pills wouldn't work, I wanted something as brisk as a pill. You, as a reader who has chosen a book about depression and anxiety, probably want the same.

When I discussed some of the ideas I was putting forward in this book, one person I know said I'd just been taking the wrong pill—you should, he said, try Xanax instead. I was tempted. But then I realized— how can we say the solution to all the understandable pain and distress I've been describing is to take a tranquilizer, and for millions more people to take it, forever?

Yet if I'm honest, that's the kind of solution I craved. Something individual; something you can do alone, without any effort; something that takes twenty seconds to swallow every morning, so you can get on with life as it was before. If it couldn't be chemical, I wanted some other trick, some switch I could flip to make it all fine.

What this evidence was telling me was that this search for quick individual solutions is a trap. In fact, this search for individual solutions is part of what got us into this problem in the first place. We have become imprisoned inside our own egos, walled off where true connection cannot reach us.

I started to think of one of the most banal, obvious clichés we have: Be you. Be yourself. We say it to one another all the time. We share memes about it. We say it to encourage people when they are lost, or down. Even our shampoo bottles tell us—because you're worth it.

But what I was being taught is—if you want to stop being depressed, don't be you. Don't be yourself. Don't fixate on how you're worth it. It's thinking about you, you, you that's helped to make you feel so lousy. Don't be you. Be us. Be we. Be part of the group. Make the group worth it. The real path to happiness, they were telling me, comes from dismantling our ego walls—from letting yourself flow into other people's stories and letting their stories flow into yours; from pooling your identity, from realizing that you were never you—alone, heroic, sad—all along.

No, don't be you. Be connected with everyone around you. Be part of the whole. Don't strive to be the guy addressing the crowd. Strive to be the crowd.

So part of overcoming our depression and anxiety—the first step, and one of the most crucial—is coming together, as they did at Kotti, and saying, in effect: What we've had up to now isn't enough. The lives we're being pressured and propagandized to live don't meet our psychological needs—for connection, security, or togetherness. We demand better, and we're going to fight for better, together. The key word in that sentence—and in how they thought—is "we." The collective struggle *is* the solution, or at least the essential foundation for it. At Kotti they got some of what they demanded at the start—but not everything. And yet the process of coming together to fight for it gave them a sense that they weren't broken-up individuals, but a collective.

I'm conscious that in some bookstores, this book will be shelved in the Self-help section. But I now saw that that whole way of thinking is part of the problem. When I have felt down, up to now, most of the time, I tried to help myself. I turned to the self. I thought there was something wrong with the self, and the solution would come from repairing and aggrandizing the self. I puffed it up. But it turns out—the self isn't the solution. The only answer lies beyond it.

My desire for a solution that was private and personal—the psychological equivalent of a pill—was in fact a symptom of the mindset that had caused my depression and anxiety in the first place.

~

After I learned this, I made a conscious decision to do something differently. Until I learned this, when I felt depression and anxiety start to set in, I felt a panicked need to keep my head above water—so I would try to do something for myself. I would buy something, or watch a film I like, or read a book I like, or talk to a friend about my distress. It was an attempt to treat the isolated self, and it didn't work very often. In fact, these acts were often the start of a deeper slide.

But once I knew about Brett's research, I saw the error I had been making. Now, when I feel myself starting to slide down, I don't do something for myself—I try to do something for someone else. I go to see a friend and try to focus very hard on how they are feeling and making them feel better. I try to do something for my network, or my group—or even try to help strangers who look distressed. I learned something I wouldn't have thought was possible at the start. Even if you are in pain, you can almost always make someone else feel a little bit better. Or I would try to channel it into more overt political actions, to make the society better.

When I applied this technique, I realized that it often—though not always—stopped the slide downward. It worked much more effectively than trying to build myself up alone.

~

Around this time, I learned about another area of research that had implications for this question—so I decided to go see its subjects for myself.

I saw my first Amish buggy on the wide, flat plains of Indiana as I whooshed past in a car going seventy miles per hour. By the side of the highway, a man with a long beard and black robes was sitting on top of a horse-drawn carriage. Behind him there was a child, and two women in bonnets who looked to me like refugees from a BBC historical drama set in the seventeenth century. Against the vast flatness of the American Midwest, where there is nothing on the horizon except more horizon, they looked almost like ghosts.

We had been driving for two hours out of Fort Wayne, the nearest city, and now Dr. Jim Cates and I had arrived in an Amish town called Elkhart-LaGrange. Jim is a psychologist who carries out psychological assessments on Amish members who've broken the law. Although he's "English"—the Amish term for everyone outside their group—he's a rare outsider who has been part of the community for years. He agreed to introduce me to people there.

We started to walk through the town, past a lot more horses, and women dressed in the exact same style of clothing their ancestors had worn three hundred years ago. When the Amish came to the United States back then, they were determined to live by a simple fundamentalist vision of Christianity and to reject any new developments that might interfere with it. That determination has persisted. So the people I was about to meet take no electricity from the grid. They have no TV, no Internet, no cars, almost no consumer goods. They speak a language that's a variant of German as their mother tongue. They rarely mix with non-Amish. They have a separate school system, and a radically separate value system from the rest of the United States.

When I was a kid, I lived not far from a community of ultra-Orthodox Jews who are like this in some ways, and as I passed them in the street, I was always baffled: Why would anyone live that way? As I got older, I developed—if I'm honest—a contempt for any group that rejected the benefits of the modern world. I saw them as crazy anachronisms. But now, as I was reflecting on some of the flaws in how we live, I wondered if they might have something to teach me after all—especially because of one key piece of research.

Freeman Lee Miller was waiting to meet us, outside a diner. He was in his late twenties and he had a medium-length beard: Amish men start to grow it when they get married. Almost before we started speaking, he pointed to something a little distance away—"Right over there, that red-green roof, that barn right there? That's where I grew up," he said. As a kid, he lived there, in a little collection of houses arranged around one another, together with four generations of his family running right up to his great-grandparents. Their electricity came from batteries or from propane gas, and they could travel only as far as they could get on foot or by buggy.

This meant that if one adult wasn't around, "you had another party to steer you the right way." You were constantly surrounded by adults and other kids: "So yeah, I definitely got enough attention," he said. They didn't have a concept of spending time with the family, because you were *always* with the family. Often, "spending time with the family was going out and working in the fields or milking the cows." Other times, it meant the constant family time of eating and social events. An Amish family isn't like an English family, he explained. It's not just your mom and dad and siblings. It's a big interconnected tribe of about 150 people—all the Amish, in fact, who live within walking or buggy distance of your home. There's no physical church for the Amish. You take turns gathering in different people's homes for the Sunday service. There's no permanent hierarchy at all—people also take turns serving as pastor, and it's allocated randomly.

"We're going to have church in our house Sunday," he said, and there will be his immediate family, but also all the other rings of Amish members, some of whom he knows very well, some of whom he knows only a little, "so it just builds another relationship . . . It's all about connection. Affection, in our community. And I guess that's where we go in a crisis—all of a sudden, you've got people showing up."

When they turn sixteen, all Amish have to go on a journey—one that makes them curiously well equipped to comment on our culture. They have to go and live in the "English" world for a few years. It's called going on Rumspringa, and out there, they don't follow the strict Amish rules for an average of two years. They get drunk, they go to strip clubs (at least, Freeman Lee did), they use phones and the Internet. (Lee told me he always thought somebody should launch a brand of rum named Rumspringa.) And then—at the end of their youth spurt—they have to make a choice. Do you want to leave all that behind and come home to join the Amish Church—or do you want to stay out in the world? If you stay out in the world, you can still come back and visit, but you'll never be an Amish. Around 80 percent choose to join the Church. This experience of freedom is one of the reasons why the Amish are never regarded as a cult. It is a genuine choice.

Freeman Lee loved a lot of things about the outside world, he told me—he still misses watching baseball games on TV, and listening to the latest pop songs. But one of the reasons he came back is because he believed an Amish community was a better place to have children, and to be a child. Out in that world, he felt like "you're always just hustling. You have no time for family. You have no time for kids." He couldn't understand what happens to kids in a culture like that. How do they grow up? What kind of life is it? I asked him how his relationship with his kids would change if (say) he got a TV. "We could watch it together," he says, shrugging. "We could enjoy TV time together. It still doesn't do justice [compared] with going out in the backyard. Even if just going to clean the buggy together. It doesn't do justice."

Later, I went to see Lauron Beachey, an Amish man in his early thirties, who works as an auctioneer, often selling off things taken from repossessed homes. We sat in his front room, surrounded by books (he loves William Faulkner the most), and he explained to me that you can only understand the difference between the Amish world and the outside world if you understand that the Amish have consciously chosen to slow down—and they don't see that as a deprivation. He knew I had just flown in from thousands of miles away, he said, and he explained: "I'd like to fly to the Holy Land, but our church has agreed we don't fly. It keeps us slower. It keeps the family more together—because if we fly, then I can fly to California to do an auction and then fly back, whereas now that's not practical, so we're at home more."

But why, I wanted to know, would you choose slowness? You lose something when you slow down, Lauron said—but he thinks you gain more. You gain "that sense [of] the local next-door-neighbor community. If we had cars, then our church district is going to be scattered across twenty miles. We wouldn't live right beside each other. The neighbors wouldn't come over for supper so often . . . There's a physical closeness, and as a result of that a spiritual or mental closeness, too. The automobiles and airplanes are ever so convenient, and we see the convenience to that speed, but as a group I suppose we decided to resist it, [so we can instead have] a close-knit community."

If you can be everywhere—in vehicles, or online—you end up, he believes, being nowhere. The Amish, by contrast, always have a "sense of being at home." He gave me an image to describe this. Human life, he says, is like a big warm coal fire that is glowing. But if you take out one coal and isolate it, it'll burn out quickly. We keep each other warm, he stays, by staying together. "I would have loved to be an over-the-road trucker and see the country and get paid and not have to sweat," he says. "I would have loved to watch the NBA playoffs every night. I like watching *That '70s Show*—I think they're hilarious. But they're not hard to give up."

As we talked longer, he started to compare the Amish to the groups out in the English world all around them, like Weight Watchers, where you gather together to lose weight and support each other. You'd never be able to resist all that food on your own; but as a group, banding together, checking each other, encouraging each other, you find you can. I looked at him, trying to process what he was saying.

"So," I asked, "you're saying the Amish community is almost like a support group for resisting the temptations of an individualist civilization?"

Lauron thought about it for a moment, smiled, and said: "That's one big benefit, yes."

~

After everything I had been learning, I found being among the Amish disorienting. As a younger man, I would have dismissed all this as just backwardness. But a major scientific study carried out on Amish mental health in the 1970s found that they have significantly lower levels of depression than other Americans. Several smaller studies since have backed up this finding.

It was in Elkhart-LaGrange that I felt I could see most clearly what we have lost in the modern world—and, at the same time, what we have gained. The Amish had a profound sense of belonging and meaning. But I could also see that it would be absurd to see the way they lived as a panacea. Jim and I spent an afternoon with an Amish woman who begged the community to help her when her husband was violently abusing her and their sons. The church elders told her it is the job of an Amish woman to submit to her husband, no matter what. She continued to be violently abused for years, before she finally left—scandalizing many in the community.

The group was united in ways that were inspiring—but it was also united by an often extreme and brutal theology. Women are subordinated; gay people are treated appallingly; the beating of children is seen as a good thing. Elkhart-LaGrange reminded me of my father's village back in the Swiss mountains. It had a profound sense of community and home; yet that home had often vicious house rules. It's a sign of how potent community and meaning are that when they were added to the scale, they could even, for some people, seem to outweigh the real and terrible pain these problems cause.

Is this, I wondered, an inevitable trade-off? Does gaining individuality and rights inevitably undermine community and meaning? Do we have to choose between the beautiful but brutal togetherness of Elkhart-LaGrange and the open but depressed culture of Edgware, where I grew up? I don't want to abandon the modern world and go back to a mythical past that was more connected in many ways but more brutal in many more. I want to see if we can find a synthesis in which we move closer to the togetherness of the Amish without suffocating ourselves or turning to extreme ideas that are often abhorrent to me. To get there, what would we have to give up, and what would we gain?

As I continued to travel, I began to find places and techniques that I think might offer the beginning of an answer.

~

Sitting in the middle of Amish country, Freeman Lee told me he knew his world would seem strange to me. "I understand how you guys would look at it," he said. "But our thought is—you can have a little bit of heaven here on earth, if you just interact with other people. Because that's how we imagine it to be, you know—when life comes to an end, if you get to heaven, it's interacting with people. That's how we look at it." If your picture of a perfect afterlife is being with the people you love all the time, he asked me, why wouldn't you choose today—while you're still alive—to be truly present with the people you love? Why would you rather be lost in a haze of distractions?

CHAPTER 17

Reconnection Two: Social Prescribing

I could see why so many people at Kotti were released from depression and anxiety—but their circumstances seemed unusual. How, I kept wondering, could you replicate their move from being isolated to being connected? It turned out the answer—or at least the first hints of one— had been just a few miles away from me all through my depression, in a little clinic in the poorest part of London. They have, they believe, found a model for how to spread it much more widely.

~

Lisa Cunningham sat down in her doctor's office in East London and explained that she couldn't be depressed. Then she burst into tears, and realized she couldn't stop. "Oh my goodness," her doctor said, "you *are* depressed, aren't you?" As the pain seeped out of Lisa, she thought—This can't be happening to me. I'm a mental health nurse. It's my job to solve problems like this, not succumb to them.

She was in her midthirties and she couldn't take it any more. For several years, up to this day in the mid-1990s, she had been working as a nurse on a psychiatric ward in a leading London hospital. That summer was one of the hottest in the city's history, and there was no air conditioning on her ward—they were trying to save money, apparently—and she had been sweatily watching as things went more and more wrong. Her ward treated people with all sorts of mental health problems serious enough to require hospitalization, from schizophrenia to bipolar disorder to psychosis. She had become a nurse because she wanted to help those people—but it was becoming clear to her that the hospital she was in just drugged people to the eyeballs.

One young man was brought in with psychosis, and he was drugged so heavily that his legs were shaking all the time and he couldn't walk. Lisa watched as the man's brother had to carry him on his back from his bedroom so he could sit and be fed his lunch. One of Lisa's colleagues mocked him by referring to an old Monty Python sketch: "Oh, it's a Ministry of Funny Walks around here, isn't it? Look at his legs!" she said. Another time, a patient became incontinent and another nurse reprimanded her in front of all the other patients. "Oh look—she's pissed herself," she said. "Oh god, can't you get to the toilet in time?"

When Lisa complained that they were not treating the patients like human beings, she was told she was being "oversensitive," and before long, the other nurses started to turn on her. Lisa had grown up in a home where there was a lot of aggression, so for her, this dynamic of being picked on and put down felt both familiar and unbearable. "I went into work one day, and I thought—I can't face being here," she told me. "I'm sitting at my desk looking at the computer screen. I couldn't do anything. Physically, couldn't do anything. And I said—Oh, I don't feel very well, I'm going to have to go home." When Lisa got home, she shut the door to her house, crawled into bed, and wept. She stayed there, essentially, for the next seven years.

A typical day for Lisa during her long depression was to wake up at midday, sick with anxiety. "Real, real anxiety," she says. She would obsessively think—"What do people think of me? Could I go out? You know, I lived in the East End of London. You couldn't go out your front door without seeing people." Day after day, she would put on makeup, try to steel herself to go out the door, and then take it all off and collapse back into bed. If it wasn't for the fact that her cats needed food, she might just have stayed at home and wasted away. Instead, she would bolt to the little shop five doors down, stock up on cat food and massive quantities of chocolate and ice cream, and hurry back home. Just before she was signed off sick, she had started taking Prozac, and on the drugs she began to put on enormous amounts of weight. She ballooned to sixteen stone (224 pounds). She was obsessively eating—"chocolate ice cream cake, bars of chocolate, and not a lot else really during the daytime," she says.

When I sat with Lisa, years later, she still found it hard to describe those years. "I was completely disabled by it. All the things that I had been confident doing up until that point [went away]. I used to love dancing. When I first moved to London, I got a reputation as being the first person to get up and dance, so I used to get into clubs for free. 'Oh, is it Lisa? Let her in for free. She'll be dancing soon.' But all that went with depression. I felt I'd lost me . . . I lost my identity completely."

Then one day her doctor told her about a new idea somebody had come up with, and asked if she would consider taking part.

~

One afternoon in the mid-1970s, on the gray western coastline of Norway, two seventeen-year-old boys were working in a shipbuilding yard. They were part of a team constructing a large boat. The night before, there had been high winds, and to prevent the crane from toppling, they had attached it, using a grappling hook, to a large immovable rock. But the next morning, somebody forgot that the crane was still attached—so when a workman tried to move it, the boys heard a loud creaking sound, and the crane suddenly began to fall in their direction. One of them—Sam Everington—managed to throw himself out of the way. He watched as the young man next to him disappeared beneath the crane.

"There's key moments in life when you think—shit, I'm going to die," Sam told me. After that moment watching his friend die, he made himself a promise. He wasn't going to sleepwalk through life. He was going to live fully. And that meant refusing to follow other people's scripts—to try to cut through to what really matters.

Sam thought of that moment when, as a young doctor in East London, he felt uncomfortable because he kept noticing something that he wasn't meant to notice. Many patients came to him with depression and anxiety, and he had been told by his training how to respond. "When we went to medical school," he explains, "everything was biomedical, so what you described as depression was [due to] neurotransmitters—it was a chemical imbalance." The solution, then, was drugging. But that didn't seem to match the reality of what he was seeing. If Sam sat and talked with his patients and really listened, the initial problem—the idea of something going wrong inside their brains—"very rarely ended up being the real issue that mattered to them." There was almost always something deeper, and they would talk about it if he asked them.

One day, a young Eastender came in who was feeling really down. Sam took out his pad, to give this man pills or refer him to a social worker. The man looked at him and said: "I don't need a fucking social worker. I need a social worker's wage." Sam looked at him and thought—"He's right. I'm wrong." He thought back over his training and realized: "I'm missing something." Everything he had been trained for was, he said to me later, "missing a massive part of the solution." His patients were often depressed, he realized, because their lives had been stripped of the things that make life worth living. And he remembered his pledge to himself, as a young man. So he thought—If we are going to respond to depression honestly, what do I do now?

~

Lisa walked, for the first time, into the doctor's center that Sam was helping to run. The Bromley-by-Bow Center is located in a concrete crevice of East London, sandwiched between some ugly housing projects, close to the end of a huge traffic tunnel. She felt painfully self-conscious. She had barely ever left the house for years. Her hair had grown out and become curly and unkempt: she thought she looked like Ronald MacDonald. She was skeptical that this new program would help, or that she would be able to bear being around people for long.

Sam's plan—working with a group of like-minded people—had been simple. He believed that something was going wrong for his depressed patients not primarily in their brains or their bodies, but in their lives, and if he wanted to help make them better, he had to help his patients change their lives. What they needed was to reconnect. So he was part of a team who helped to turn this doctor's office suite into a hub for all the volunteering groups in East London, as part of an unprecedented experiment. When you went to see your doctor, you didn't just get pills. You were prescribed one of over a hundred different ways to reconnect—with the people around you, with the society, and with values that really matter.

What Lisa was prescribed was something that seems almost stupidly modest from the outside. Around the corner from the medical center was an ugly scratch of scrub and concrete that the locals dubbed "Dog Shit Alley"—a messy place that contained nothing but weeds and a broken bandstand and (as the name suggests) dog shit. One of the programs Sam helped set up was to turn this ugly wasteland into a garden, full of flowers and vegetables. They had one member of the staff to coordinate, but otherwise it was up to a group of around twenty volunteer-patients who were depressed or suffering from other forms of distress. It's yours, they said. Help us to make it beautiful.

On that first day, Lisa looked at the scrubland, and looked at the other volunteers, and the thought that they were responsible for this made her seize up with anxiety. How, in two days a week, were they going to make anything work? Her heart began to thump.

She made very nervous and halting conversation with the other members of the group. She met a white working-class man who told her he had dropped out of school when he was really young. Later, the doctors told Lisa that for years he had come in to see them and been threatening and aggressive and they thought twice before even letting him in the program. She met Mr. Singh, an elderly Asian man who said he had traveled the world and began to tell fantastical stories about where he had been. There were two people with serious learning difficulties. And there were some middle-class people who couldn't shake off their own blues. Lisa looked at them and thought—There's nowhere else in London where we would all be talking to each other. But they agreed they had a common goal—to make this park nice for people to walk through.

In those first few months, they began to learn about seeds and plants, and they discussed what they wanted the park to look like. They were city people—they didn't have a clue. They had, they realized, to learn about nature. It was a slow process. One week they'd plant something and expect it to grow—but nothing came. It was only when they sank their fingers into the earth, and realized that in one part of the alley they had been planting on clay, that they saw their mistake. They began, as the weeks passed, to see they would have to learn the rhythms of the seasons and the earth beneath their feet.

They decided to plant daffodils, and key shrubs, and seasonal flowers. At first it was slow, and difficult. They realized "there's something about nature," Lisa told me. "You can't change how nature is—because the weather will do that. The seasons will do that. So you can plant things, and either they'll fail, or they'll succeed. You have to learn how to do that. You have to learn to be patient. It's not a quick fix. Creating a garden takes time and investment of energy and a commitment . . . You might not feel you've made much impact in one gardening session, but if you do that every week, over a period of time, you'll see a change." She was going to learn "it's about commitment to something that might take a long time, and having the patience to do that."

Normally, depressed or anxious people—when they are offered treatment beyond drugs—are put in a position where they have to talk about how they feel, but often that's the last thing they want to do. Their feelings are unbearable. Here they had a place where there was something slow and steady to do, and there was no pressure to talk about anything but that. But as they began to trust one another, they would talk about how they felt—at a pace they felt comfortable with. Lisa began to explain her story to the members of the group she liked. In turn they began to explain things back to her.

And what Lisa realized is that everyone there had understandable reasons to feel terrible. One of the men who came to the group was, he told Lisa quietly, sleeping on the Number 25 bus every night: the drivers knew he was homeless, so they didn't throw him off. Lisa looked at him and thought—how could you *avoid* depression in a situation like that? Just like the doctors in Cambodia who realized the farmer needed a cow, Lisa realized that many of the depressed members of the gardening group needed practical solutions. So she started to phone and harass the council until they finally agreed to house this man. In the months that followed, he became less depressed.

As time passed, the group began to see their flowers bloom. People started to walk through the park, and they would thank this group—who had been shut away, feeling useless, for so long—for what they were doing. One old white woman would always stop on her way home from shopping and give some of the Bengali women in the group money to plant more flowers. Mr. Singh, the elderly Bengali man, would talk to the group about how these plants were connected to everything in the universe—part of a cosmic plan. They began to feel, in their modest ways, that they had a purpose—that they could do something.

One day, another member of the group asked Lisa how she had become depressed, and when she explained, he said, "You were bullied at work? I was bullied at work." Later, he told her it was a key moment in his life: "I realized you are the same as me," he said.

As she told me that, Lisa teared up: "Oh, Jesus Christ, but that's what the project was about, really."

For many members of the group, two forms of deep disconnection were being healed. The first was disconnection from other people. There's a café in the Bromley-by-Bow Center that Sam runs, and they would sit there together after the gardening sessions, and after a few months, Lisa realized she was almost shouting, because it was such a relief—after so long—to be really talking to people again. She had been terrified to leave her front door, and crushingly self-conscious in front of people; but now she had been helped over that initial threshold, she realized. She says, "I was really almost desperate to reconnect with people." As she engaged with their problems and their joy, "I stopped obsessing about me so much. I had other people to worry about."

Phil, the angry young white guy, who the doctors had been a little afraid of—who they were wary of putting into the program at all—took the two people with learning difficulties under his wing. He was the first to make sure they were included in everything, and to help them. And he was the one who suggested that they should all study for a certification in horticulture—which the group then embarked on together.

The second form of disconnection that was being healed, Lisa believes, was from nature. "There's something about engaging in the natural environment, even if it's a little scrubby patch in a really urban area," she says.

"I just was reconnecting with the earth and noticing little things. You stop hearing the airplanes and the traffic, and you get a sense of just how tiny we are, our insignificance." Later, she said: "It was actually getting my hands dirty, literally getting them dirty" that helped her to discover "a sense of place. It wasn't just me. There's the sky. Out there's the sun . . . It isn't all about me, right? It isn't about my battle with injustices. There's a wider picture here, and I need to be part of that again. That's how I felt sitting on the paving in this garden with my hands in the flowerbed."

Because of this modest little program, "those two things that I had completely lost contact with"—people, and nature—"had come back into my life again."

It felt to Lisa like, as the garden came to life, the members of the group came back to life. They felt proud of something they'd done, for the first time in years. They'd made something beautiful. When I went to walk through the garden they had built, I felt a sense of serenity in this little green oasis, with a bubbling fountain, in this lumbering polluted lump of East London where I had lived for so long.

After she had been in the gardening program for a few years, Lisa stopped taking Prozac, and over the next few years, she lost four and a half stone (62 pounds) in weight. She had met a gardener who she fell in love with, a man named Ian, and after a few years more, she moved away to a village in Wales, where by the time I met her, she was about to open a gardening center of her own. She is still in touch with some of the people from the gardening group. They saved each other, she told me. Them, and the soil.

~

As I talked with Lisa for hours over an East London breakfast of sausages and chips, she told me that some people might misunderstand the lesson from the gardening group. "It isn't something that just happens. I think if you're depressed, you can't just go out and find a bit of garden and get stuck in it and you'll feel better. It has to be managed and supported." If people merely say "Oh, just go sit in a park, you'll feel better; go for a walk in the woods, you'll feel better," she says: "Yeah, of course that's true, but someone has to help you do it."

She could never have done it alone. It took a doctor to prescribe it—to talk her gently through its medical value, and to urge her on—for it to happen. Without it, she fears she might still be shut away in that house, guzzling Ben and Jerry's, afraid to be seen, slowly shutting down.

~

When you arrive at the reception desk of the Bromley-by-Bow Center, you will see that you have several choices. You can be referred to a doctor—or you can be referred to one of the more than a hundred social programs that work out of here, offering everything from pottery to exercise classes to going out into the community to help other people. If you go in to see a doctor, you find it looks a little different from any other doctor's office I've been to. The doctor doesn't sit behind a desk, with a screen in front of him or her. You sit side by side, together. This, Sam tells me, is one small expression of a subtly different way of thinking about health.

He was trained, as a doctor, to act as "the person who had the knowledge." The patient comes in, describes some symptoms, you do some tests, and then you pronounce what's wrong and how to solve it. There are some instances where that's the right approach, he says—"You've got a chest infection, you need an antibiotic, bang, bang, there's clarity"—but "the vast majority of the time" it's not like that. Most people come to their doctor because they are distressed. Even when you have a physical pain—like a bad knee—that will feel far worse if you have nothing else in your life, and no connections. Almost all his consultations, he says, are in part about the emotional health of the patient. The biggest job of the doctor is to listen.

He says he has learned, especially with depression and anxiety, to shift from asking "What's the matter with you?" to "What matters *to* you?" If you want to find a solution, you need to listen to what's missing in the depressed or anxious person's life—and help them to find a way to resolving this, the underlying problem.

The doctors at Bromley-by-Bow do prescribe chemical antidepressants, and they defend them and believe they work. But they only see that as one small part of the picture, and not a long-term solution. Saul Marmot, another doctor there, told me "there's no point . . . putting sticking plasters over" the patient's pain. No: "What you've got to do is tackle the reasons why they're there in the first place." Later, he said: "There's no point in using antidepressants if nothing has changed, so that when they come off the antidepressant they're still in the same place they were before . . . Something's got to change, or you're going to go back."

Often, the patients come in—just as I did—believing their depression is purely physical, a brain malfunction. Sam starts by explaining two things to them, both of which can be surprising. First he tells them that there's a lot doctors don't know about depression and anxiety, and that this is a complex question, so they'll have to work with the patient to get to the bottom of it. "It's [our] fundamental philosophy—having the humility to say 'I don't know.' It's really important. It's the most important thing you could say. And by the way, you will increase the trust a patient has in you by saying that."

And then he tells them about how, after he got divorced a few years ago, he became profoundly anxious all the time, for several years. It can, he says, happen to anyone. You're not alone. "There's something about saying 'It's okay,' " Sam says. "I hesitate to use the word 'normal,' but it's normal."

If, by contrast, Sam told you just that you have a problem inside your brain, he said, then "you have no control over it, and there's nothing you can do about it. That's clearly utter nonsense. And how does that set you up in the longer term?" he asks. "When you're depressed," he says, "you're in a very dark place, and if you can give somebody a taste of recovery, even if it's a small taste, just that small hope, a bit of hope, [it's] absolutely critical, and you never quite know where that hope is going to come from." So he lays out a big, broad menu of small steps they can take back to reconnection.

He tries to model that connection when he talks to his patients. Part of his job, he says, "is to be a friend." He lives just a few hundred yards from the center. He's available. And he says another key part of the center's philosophy is: "Any excuse for a party." They're always finding some reason to have a celebration, with all their patients invited.

Sam calls this approach "social prescribing," and it's spurred a real debate. The potential advantages are obvious. Sam's health trust alone spends £1 million a year (around $1.2 million) providing chemical antidepressants to seventeen thousand patients, with limited results. Sam suspects that social prescribing can get the same or better results for significantly less money. So for years, the Bromley-by-Bow Center—and other groups doing social prescribing—have been patiently gathering data, hoping that academics would come to study what they're doing. But little research has been done so far.

Why? It was the same story I had been hearing everywhere. Giving people drugs for depression and anxiety is one of the biggest industries in the world, so there are enormous funds sloshing around to finance research into it (and that research is often distorted, as I learned). Social prescribing, if it is successful, wouldn't make much money. In fact, it would blast a hole in that multibillion-dollar chemical market—there would be less profit. So none of the vested interests want to know.

There has, however, been a series of scientific studies of "therapeutic horticulture"—getting people to try gardening to improve their mental health. None of the studies have been carried out on especially big groups or for a long time, and the studies aren't perfectly designed, so we should handle them with some skepticism—but the results suggest there's something here we should be looking at more. One study of depressed people in Norway found that a program like this moved people on average 4.5 points on the depression scale—more than double the effect of chemical antidepressants. Another study of young women suffering from severe anxiety found similar effects. This suggests, at the very least, that it is a good place to start planting the seeds of research.

~

I went back to see Michael Marmot, the social scientist who first discovered that meaningless work makes us depressed. He had begun on his journey—as you might remember—in a clinic in Sydney, where he watched while people came in to his hospital depressed because their lives were lousy, only to be given a bottle of white mixture and told to go home. Michael, I knew, had visited and informally advised the Bromley-by-Bow Center over the years, and I wanted to hear what he had to say about it. He told me that what they are doing is simple. When people come to them with a physical problem, they treat the physical problem. But much—perhaps most—of the reasons we visit the doctor are not like that. "When people come to them with a problem in living," he said, "they try to address the problem in living."

~

Sam, the doctor who helped transform this clinic, told me he suspects that a century from now we will look back on the discovery that you need to meet people's emotional needs if you want them to recover from depression and anxiety as a key moment in medical history. Until the 1850s, nobody knew what caused cholera, and it killed enormous numbers of people. Then a physician named John Snow discovered (just a few miles from Sam's clinic, coincidentally) that the disease is carried in water—and we started to build proper sewage systems. As a result, cholera outbreaks in the West stopped.

An antidepressant, they have learned, isn't just a pill. It's anything that lifts your despair. The evidence that chemical antidepressants don't work for most people shouldn't make us give up on the idea of an antidepressant. But it should make us look for better antidepressants—and they may not look anything like we've been trained to think of them by Big Pharma.

Saul Marmot, one of the general practitioners there, told me that the benefits of the approach they have developed at Bromley-by-Bow are "so obvious I don't know why I couldn't see it before, and I don't know why the whole of society can't see it."

~

While we talked, Sam Everington and I were sitting in the center's busy café, and people kept interrupting us, to talk to him, or hug him. That's the woman who teaches people how to paint windows, he said to me at one point. That's the man who used to be a police officer, who came here as part of his job, fell in love with it, and now works here. It's funny, he says, to see the teenagers come and ask his advice for what somebody should hypothetically do to avoid a hypothetical crime.

As Sam waved to yet another person, he told me something. What he has learned is that when you can become connected to the people around you, "it's restoring of human nature." Sitting in this web of reawakened connections, a woman at the table next to us, who had been listening to our conversation, smiled, at him, and to herself.

Sam looked at her, and he smiled back.

CHAPTER 18

Reconnection Three:
To Meaningful Work

Whenever I became optimistic about the chances of this reconnection spreading beyond isolated points of light like Kotti in Berlin or the Bromley-by-Bow clinic in East London, I came back to a huge obstacle, and for a long time I couldn't see how we get beyond it. We spend most of our waking lives working—and 87 percent of us feel either disengaged or enraged by our jobs. You are twice as likely to hate your job as love it, and once you factor in e-mails, those work hours are spreading over more and more of our lives—fifty, sixty hours a week. This isn't a molehill. It's the mountain at the center of almost all our lives. This is where our time goes, and our lives go.

So yes, you can tell people to try alternatives—to reach out—but when, exactly, are they meant to do it? In the four hours when they collapse onto the sofa and try to engage with their kids before they clamber into bed before it starts all over again?

But that's not the obstacle I was thinking of. The obstacle is that meaningless work has to be done. It's not like some of the other causes of depression and anxiety I've been talking about, like childhood trauma, or extreme materialism, which are unnecessary malfunctions in the wider system. Work is essential. I thought about the jobs all my relatives have done. My maternal grandmother cleaned toilets; my maternal grandfather worked on the docks; my paternal grandparents were farmers; my dad was a bus driver; my mother worked in a shelter for victims of domestic violence; my sister is a nurse; my brother orders stock for a supermarket. All of these jobs are necessary. If they stopped being done, then key parts of our society would cease to function. And if that work—being bossed around, being made to do it, being disciplined by the market into doing stuff that's tedious but necessary—is essential, then even if it causes depression and anxiety, it must continue. It felt like a necessary trap.

On an individual level, a few of us might escape. If you can move to a job where you are controlled less, and have more autonomy, or are doing something you believe matters—do it. Your anxiety and depression levels will likely dip. But in a landscape where only 13 percent of people have jobs they find meaningful, that advice seems almost cruel. Most of us aren't—in this environment, as it stands today—going to get to work that we find personally meaningful. As I type this, I am picturing one person I know and love, who is a single mother, working a low-paid job she hates in order to keep her three kids in their apartment. Telling her she needs a more fulfilling job when she's battling to keep a job at all would be both mean, and meaningless.

I began to think about this obstacle differently—and to see a way beyond it—only when I went to a rather prosaic place. It is a small store in Baltimore that sells and repairs bikes. They told me a story. And that story opened me up to a much wider debate, and to the evidence that suggests we can infuse our work with greater meaning and make it radically less depressing—not just for a few privileged individuals, but for the whole society.

The day that Meredith Mitchell handed in her resignation, she wondered if she was doing something crazy. She worked at the fundraising arm of a not-for-profit campaign group in Maryland. It was a typical office job: she was given assignments with a deadline, and her role was to keep her head down and do what she was told. Sometimes she would have ideas about how they could do things better. If she tried to put them forward, she was told to get on with what she'd been assigned. She had a boss who seemed like a nice person, but she was volatile, and Meredith never really knew how to read her moods. Meredith knew that in the abstract her work was probably doing some good, but she never felt any connection to it. It felt like a karaoke life—her job was to sing along to a song sheet written by somebody else. It wasn't a life where she would ever get to write her own song. At the age of twenty-four, she could see this stretching out before her for the next forty years.

Around this time, Meredith started to feel a pervasive sense of anxiety she couldn't quite understand. On Sunday nights, she'd feel her heart pounding in her chest, and a sense of dread about the week to come. Before long, she found she couldn't sleep during the week, either. She kept waking up feeling cripplingly nervous, but she didn't know why.

Yet when she told her boss she was quitting, she wasn't at all sure she was doing the right thing. She had grown up in a politically conservative family, and what she was about to embark on seemed radical, and strange, to them—and, if she was honest, to herself.

Meredith's husband, Josh, had a plan. He had started working in bike stores when he was sixteen years old, and he'd been riding bikes as a hobby for years before that: he loved the 20-inch trick bikes, on which you could whirr around the city and carry out stunts off the sides of sloped buildings. But working in bike stores, he learned, is a really hard way to make a living. It's low-wage work. You don't get a job contract, or sick pay, or vacations. It can be monotonous at times. And you're pervasively insecure. You can't plan for anything, and there's no path up—you're basically stuck on the bottom rung. If you ever wanted a raise, or a day off, or to stay home when you were ill, you had to beg the boss.

Josh had been working for a few years in a typical bike store in the city. The owner wasn't, on a personal level, a bad guy, but life working in his bike store was—for all these reasons—pretty miserable. You could bear it as a teenager, but as you got into your twenties and started to think about the future, you found there was just a big hole ahead of you.

At first, Josh's solution was to try something that has largely faded from life in the United States. He approached his colleagues—there were ten people working in the store—and asked them if they would consider, together, setting up a labor union, to formally demand better conditions. It took some time to persuade people, but Josh is an enthusiastic guy, and everyone who worked there agreed to sign on. They drew up a list of pretty basic demands that they felt would make their lives better. They wanted written contracts. They wanted pay raises for two of the workers, to bring them up to the level of everyone else. And they wanted annual meetings to discuss salaries. It wasn't much, but it would, they felt, make them less anxious, and more secure.

But the list of demands was—in truth—more than that. It was a way of saying—we're not just cogs in a machine, like the screws we put into the bikes when we fix them. We're people, with needs. We're partners, and we deserve respect. He didn't quite think of it this way then, but it was about restoring dignity, Josh told me later, to working-class people who were being told that they were, basically, not worth much, and could be tossed aside at any time. Josh felt they were in a strong position, though, because he knew the business couldn't function without them.

When he was presented with the demands, Josh's boss looked really surprised, but he said he'd think about it. A few days later, he employed a tough labor-busting lawyer, and a long process of trying to deny them the right to organize began. It dragged on for months, and the whole U.S. legal system is designed to make it hard to organize a union and easy to break one up. The workers couldn't afford any kind of lawyer. His boss started to bring in new workers to undermine the unionized ones. Josh knew that, technically, it would be illegal for his boss to fire him or the other workers—but both sides knew the workers couldn't afford a long legal fight to assert that right.

That's when Josh had an idea. He knew how bike shops were run. The workers knew how it operated—because they literally did almost all the work. He thought—we could do this. We could run a store like this, ourselves, without the boss. If this was a conventional American story, Josh would now break away and set up his own business and rise to become the Jeff Bezos of bikes (or at least end up owning his own beach house on the Jersey Shore). But Josh didn't want to become the guy who orders everyone else around. In his years working in bike shops, he had noticed some things. The boss is isolated. Even when he's a nice guy, he's pushed into this weird position, controlling other people, which makes it hard for him to connect in ordinary ways. And this system—of having one guy at the top, giving orders—seemed to Josh to be quite inefficient. The guys working on the shop floor had loads of good ideas about how to make the business better. They could see things the boss couldn't see. But it made no difference. Their thoughts were irrelevant. And that actually harmed, Josh suspected, the business itself.

No—what Josh wanted was to be part of a business that ran on a different American ideal: democracy. He read up on the history of something called cooperatives. It turns out the way of working that we all take for granted now—a corporation that's run like an army, with one person at the top giving orders to the troops below, who have no say—is actually quite recent. It was only in the late nineteenth century that it became standard for human beings to work this way. When the boss-run corporation first started to take over, it was resisted intensely. Lots of people pointed out that it would create a system of "wage slavery" in which people would be controlled all the time and would end up feeling miserable. Some of them, Josh learned, had proposed organizing our work on totally different principles. They were called democratic cooperatives— and Josh learned that some had been really successful.

So Josh talked with some of his close friends, people he had worked alongside for a long time, and with his wife, Meredith, about an idea. Let's run our own bike store, and do it as a cooperative. That means we'll share the work, and we'll share the profits. We'll make the decisions democratically. We won't have a boss—because we'll all be the boss. We're going to work hard—but we'll work differently. And it might just make us feel better. Meredith thought it sounded appealing—but as she quit her old job, she kept wondering: Was it realistic? How would it work?

∼

As I approached Baltimore Bicycle Works on its corner in the downtown of the city, it looked like any other bike store. On the ground floor, there are bright bikes and accessories all around, on a cement floor, and there's a cash register, where Meredith was working when I arrived. When she took me upstairs, I saw there was a row of bikes lifted up as if on pulleys, and guys were standing next to them, looking as though they were performing some kind of primitive surgery. The bikes were partly dismantled, and they were being altered with screwdrivers and some tool I'd never seen before. Images of George Clooney repairing somebody's heart on *ER* flickered through my mind.

Alex Ticu, a guy in his late twenties with a big bushy mustache, carried on working on the bike as he told me about his life before he became a partner there, when he worked for a catering firm. He would hear from his boss once every two weeks, and "it would be a phone call in the morning, of her either yelling at me, or expressing disappointment, and then a phone call at the end of the night either yelling or expressing disappointment . . . But she had no idea what I was doing, so I never understood how she knew to be disappointed in me." Like a lot of people in standard jobs, he says, "I would wake up stressed in the middle of the night. It was pretty bad. It was affecting everything."

Here, he said, it works differently. At Baltimore Bicycle Works, they have a meeting every Thursday morning to discuss together the decisions they have to make as a business. They've divided the work of the business into seven different chunks—from marketing to servicing broken bikes—and everyone takes joint responsibility for at least two of them. If anyone has an idea for how to do something better, or to stop doing something that's failing, they can propose it at that meeting. If somebody seconds it, they discuss it as a group, and then they vote on it. So—for example—if somebody wants to start carrying a new brand of bicycles, that's the process they go through.

There are six full partners in the business, who all share the proceeds, and when I was there, there were also three apprentices who were spending a year as part of the process and—if everyone felt they were a good fit—would then become full partners. At the end of each year, everyone does an annual review on everyone else. The goal is for everyone to feel equally committed to the cooperative, and able to find a way to make the best contribution they possibly can to it.

It was a tough job to set up a new business, and Meredith explained to me that she was working ten hours a day, every day, for the first year. She had more responsibility in this job than in her old one. But Meredith noticed something surprising. After she'd been there a short time, that heart-thumping, wake-in-the-night anxiety went away, and it's never come back.

I asked her—why? She has some ideas, and they fit closely with what I'd learned about the science of depression and anxiety earlier. Every previous job she had was, she says, "an out-of-control experience." There, "it didn't matter if you had a good idea—if that was outside of your job's scope, nobody was really interested in it. You got into your position and you did that job, you waited in line, and you would get promoted maybe after five years, and you did that next job for like five more years." But here, she says, her ideas—and everyone's ideas—count. "I feel like it's different because if I have a good idea or want to explore something further, I feel like I have the liberty and the freedom to do that, and to see these ideas come to fruition." When she suggests a different publicity strategy, or figures out a mistake they've been making in fixing one particular kind of bike, or thinks of a whole new item to stock—it can happen, and she can see the results.

As I sat with Meredith and watched the bike repairs happening all around us, I remembered what I had learned from Michael Marmot, the social scientist who carried out the research into British civil servants that showed the ways in which our work can make us sick, physically or mentally. He had explained to me: It's not the work itself that makes you sick. It's three other things. It's the feeling of being controlled—of being a meaningless cog in a system. It's the feeling that no matter how hard you work, you'll be treated just the same and nobody will notice—an imbalance, as he puts it, between efforts and rewards. And it's the feeling of being low on the hierarchy—of being a low-status person who doesn't matter compared to the Big Man in the corner office.

Everyone at Baltimore Bicycle Works said they were dramatically happier, less anxious, and less depressed than they had been working in the kind of top-down organizations that dominate our society.

But here's the thing that most fascinated me—and showed me a way beyond the obstacle I thought was insurmountable. The actual day-to-day work, for most of the people here, hasn't changed radically. The guys who fixed bikes before fix bikes now. The guys who did publicity before do publicity now. But changing the structure radically changed how they felt about the work itself. Josh, when I interviewed him on another day, told me why he thinks that is. "I can certainly see depression and anxiety being related to the fact that people feel really, really confused and helpless . . . I think it's hard for people to live in a society where you have got no control over anything... You don't control your economic life, from the standpoint that it's precarious whether you've got work at all, and then if you do have a job, you walk into the place, spend forty, fifty, sixty, eighty hours a week in this place. You don't have free speech. You don't have any sort of voting." Anxiety and depression seem to him, he says, "rational reactions to the situation, as opposed to some kind of biological break."

This way of living and working is, he explains, an attempt to deal with that problem. When you have no say over your work, it becomes dead and meaningless. But when you control it, you can begin to infuse it with meaning. It becomes yours. And if there's something about the work that depresses you, you can argue for it to be broken up, or alternated with something more meaningful—and you have a good chance of being listened to.

This might sound like a pretentious way to describe a bike shop, but it seemed to me they had found a way of working that more closely resembled the participative tribes that human beings evolved to live in on the savannas of Africa millennia ago—one in which everyone is needed and everyone has a role that is meaningful to them. (It also has lots of advantages those early humans didn't have—no large animals are going to come into Baltimore Bicycle Works and eat them, and they are going to live well beyond their thirties.)

This way of working provides, it occurred to me, several forms of reconnection at the same time. You are reconnected to your work—because you feel you are choosing it, you can see the difference it makes, and you directly benefit from the work you do. You are reconnected to a sense of status—you aren't humiliated by having anyone order you around or tell you what to do. And you are reconnected to the future—instead of knowing you could be fired at any moment, you know where you'll be a year or five years from now, if you choose it and keep working hard.

Of course, they all told me, they still have bad days. They have days when they have to prod each other to do something; they have days when they don't feel like being at work; there are aspects of the job that feel like a chore. One of the original partners explained that it felt like too much responsibility—to be partly in charge of the whole business—and went back to a more conventional office job. This isn't a magical solution. But "when I started working here, I didn't have trouble sleeping anymore," Meredith says, and she's echoed by several of her colleagues.

They also feel it's more efficient—that they literally have a better bike shop. In the old system, you have one person's brain on every problem, and he might listen to others if they're lucky. Here, you have nine people's brains on every problem.

~

At bars and parties, when Meredith tells people about this work, they're often incredulous. "People are constantly amazed—[they] don't understand how you could possibly run a business like this," she explains. But she tells them—Everyone's been in a group environment. Everyone's been in a family, or on a team. You know how it works. "But all of a sudden, when you think about it in the context of making money or running a business, everyone's head explodes about it. But I don't feel like it's that complicated. People want it to be a lot more complicated than it really is . . . They can't even imagine how people would work together to make simple decisions . . . I like to explain that it's a democratic organization. This isn't a foreign concept. You live in America. We say we're a democracy, but people are so far removed from the concept."

Our politicians are constantly singing hymns to democracy as the best system—this is simply the extension of democracy to the place where we spend most of our time. Josh says it's an amazing victory for their propaganda system—to make you work in an environment you often can't stand, and to do it for most of your waking life, and see the proceeds of your labor get siphoned off by somebody at the top, and then to make you "think of yourself as a free person."

Those people at parties tell Meredith that without a boss, everyone would surely just sit around doing nothing. But, she explains, "the business is our livelihood, so if we all just sat around and did nothing, then it would be nothing and we would get nothing out of it." But she thinks it goes deeper than that. From this experience, she has learned that "people want to work. Everybody wants to work. Everybody wants to feel useful, and have purpose." The humiliation and control of so many workplaces can suppress that, or drive it out of people, but it's always there, and it reemerges in the right environment. People "want to feel like they've had an impact on other humans—that they've improved the world in some way."

In fact, there's good evidence that this increases effectiveness in the long term. A major study by scientists at Cornell University investigated 320 small businesses. Half had top-down control, and half let the workers set their own agenda in a model that was closer to the democratic system at Baltimore Bicycle Works. The businesses closer to the democratic model grew, on average, four times more than the others. Why? Alex Ticu, who was still performing surgery on a bike, told me that here, for the first time, "I feel proud of the work I do." Another one of the bike mechanics, Scott Myers, told me: "It definitely feels very rewarding when you show up and see the building and don't think of it as the place where you come in to put your hours, but as the thing you've contributed to making."

Sometimes, Meredith says as we look out over the floor of bikes, she feels that "we're on the beginning of a cultural change." Why would anyone work in the old way, the people at Baltimore Bicycle Works wonder, when they can take back control of their work and make it meaningful again?

~

I learned there are tens of thousands of democratic workplaces like Baltimore Bicycle Works, all over the world. Several distinguished social scientists have tried to get grants to study what happens to your mental health in democratic workplaces, and they have all been turned down, so we don't have much data. But there is a large amount of evidence—as I discussed before—that feeling controlled and ordered around at work, and feeling you're at the bottom of a hierarchy, makes you more depressed, and more anxious. It seems fair, then, to assume that a spread of cooperatives would have an antidepressant effect—although this is something that needs to be studied a whole lot more.

I realized that this recipe for mental health could be distilled down to the three words that everyone in our culture instinctively understands: Elect Your Boss. Work wouldn't be an ordeal that's done to you, something to endure. It'd be a democratic tribe that you are part of, and that you control as much as anyone else. One of the most popular political slogans of the past few years has been "Take Back Control." People are right to connect with this slogan—they have lost control, and they long to regain it—but that slogan has been used by political forces, like those backing Brexit or Donald Trump, that will give them even less control. This, I came to think, is a way to reclaim that slogan, and help people to gain what they are rightly hungering for.

∼

Before I left her for the last time, Meredith told me that she believes this longing for meaningful work—to have a say over what you spend most of your life doing—is there, just below the surface, in everyone. "Happiness is really feeling like you've impacted another human positively. I think a lot of people want their work to be like that," she said. And she looked around the workplace she built and controls with her colleagues, then she looked back at me and said: "You know?"

CHAPTER 19

Reconnection Four:
To Meaningful Values

When I was trying to apply everything I had learned—to change, in order to be less depressed—I felt a dull, insistent tug on me. I kept getting signals that the way to be happy is simple. Buy stuff. Show it off. Display your status. Acquire things. These impulses called to me, from every advertisement, and from so many social interactions. I had learned from Tim Kasser that these are junk values—a trap that leads only to greater anxiety and depression. But what is the way beyond them? I could understand the arguments against them very well. I was persuaded. But there they were, in my head, and all around me, trying to pull me back down.

But Tim, I learned, has been proposing two ways, as starters, to wriggle free. The first is defensive. And the second is proactive—a way to stir our different values.

~

When there is pollution in the air that makes us feel worse, we ban the source of the pollution: we don't allow factories to pump lead into our air.

Advertising, he says, is a form of mental pollution. So there's an obvious solution. Restrict or ban mental pollution, just like we restrict or ban physical pollution.

This isn't an abstract idea. It has already been tried in many places. For example, the city of São Paulo, in Brazil, was being slowly smothered by billboards. They covered every possible space—gaudy logos and brands dominated the skyline wherever you looked. It had made the city look ugly, and made people feel ugly, by telling them everywhere they looked that they had to consume.

So in 2007 the city's government took a bold step—they banned all outdoor advertising: everything. They called it the Clean City Law. As the signs were removed one by one, people began to see beautiful old buildings that had long been hidden. The constant ego-irritation of being told to spend was taken away, and was replaced with works of public art. Some 70 percent of the city's residents say the change has made it a better place. I went there to see it, and almost everyone says the city seems somehow psychologically cleaner and clearer than it did before.

We could take this insight and go further. Several countries, including Sweden and Greece, have banned advertising directed at children. While I was writing this book, there was a controversy after a company marketing diet products put advertisements in the London Underground asking ARE YOU BEACH BODY READY? next to a picture of an impossibly lithe woman. The implication was that if you are one of the 99.99 percent of humans who look less buff than this, you are not "ready" to show your flesh on the beach. There was a big backlash, and the posters were eventually banned. It prompted a wave of protests across London, where people defaced ads with the words "Advertising shits in your head."

It made me think: Imagine if we had a tough advertising regulator who wouldn't permit ads designed to make us feel bad in any way. How many ads would survive? That's an achievable goal—and it would clear a lot of mental pollution from our minds.

This has some value in itself—but I think the fight for it could spur a deeper conversation. Advertising is only the PR team for an economic system that operates by making us feel inadequate and telling us the solution is to constantly spend. My hunch is that, if we start to really talk about how this will affect our emotional health, we will begin to see the need for more radical changes.

There was a hint of how this might start in an experiment that tried to go deeper—not just to block bad messages that divert our desires onto junk, but to see if we can draw out our positive values. This led to the second—and most exciting—path back that Tim has explored.

~

The kids were telling Nathan Dungan one thing, over and over again. They needed stuff. They needed consumer objects. And they were frustrated—outright angry—that they weren't getting them. Their parents were refusing to buy the sneakers or designer clothes or latest gadgets that they needed to have, and it was throwing them into an existential panic. Didn't their parents know how important it is to have all this?

Nathan didn't expect to be having these conversations. He was a middle-aged man who had worked in financial services in Pennsylvania for years, advising people on investments. One day, he was talking to an educator at a middle school and she explained that the kids she was working with—middle-class, not rich—had a problem. They thought satisfaction and meaning came from buying objects. When their parents couldn't afford them, they seemed genuinely distressed. She asked—could Nathan come in and talk to the kids about financial realities?

He agreed cautiously. But that decision was going to set him on a steep learning curve—and lead him to challenge a lot of what he took for granted.

~

Nathan went in believing his task was obvious. He was there to educate the kids, and their parents, about how to budget, and how to live within their financial means. But then he hit this wall of need—this ravenous hunger for stuff. To him, it was baffling. Why do they want it so badly? What's the difference between the sneakers with the Nike swoosh and the sneakers without? Why would that gap be so significant that it would send kids into a panic?

He began to wonder if he should be talking not about how to budget, but why the teenagers wanted these things in the first place. And it went deeper than that. There was something about seeing teenagers craving apparently meaningless material objects that got Nathan to think—as adults, are we so different?

Nathan had no idea how to start that conversation—so he began to wing it. And it led to a striking scientific experiment, where he teamed up with Tim Kasser.

A short time later, in a conference room in Minneapolis, Nathan met with the families who were going to be the focus of his experiment. They were a group of sixty parents and their teenage kids, sitting in front of him on chairs. He was going to have a series of long sessions with them over three months to explore these issues and the alternatives. (At the same time, the experiment followed a separate group of the same size who didn't meet with Nathan or get any other help. They were the experiment's control group.)

Nathan started the conversation by handing everyone worksheets with a list of open-ended questions. He explained there was no right answer: he just wanted them to start to think about these questions. One of them said: "For me, money is . . ." and you had to fill in the blank.

At first, people were confused. They'd never been asked a question like this before. Lots of the participants wrote that money is scarce. Or a source of stress. Or something they try not to think about. They then broke into groups of eight, and began to contemplate their answers—haltingly. Many of the kids had never heard their parents talk about money worries before.

Then the groups began to discuss the question—*why* do I spend? They began to list the reasons why they buy necessities (which are obvious: you've got to eat), and then the reasons why they buy the things that aren't necessities. Sometimes, people would say, they bought nonessential stuff when they felt down. Often, the teenagers would say, they craved this stuff so badly because they wanted to belong—the branded clothes meant you were accepted by the group, or got a sense of status.

As they explored this in the conversation, it became clear quite quickly—without any prompting from Nathan—that spending often isn't about the object itself. It is about getting to a psychological state that makes you feel better. These insights weren't deeply buried. People offered them quite quickly—although when they said them out loud, they seemed a little surprised. They knew it just below the surface, but they'd never been asked to articulate that latent feeling before.

Then Nathan asked people to list what they really value—the things they think are most important in life. Many people said it was looking after your family, or telling the truth, or helping other people. One fourteen-year-old boy wrote simply "love," and when he read it out, the room stopped for a moment, and "you could hear a pin drop," Nathan told me. "What he was speaking to was—how important is it for me to be connected?"

Just asking these two questions—"What do you spend your money on?" and "What do you really value?"—made most people see a gap between the answers that they began to discuss. They were accumulating and spending money on things that were not—in the end—the things that they believed in their heart mattered. Why would that be?

~

Nathan had been reading up on the evidence about how we come to crave all this stuff. He learned that the average American is exposed to up to five thousand advertising impressions a day—from billboards to logos on T-shirts to TV advertisements. It is the sea in which we swim. And "the narrative is that if you [buy] this thing, it'll yield more happiness—and so thousands of times a day you're just surrounded with that message," he told me. He began to ask: "Who's shaping that narrative?" It's not people who have actually figured out what will make us happy and who are charitably spreading the good news. It's people who have one motive only—to make us buy their product.

In our culture, Nathan was starting to believe, we end up on a materialistic autopilot. We are constantly bombarded with messages that we will feel better (and less stinky, and less disgustingly shaped, and less all-around worthless) only if we buy some specific product; and then buy something more; and buy again, and on and on, until finally your family buys your coffin. What he wondered is—if people stopped to think about this and discussed alternatives, as his group was doing, could we turn off the autopilot, and take back control for ourselves?

At the next session, he asked the people in the experiment to do a short exercise in which everyone had to list a consumer item they felt they had to have right away. They had to describe what it was, how they first heard about it, why they craved it, how they felt when they got it, and how they felt after they'd had it for a while. For many people, as they talked this through, something became obvious. The pleasure was often in the craving and anticipation. We've all had the experience of finally getting the thing we want, getting it home, and feeling oddly deflated, only to find that before long, the craving cycle starts again.

People began to talk about how they had been spending—and they were slowly seeing what it was really all about. Often—not always—it was about "fill[ing] a hole. It fills some sort of loneliness gap." But by pushing them toward that quick, rapidly evaporating high, it was also nudging them away from the things they really valued and that would make them feel satisfied in the long run. They felt they were becoming hollow.

There were some people—both teens and adults—who rejected this fiercely. They said that the stuff made them happy, and they wanted to stick with it. But most people in the group were eager to think differently.

They began to talk about advertising. At first, almost everyone declared that ads might affect other people but didn't hold much sway over them. "Everyone wants to be smarter than the ad," Nathan said to me later. But he guided them back to the consumer objects they had longed for. Before long, members of the group were explaining to each other: "There's no way they're spending billions of dollars if it's not having an impact. They're just not doing that. No company is going to do that."

So far, it had been about getting people to question the junk values we have been fed for so long.

But then came the most important part of this experiment.

Nathan explained the difference that I talked about before between extrinsic and intrinsic values. He asked people to draw up a list of their intrinsic values—the things they thought were important, as an end in themselves and not because of what you get out of it. Then he asked: How would you live differently if you acted on these other values? Members of the groups discussed it.

They were surprised. We are constantly encouraged to talk about extrinsic values, but the moments when we are asked to speak our intrinsic values out loud are rare. Some said, for example, they would work less and spend more time with the people they loved. Nathan wasn't making the case for any of this. Just asking a few open questions took most of the group there spontaneously.

Our intrinsic motivations are always there, Nathan realized, lying "dormant. It was brought out into the light," he said. Conversations like this, Nathan was realizing, don't just happen "in our culture today. We don't allow space or create space [for] these really critical conversations to take place—so it just creates more and more isolation."

Now that they had identified how they had been duped by junk values, and identified their intrinsic values, Nathan wanted to know: could the group choose—together—to start to follow their intrinsic goals? Instead of being accountable to advertising, could they make themselves accountable to their own most important values, and to a group that was trying to do the same thing? Could they consciously nurture meaningful values?

Now that each person had figured out his or her own intrinsic goals, they would report back at the next series of meetings about what they'd done to start moving toward them. They held each other accountable. They now had a space in which they could think about what they really wanted in life, and how to achieve it. They would talk about how they had found a way to work less and see their kids more, for example, or how they had taken up a musical instrument, or how they had started to write.

Nobody knew whether all this would have any real effect, though. Could these conversations really reduce people's materialism and increase their intrinsic values?

Independent social scientists measured the levels of materialism of the participants at the start of the experiment, and they measured them again at the end. As he waited for the results, Nathan was nervous. This was a small intervention, in the middle of a lifetime of constant consumerist bombardment. Would it make any difference at all?

When the results came through, both Nathan and Tim were thrilled. Tim had shown before that materialism correlates strongly with increased depression and anxiety. This experiment showed, for the first time, that it was possible to intervene in people's lives in a way that would significantly reduce their levels of materialism. The people who had gone through this experiment had significantly lower materialism and significantly higher self-esteem. It was a big and measurable effect.

It was an early shot of proof that a determined effort to reverse the values that are making us so unhappy works.

The people who took part in the study could never have made these changes alone, Nathan believes. "There was a lot of power in that connection and that community for people—removing the isolation and the fear. There's a lot of fear around this topic." It was only together, as a group, that they there were able to "peel those layers away, [so] you could actually get to the meaning, to the heart: their sense of purpose."

I asked Nathan if we could integrate this into our ordinary lives—if we all need to form and take part in a kind of Alcoholics Anonymous for junk values, a space where we can all meet to challenge the depression-generating ideas we've been taught and learn to listen instead to our intrinsic values. "I would say—without question," he said. Most of us sense we have been valuing the wrong things for too long. We need to create, he told me, a "counter-rhythm" to the junk values that have been making us mentally sick. From his bare conference room in Minneapolis, Nathan has proven something—that we are not imprisoned in the values that have been making us feel so lousy for so long. By coming together with other people, and thinking deeply, and reconnecting with what really matters, we can begin to dig a tunnel back to meaningful values.

CHAPTER 20

Reconnection Five: Sympathetic Joy, and Overcoming Addiction to the Self

I hadn't seen my friend Rachel for nearly three years when she walked into my hotel room in a small town in the American heartland, lay down on the bed, and laughed.

When I first moved to New York, Rachel Shubert was one of the first people I bonded with. We sat next to each other when we took a class at NYU and we were both a bit disoriented, by the city and by life. Rachel was in a marriage that wasn't working out, for all sorts of reasons. She was trying to build a career for herself, and she was, as it turned out, about to become pregnant with her first child. I was ragged and worn from a series of crises. We bonded over several things—and one of them was bitching. She had lived in Switzerland for two long years; my dad is from Switzerland and I used to be banished there for the summers as a kid; so we bitched about the Swiss. We bitched about some of the other people in the class. We bitched about our teacher. We laughed a lot. But it was often—though not always—bitter laughter, the kind that doesn't leave you feeling good. There was a lot of joy in our friendship—her love of British comedy bonded us for life—but there was also a lot of rage when we met.

After her marriage finally Hindenburged, Rachel moved back to the small town she's from in rural Illinois, and we lost touch for a while. But when I went to see her, I saw—quite quickly—that there had been a change in her character. She seemed lighter in spirit, and she was clearly less depressed. I asked her what had happened. She told me that when she got back home, she tried taking antidepressants and had an initial bump—but then felt just as bad. Rather than jack up her dose as her doctor advised, she had started thinking a lot about the way she approached life. She explained that after reading widely, she had found some tools that were helping her to live differently, and for which there was some scientific evidence.

Rachel had come to realize that she was angry and envious a lot of the time. She was embarrassed to say it, because she knew it made her sound bad—but, to give one example, she had a relative who had been driving her crazy for years. She was nice, and Rachel had no reason to dislike her. But her every success—in work, in her family—felt like a put-down to Rachel, and it made her dislike the relative, and that in turn made her dislike herself. This envy had spread through her life, tugging her mood down every day. It felt like a major cause of her depression and anxiety. She began to find Facebook unbearable: it felt as if everyone was flaunting their superiority, and what she came to think of as her "envy monster" was running wild.

Over the years, she tried, alone, to find little tricks that would make her feel better. When she saw someone who had something she envied, she would think of a reason why they in fact sucked. Okay, so you're gorgeous—but your husband is ugly. Okay, so you have a great career—but you never see your kids. It was, she told me, her "unskilled way of trying to reduce envy." This would give her relief, but only for a moment.

She thought there was something wrong with her. But as she began to read about envy, she realized that our culture was priming her to feel this way. She had been raised to constantly compete and compare, she said. "We're highly individualistic," she explained, and we're constantly told that life is a "zero sum game. There's only so many pieces of the pie, so if somebody else has success, or beauty, or whatever, somehow it leaves less for you. Or if you can get it, too, it's less meaningful if all these other people have it." We are trained to think that life is a fight for scarce resources— "even if it's for something like intelligence, when there's no limit to how much human intelligence can grow across the world." If you become smarter, it doesn't make me less smart—but we are primed to feel that it does.

So Rachel knew that if (say) she sat down and wrote a wonderful book, and at the same time the relative she envied sat down and also wrote a wonderful book, "it would almost take the wind out of my sails—even though it hasn't done anything to diminish my completely different book." We end up on a seesaw of feeling envy and then trying to make others envious. "It's like we've learned so well from the advertisers over the years, we're marketing experts ourselves, and now we just know how to curate and market our own lives, without any conscious process. We just culturally learn it." So you display your life on Instagram and in conversations as if you are the Chief Marketing Officer of Me, "not trying to get other people to buy anything other than the idea that we're awesome and worthy of envy ourselves. You know?"

She realized something was wrong when she heard one day through the grapevine that somebody was envious of her, and she was thrilled. "I am ashamed to tell you that," she said.

Rachel didn't want to be this way. Like me, she's a strong proponent of skepticism and rationality, so she looked for techniques that scientific studies had suggested might have some basis in fact. And she discovered an ancient technique called "sympathetic joy," which is part of a range of techniques for which there is some striking new scientific evidence.

It is, she says, quite simple. Sympathetic joy is a method for cultivating "the opposite of jealousy or envy . . . It's simply feeling happy for other people." Rachel guided me through how it works.

You close your eyes and picture yourself. You imagine something good happening to you—falling in love, or writing something you're proud of. You feel the joy that would come from that. You let it flow through you.

Then you picture somebody you love, and you imagine something wonderful happening for them. You feel the joy from that, and you let that, too, flow through you.

So far, so easy. Then you picture somebody you don't really know—say, the clerk who serves you in the grocery store. You imagine something wonderful happening to her. And you try to feel joy for her—real joy.

Then it gets harder. You picture somebody you don't like, and you try to imagine something good happening for that person. And you try to feel joy for that person. You try to feel the same joy you'd feel for yourself, or for somebody you love. You imagine how good they'd feel, and how moved they'd be.

Then you picture somebody you really dislike, or someone you really envy—Rachel pictured the relative she's been jealous of. And you try to feel joy for them. Real, true joy. "When you're meditating, you may not feel that way at all. It might actually be almost killing you to say those things," she explained. "You might hate the person and their success—but you say it."

You do this every day, for fifteen minutes. For the first few weeks, Rachel thought it felt pointless. Nothing changed. But then she started to notice, over time, "I don't feel that same churning punch in the gut. It's just not there." She felt the toxic feelings slowly abate. Envy wasn't puncturing her several times a day in the same way. The longer she did it, the more these feelings ebbed. Thinking about the relative she had a particular problem with, she says, "It doesn't mean that I don't feel envy at all about her ever again. It just means that it's been taken down so many notches that I don't experience the same pain."

This kind of meditation is about "setting the intention to feel different," she told me—"almost like saying 'I want to feel differently about you,' and saying it enough times, until you really do. I think it works on you below the level of ordinary consciousness."

As she kept on practicing, she started to feel something more. Part of the point of sympathetic joy meditation is that you feel less envy, but an even more important part is that you start to see the happiness of others not as a rebuke, but as a source of joy for yourself, too. One day Rachel was in a park and she saw a bride in her wedding dress, with her groom, posing for pictures. Before, she would have felt envy, and comforted herself by finding some flaw in the bride or groom. This time, she felt a rush of joy, and it really lifted her for the rest of the day. She didn't feel that the bride's happiness took away from her happiness—she felt it added to it. She didn't start mentally comparing this bride to how she looked on her own wedding day. She would never see this couple again, but her eyes welled up with sympathetic joy.

I asked her what it feels like. "It's happiness. It's warmth—and it has a tender quality to it," she said. "It's almost like people become your children. That same tender, warm happiness you have for your child when they're having fun and they're happy or they get something they like, you can feel that for a complete stranger, and it's quite incredible. It's almost like looking at them through the eyes of a loving parent that just wants someone they love to be happy and have good things, and there's a tenderness to it for me."

She was surprised that she could change in this way. "You think that certain things aren't malleable," she says, but "they completely are. You can be a total jealous monster, and you think that's just part of who you are, and you find you can change it [by just] doing some basic thing."

As Rachel and I spent a few days together, wandering around, eating in diners, I could see a real change in her, and—I could see the irony right away—I started to envy it. Rachel looked at me and said: "I've pursued happiness for myself my whole life, and I'm exhausted, and I don't feel any closer to it—because where does it end? The bar just keeps getting moved." But this different way of thinking, she said, seemed to offer a real sense of pleasure, and a path away from the depressing, anxiety-provoking thoughts she'd been plagued by. "There's always going to be shit coming into your life to be unhappy about. If you can be happy for others, there's always going to be a supply of happiness available to you. Vicarious joy is going to be available millions of ways every single day. If you want to look at other people and be happy for them, you can be happy every single day, regardless of what's happening to you."

As she began to practice this, she realized it was really a radical break with what she'd been taught. She's conscious that to many people, this would sound like a philosophy for losers—you can't make it, so you have to get a thrill when somebody else does. You'll lose your edge. You'll fall behind in the constant race for success. But Rachel thinks this is a false dichotomy. Why can't you be happy for other people *and* for yourself? Why would being eaten with envy make you stronger?

She felt she was slowly realizing that the things she had been trained by the culture to envy were in fact the least valuable things we have: "Who's envious of someone else's good character? Who's envious of somebody else's wonderful treatment of their spouse? You're not envious of that. You might admire that. You're not envious of it. You're envious of other shit: you're envious of what people have materially, or status-wise." As the meditation progressed across the years, Rachel began to see that even if she got those things, they wouldn't make her happy. They're not what matters.

"I think this concept could help tons of people with depression," Rachel said, pointing me to the scientific evidence, which I then studied in detail. The largest scientific study of using meditation as a treatment for depression found something really interesting. It turned out that depressed people were significantly more likely to recover from depression if they went into an eight-week meditation training program than people in a control group who didn't. Some 58 percent of the control group became depressed again, while only 38 percent of the newly trained meditators did—a huge gap. Other studies have found that meditation is similarly helpful for people with anxiety. One different study honed this effect a little and found that meditation works particularly well for people who've developed depression as a result of abusive childhoods—they have a 10 percent higher improvement rate than others.

But I was especially keen to read the scientific evidence about the particular style of meditation Rachel had been teaching me, to find out whether it actually changes people. If you took part in the major study that's been conducted into a technique like this, you were randomly assigned to one of two groups—one group did loving-kindness meditation, and the other got no help. If you were in the first group, you did a style of meditation similar to Rachel's every day for a few weeks. Then, at the end, both groups were tested. The test took a particular form: you took part in games, which you were told were a warm-up. You didn't know that some of the people taking part were in fact actors. During the games, subtly and unexpectedly, one of them would drop something, or clearly need help in some other way. What the researchers wanted to find out was—Would there be any difference between the people who'd been practicing this technique and the people who hadn't when it came to offering help?

It turned out if you'd done the loving-kindness meditation, you were almost twice as likely to help somebody else than the people who hadn't. This is an early sign suggesting Rachel was right: you could double your compassion through doing this practice even for a short time. And that in turn would lead to greater connection to other people. It's as though the loving-kindness meditation works a muscle that helps us resist and counteract the worst of our culture. It's not so much what happens in those fifteen minutes—Rachel has come to feel that "you're planting seeds during the meditation, [and] it flowers spontaneously during your day, and your life."

~

All through this book, I've been talking about how the evidence shows there are three different kinds of causes of depression—biological, psychological, and social. Right at the start I talked about how the biological interventions we currently have—antidepressants—don't do much for most of us. Then, up to now, I've been talking about the environmental or social changes that might be able to help us.

But what Rachel was teaching me was something different. She was proposing a psychological change.

There are other kinds of psychological changes people can try, too. One is prayer—there's evidence that people who pray become less depressed. (I'm an atheist, so that's not on the table for me.) Another is Cognitive Behavioral Therapy (CBT), which encourages people to train themselves out of negative patterns or thoughts and to move to more positive ones. The evidence suggests that this kind of therapy has a small effect, and it doesn't last very long—but its effect is real nonetheless. (To be fair, the main champion of CBT, Professor Richard Layard, says it should be combined with social change if you want the best results.) And another is psychotherapy. It's hard to scientifically measure whether that helps you—you can't set up a clinical trial in which you give someone fake therapy and compare it to real therapy. But there is some striking evidence about the value of therapy for people who've had a traumatic childhood—which I'll come to in the next chapter.

So it's worth underscoring—it's not only environmental change that can help people. Even if you really believe you are trapped and you genuinely can't change your environment, some of these methods might help. And my strong suspicion is that if they do help you ease your depression and anxiety, you will realize you can change your environment—by banding together with other people—more than you think.

Until I had this experience with Rachel, I had been wary about meditation. There were, I realized, two reasons. The first is that I was afraid of being still and alone with my thoughts—I associated that with depression and anxiety.

The second is that I found many of the reasons why meditation has been promoted over the past few years problematic. There are self-help gurus who have made a fortune telling people that meditation can make you a better little worker-bee, more able to cope with working constantly and being loaded with stress. This seemed to me to be just another individualistic "solution" that misses the point—why do so many people feel overloaded and stressed out in the first place, and how do we stop it happening?

But I now knew there are lots of different kinds of meditation. Rachel's school of meditation is the opposite of this individualistic meditation that disturbed me. It's not about dealing with the distress and strain of disconnection a little better. It's about finding a way back to reconnection.

~

The thing that most fascinated me about Rachel's transformation was the way she talked about changing her relationship with her own ego. She didn't seem rattled by the constant ego-jabbing that assaults us all the time in our culture—from advertising, from social media, from competitive people all around her. She had found a way to protect herself from it.

Once I saw this, I asked myself—what more could we do to protect ourselves from the depressants that are polluting our atmosphere? What else could we do to shrink our egos and strengthen our connections? As

I read more about the science of meditation, I started to delve into a different but related series of studies that—frankly—I was pretty skeptical of at first. If you've read my previous book, *Chasing the Scream*, you'll know I referred to some aspects of this quite dismissively.

And yet I kept looking at the latest scientific results, and they were startling, so I went on a journey into this field. What I learned may sound weird to you at first. It sounded weird to me. But stick with me.

~

Roland Griffith was trying to meditate, but he couldn't do it. If he sat there for a few minutes, it would feel like hours, stretching out agonizingly before him. All he felt at the end of it was frustration, so he gave it up. He would not meditate again for twenty years—when he became part of unlocking something crucial not just for himself, but for all of us.

He had been a young grad student when his attempts at meditation flickered out, and Roland was at the start of a stellar career in academic psychology. He rose through this field to become a leading professor at Johns Hopkins University School of Medicine in Maryland, one of the best academic institutions in the world. When I met him, he was one of the most respected figures internationally when it came to the study of drug use, especially the effects of caffeine. As we sat in his office, he explained to me that after twenty years of rising to this position, "if I hadn't been certifiably workaholic, I was pretty close to it.

"My career had gone well," he said, but he felt something was lacking. "I felt as though in some respects I was going through the motions of being a scientist and having a career in science." He realized he was starting to think again—he didn't quite know why—about the flailing attempts at meditation he had made all those years before. It was heresy in his field to think about the deep inner self. He was a specialist in a field of psychology that regarded all this as hippieish nonsense, and not something serious academic psychologists should think about at all. But, he said, "it seemed quite apparent to me there was something fascinating about this methodology of meditation that had been focused, for thousands of years, on trying to plumb the depths of these deeper experiences of mind, self, consciousness—whatever that means."

He had a friend who went regularly to an ashram—a spiritual retreat—in upstate New York to meditate as part of a group, and one day, Roland asked to go along. Unlike his attempts all those years before, he had somebody there to guide him in his meditation, and to talk him through how to do it. This time, he found he could meditate after all. As he kept doing it, day after day, he found, to his surprise, "this inner world started to open up—and I started to open up," he said. "That became, frankly, enthralling to me." The people he was meeting who had been meditating for years seemed to have a spiritual dimension to their lives that really benefited them in all sorts of ways. They appeared calmer, and happier, and less anxious. Roland began to feel there were dimensions to his own character—and to everyone's character—that he had neglected in his own life, and that weren't being properly studied by academics.

He asked himself some basic questions. What is happening when a person meditates? What changes in them? If you meditate in a dedicated way, for long enough, most people—like my friend Rachel—say that they start to experience a spiritual change: they value things differently. They see the world differently. Why, Roland wanted to know, would that be? Why did meditation make people feel they were being changed in a way that was mystical—and what did that even mean?

He looked for scientific studies that might have looked at people who feel they are having mystical experiences—and he discovered there was quite a large literature on it, although it was rather peculiar. From the mid-1950s to the late 1960s, different groups of scientists working at top universities across the United States had discovered something. They found that if you give people psychedelic drugs—mostly LSD, which was legal at the time—under clinical conditions, you can fairly predictably cause them to have what feel like spiritual experiences. You can make them feel they are transcending their egos and their everyday concerns and connecting intensely with something much deeper—with other people, with nature, even with the nature of existence itself. The vast majority of people given the drug by doctors said that it made them feel this way, and that the experience seemed profound to them.

As he read through this, Roland noticed one thing in particular. The way people described feeling when they took psychedelics was strikingly similar to the way people said they felt if they had a deep, sustained program of meditation.

When all this research had been taking place, the scientists seemed to be discovering all sorts of benefits to giving people these drugs under clinical conditions. When it was given to chronic alcoholics, a startling number stopped drinking. When it was given to chronically depressed people, many of them felt radically better and left behind their depression. These scientific trials weren't conducted according to the standards that we'd use today, and the results should be viewed with some caution, but they caught Roland's eye. Yet across the United States, toward the end of the sixties, there was a panic about psychedelics. Some people had had bad experiences taking these drugs recreationally, and on top of that, there were lots of stories that were invented to demonize the drugs—for example, claims that if you took LSD, you could stare into the sun and go blind. In the midst of this controversy, LSD was banned, all scientific research on psychedelics was abruptly stopped, and the trail went cold.

Looking at these studies afresh in the 1990s, Roland was curious to learn whether there was any connection between the experiences long-term meditators were having and the experiences people have when they are given psychedelics. If these are two different routes to feeling the same thing, would that help us figure out what was really going on? So Roland applied to conduct the very first clinical trial on a psychedelic since the ban a generation before. He wanted to give psilocybin, a naturally occurring chemical found inside "magic" mushrooms, to respectable citizens who had never used it before, to see if they would have a mystical experience—and to discover what the longer-term consequences, if any, would be.

"I have to say, frankly, that I was a skeptic," he said to me as we sat together in Maryland. He didn't think one drug could trigger an experience comparable to the deep, sustained, decades-long practices of meditation he was seeing at the ashram. And he didn't think there would be many effects beyond that. No other scientist had been given permission to do this since the lockdown in the sixties—but Roland was so prestigious, and so unimpeachable, that he was, to widespread amazement, given a green light. Many people think it happened only because the authorities assumed he was going to show the drug did terrible harm to people. So dozens of ordinary professional people were recruited in Maryland. We want you, they said, to do something unusual.

~

Mark didn't know what to expect as he walked through Roland's lab into a room that had been decorated to look like a living room in an ordinary home. There was a sofa, and soothing pictures on the wall, and a carpet. He was a straitlaced forty-nine-year-old financial consultant who had seen an ad in the local newspaper. It was a new study looking at spirituality, it said. He had never taken a psychedelic before; he hadn't even smoked cannabis.

He responded because he had gotten divorced from his wife and become depressed. He had been taking an antidepressant—Paxil, the one I took—for four months, but it was just making him feel sluggish. In the year and a half since he stopped, he had become worried about himself. "What I felt was missing in my life was an ability to connect with other people," he told me. "I was just somebody who kept everybody at arm's length. Never really comfortable getting close to people." It had begun when Mark was ten years old and his father had developed a heart problem—a defect in one of his valves. One day he was in pain and taken to the hospital, and as Mark watched him leave, he knew instinctively he would never see his father again. Mark's mother had been so lost in her own grief that she couldn't discuss the death with him, and nobody else did, either. "I was left to my own devices to make sense of this and to get along in life," he said, "and I think I just stuffed it all. I think I just went into denial mode." It was the beginning of a pattern for him—of hiding how he felt in order to protect himself.

As he got older, this sense of distance caused him a lot of social anxiety. When he was asked out to (say) a party he would always confect a reason not to go. If he made himself attend, he'd stand to one side, blushing. "I was very careful about what I said, and just overmonitored myself," he says. He had a constant internal monologue saying: Was that a dumb thing to say? What should you say next? Will that be dumb? And what will you say after that?

His anxiety was understandably flaring that day as he lay on the sofa in the pretend lounge. It was to be the first of three sessions in which he was given psilocybin. As a preparation, he had been learning for a few months— with a psychologist at Johns Hopkins, Bill Richards—how to meditate. He had been given a mantra to chant to himself—*om mani padme hum*— which they felt would help to steady him if he became confused or panicked during the drug experience. Bill explained to Mark that he would be there all the way through the experience, to reassure him and to guide him.

All Mark had heard about psychedelics when he was growing up is that they drive you insane. At the Baptist church he went to, they used to give the teenagers little comic strips about a man who took LSD and thought his face was melting. He couldn't stop and had to be taken to a psych ward—and never recovered. Mark never imagined he'd be taking something like it at the heart of one of the most prestigious universities in the world.

He had been told to bring a few objects that had meaning for him, so he brought pictures of his parents, who had both died, and of his new girlfriend, Jean. He also brought a chestnut he had found on the ground the day his divorce came through, which he had kept, though he didn't know why. He lay down on the sofa, and when he was comfortable, he was handed a small psilocybin pill to swallow. Then, calmly, he looked at some pictures in a book with Bill—images of landscapes—and then Bill placed a blindfold over Mark's eyes and put some headphones on him, playing gentle music. And within forty-five minutes, Mark started to feel something different.

"I could feel my mind getting looser," he said to me. "I could sense that there was something—a change a-coming, as they say . . . I could definitely feel it coming over me."

And then, quite suddenly, Mark freaked out. He didn't know what was happening to him. He stood up and said he wanted to leave. He realized he hadn't been totally honest with his girlfriend about how he felt about her. He wanted to go and tell her.

Bill talked to him gently, and after a few minutes, Mark decided he wanted to sit back down on the sofa, and he began to chant his mantra, to center himself and to relax. He realized he had to let this experience "go deeper and deeper," he said, and to trust it. The scientists had explained to him in the long preparation process that calling these drugs "hallucinogens" is a bit of a mistake. A true hallucination involves seeing something that isn't there and thinking it's as real as this book you're reading—a physical object in the world. That's actually very rare. It's more accurate, they said, to call them "psychedelics"—which in Greek means, literally, mind-manifesting. What these drugs do is draw things out of your subconscious and bring them into your conscious mind. So you don't hallucinate—rather, you will see things in the same way you see them in a dream, except you are conscious; and at any given moment, you will be able to talk to your guide, Bill, and know he is physically present, and know that the things you are seeing as a result of the drug are not physically there.

"There's no visual experience of the walls turning or anything like that," Mark told me. "It's totally dark. And all you hear is this music as a means of grounding you—and then it's just internal visualization . . . I would say [it is like] dreaming awake," except he could remember it all afterward, vividly—"as vividly as anything in my life."

As he lay back on the sofa, Mark felt he was paddling in a great cool lake. He started wandering up and down, and he could see there were different coves around him, and that there would be inlets from those coves. He sensed intuitively—as you do in a dream—that this lake symbolized all of humankind. All of us empty out into this lake, he thought—all our feelings, all our longings, all our thoughts.

He decided he was going to explore one of these coves. He hopped from rock to rock, all the way up the stream, and he felt something was calling him to keep going, deeper, deeper. He then reached a sixty-foot waterfall and stood before it in awe. He realized that he could swim up it, and he thought that when he got to the top of the waterfall, he would be wherever he wanted to go in life, and "the answer would be there for me."

He told Bill, his guide, what was happening. "Drink it in," Bill said.

When Mark reached the top of the waterfall he saw a little fawn in the water, drinking from the stream. It looked at Mark and said, "There's some unfinished business here for you to take care of," from your childhood. "This is something that you need to take care of if you want to continue to evolve and grow." Mark felt—as a revelation—that this experience was telling him "I had been hiding some experiences that I had. I had these experiences early in my life, and I had been trying to cover them over and just get along in life as best I could."

Now, at the top of this waterfall, Mark felt for the first time in his life that it was safe to approach the grief he had hidden away since he was ten years old. He followed the fawn farther down the river and he found an amphitheater. And there, waiting for Mark, was his dad, as he had been that last time Mark saw him.

Mark's father explained that he was going to tell him some things he had wanted to be able to say to him for a long time. First of all, he wanted Mark to know that he was fine. "That he had to leave," Mark recalls, "and he felt bad about it, but [he said] 'Mark—you are perfect just the way you are, and you have everything you need.'"

Mark cried when he heard that, in a way he had never cried for his father before. His father held him, and he said: "Mark, don't hide. Go seek."

Mark knew then—"this whole journey, everything I had experienced, this whole push, was to say—life is for living. Go out and live. Go out and explore, and enjoy, and just take it all in." He had an intense sense of the beauty of being alive, of being human—"the magnificence of it, the wisdom of it, it was just overwhelming." But he also had a strong sense that "the crazy part of it is—this was not coming from outside anywhere. This is just coming from inside me—you know? This is not the drug bringing something with it. This is just the drug opening up another space in me," a space that had been there all along, beneath his loss.

And then he began to feel the drug wearing off, and it was "like you were back in your own ego," as he puts it. He had arrived at Johns Hopkins at nine o'clock, and he left at five thirty. When his girlfriend, Jean, picked him up, she asked him how it had gone, and he had no idea what to say.

In the months that followed, Mark found he was able to talk about his father in a way he never had before. He had a strong sense that "the more open I am, and the more revealing I am, the more I'm going to get from anything." He felt his anxiety had—to a significant degree—been replaced with a sense of wonder. "I felt I was able to be a little bit more human with people," and he even started to go to ballroom dancing with his girlfriend, something he would have had to be dragged to kicking and screaming before.

It was three months before his second session. That time, the same process was followed—but this time he had lots of fragmented visions that didn't seem especially significant to him. "It wasn't poetry—it was prose, you know?" he says. He felt disappointed.

But it was the third session, he says, that "just totally changed my life."

~

When you take part in these experiments, they don't tell you if you're getting the low, medium, or high dose, but Mark feels sure he got the high dose that last time.

When the effect kicked in, he felt himself to be in a very different space again. But this time, it wasn't a landscape that felt familiar, like the waterfall. It was something radically different, and far from his experience. He felt he was floating in nothingness—"like in some infinity somewhere," outer space. And then, as he was trying to figure out where he was, a being appeared next to him, who seemed like a court jester. Mark instinctively knew that this being was going to help him through the experience. Spinning out in the distance, Mark could see a great cylindrical object, and he intuitively sensed that it contained all the wisdom in the entire universe and it was coming into view—and that, if he was receptive, it would be downloaded into him.

At first Mark saw this and said: "I know. I know." But then he heard a whole chorus of other voices saying it, and he joined them: "We know. We know."

And the "we know" seemed to him so much stronger. "It was almost like this whole dance of the universe that was coming to me in this cylindrical form just stopped, and my guide said—'We need to take care of something first.' And he reached inside me, and he pulled out this shivering, anxious, fearful being that was inside me, and he took him out, and he communicated with him. [He said] 'Mark, we need to talk to this part of you.' . . . [And he said to it] 'You have done an amazing job for Mark. You have protected him. You have created incredible works of art for him—these beautiful walls you created for Mark, these trenches, this scaffolding which has protected Mark for many, many years and got him to this place. We need to make sure you're okay with taking these [walls] down so you can experience what's next.'

"And it was done with such love," Mark says. "No judgment. No sense of—'You're terrible that you're here.'" And the frightened parts of Mark consented to let his walls come down. And as he did, Mark realized that close by, he could see people he had loved, who had died—his father, and his aunt—applauding him.

And then Mark felt he was open to whatever wisdom the universe had to offer him, and he could feel it flow through him, and he felt happy.

"You know—we always have this part of ourselves which is always judging, which is always looking at ourselves or other people, over-monitoring," he told me. "And I was [at that moment] in this place where my ego was just gone. I mean, they describe [it as] ego-death. But 'I' didn't have any place in this. It was just totally shut off." And for the first time in his life, Mark could feel "there's no judgment. There's compassion, an incredible sense of compassion for yourself and everyone else in the universe." And he had an intense sense of the oneness of all living things, bonded together through nature.

As he basked in the joy of this, he turned to the jester, and to his father, and to his aunt, and asked, "Who is the one true God?" And they all looked at him and shrugged, and said: "We don't know. We know a lot. But we don't know that." And they all laughed, and Mark laughed with them.

When he came back from that experience, Mark never quite felt like the same person again. He feels, he told me, that the experience made

clear to him that people need a sense "of being accepted, to have some
sense of importance, and to be loved. And I can give that to anyone at any
time, and it's that simple. It's just paying attention. It's just being with
people. It's loving."

And then, later, something else happened with Mark.

∽

Part of the job for Roland—the skeptical scientist who was running this
experiment—was to interview everyone who had been given psilocybin,
two months after the experience. These people would come in, one by
one, and their answer was almost always the same. Routinely, they would
say it was "one of the most meaningful [experiences] of my life" and
compare it to the birth of a child, or the death of a parent. Mark was
typical. "It struck me as kind of wildly implausible at first," Roland said to
me. "My immediate thought was—what kind of life experience did
these people have [before the experiment]? But they were high-func-
tioning, mostly professional-level people. So they were really credible
respondents . . . This is something that was totally unexpected for me. I
didn't have any way of capturing it."

Some 80 percent of people who were given the highest dose of psilocybin said, two months later, that it was one of the five most important
things that had ever happened to them. Roland and his team were
measuring changes in the people who took part in the experiment. A large
majority had more "positive attitudes about themselves and about life,
better relationships with others, [and they became] more compassionate."
It's precisely what has been shown to happen with meditators too. Roland
was dumbfounded.

When I interviewed people who had gone through this program and
the other experiments like it, I found it strangely energizing. Many of
them had stories of a long-buried childhood trauma they could finally

talk about, or a sense of dread they could finally overcome. Many of them wept with joy as they described it.

He hadn't anticipated it at the start, but by conducting the first scientific research on psychedelics in a generation, Roland had crowbarred open a gate that had been closed for a long time—and, given his striking results, a lot more scientists started to stream through behind him. This was just the first of dozens of new experiments. To understand what is happening, I traveled to Los Angeles, Maryland, New York, London, Aarhus in Denmark, Oslo in Norway, and São Paulo in Brazil to meet with the teams of scientists who have restarted this research into psychedelics, to try to figure out what it means for overcoming depression and anxiety.

A team that works with Roland at Johns Hopkins wanted to see what would happen if you gave psilocybin to long-term smokers who had been trying to quit for many years without success. After just three sessions—like Mark—80 percent of them quit, and were still off cigarettes six months later. That's a higher success rate than any comparable technique anywhere. A team working at University College London gave psilocybin to people who had severe depression and hadn't been helped by any other form of treatment. It was only a preliminary study, so we shouldn't overstate it, but they found that nearly 50 percent of patients saw their depression go away entirely for the three-month period of the trial.

And—crucially—the researchers discovered something even more important. These positive effects were dependent on one thing. Your likelihood of recovering from depression or addiction was dependent on how intense a spiritual experience you had during the drug experience. The more intense the spiritual experience, the better the outcomes afterward.

All the scientists involved correctly warn against generalizing from small samples. But these were remarkable early results—and they seemed to vindicate the research that had been happening back in the sixties.

Roland was beginning to believe, he told me, that "these effects truly have the potential to be life-transformative, in a very profound way."

So what was happening? And what's the catch?

~

One of the ways the researchers tried to figure out the answer to these questions is by looking at it sideways—by seeing the similarities and differences between these experiences and deep meditation. Fred Barrett, an assistant professor at Johns Hopkins, is running a study with Roland in which they give psilocybin to people who had been deep meditators for over a decade—people who had gone on months-long retreats and had meditated for at least an hour a day for years. He explained to me that people like Mark—who hadn't meditated before and hadn't used psychedelics— usually had no words (at least at first) to describe what they had experienced on the drug, and couldn't think of any parallel in their lives. But the long-term meditators had plenty of words, because to them, the drug seemed to be bringing them, they said, to "the same place" that really deep meditation, at its highest peaks, could sometimes reach. "By and large," Fred told me, "they're saying that these places are, if not similar, identical."

So they asked: What do both these practices do? What do they have in common? As we sat over dinner in a Thai restaurant, Fred gave me an explanation that stopped me in my tracks.

They both, he said, break our "addiction to ourselves." When we're born, as babies, we have no sense of who we are. If you watch a newborn, before long, she'll hit herself in the face, because she doesn't know the boundaries of her own body yet. As she grows, she'll develop a sense of who she is. She'll build up boundaries. A lot of that is healthy, and necessary. You need some boundaries to protect yourself. But some parts of what we build up over time have a mixed effect. Mark built up walls, as an isolated ten-year-old, to defend himself against the grief for his father that he couldn't voice to anyone. But as he grew older, those protective walls became a prison, preventing him from living fully. Our ego, our sense of self, always has both these qualities—protective, and imprisoning.

But what both deep meditation and psychedelic experiences teach us is the ability to see how much of that self—that ego—is constructed. Mark could suddenly see that his social anxiety had been a way of protecting himself—but he didn't need it any more. My friend Rachel could see that her envy was a way of protecting herself from sadness— and meditation enabled her to see she didn't have to be that way: she could protect herself with positivity and love instead.

Both of these processes, Roland told me, "create a whole new relationship with mind." Your ego is part of you. It's not the whole of you. By having moments when your ego is—as he puts it—"dissolved and merged into the greater whole," into the lake of humanity that Mark saw in his vision, you can see beyond your ego. You gain a radically different sense of perspective on yourself. As Fred put it to me, these experiences teach you that "you don't have to be controlled by your concept of yourself."

"If meditation is the tried and true course for [discovering this]," Roland said, "psilocybin surely has to be the crash course."

Everyone I interviewed who worked with administering psychedelics clinically emphasized that these substances most often leave people with a profound sense of connection—to other people, to nature, and to a deeper sense of meaning. They were the opposite of the junk values we're soaked in.

"A pretty common theme when people get off the couch" after a psilocybin experience, one of the team—Fred—told me, "is love. They've recognized the connection between themselves and others . . . They feel more motivated to connect to others. They feel more motivated to care for themselves in healthy ways, rather than destructive ways." As he said this, I kept thinking about the seven social and psychological causes of depression and anxiety I'd identified, and the parallels were obvious. These experiences left people with a sense that the stuff we obsess about every day—the shopping, the status, the petty slights—really doesn't matter. They allowed people to see their childhood traumas in a different light. They offer you, as Roland put it, "a perceptual shift, where you recognize you're not enslaved to your thoughts or your emotions or your feelings—that you actually have moment-to-moment choice, and there's a joy" in that. That's why, for example, 80 percent of long-term smokers gave it up after this experience. It's not that it flipped some chemical switch in their brains. It's that if you zoom back and see the majesty of life, you think—Cigarettes? Craving? I'm bigger than that. I'm choosing life.

It also helps us to understand why the small early trial at University College London seems to have shown such remarkable results with severely depressed people. "Depression is a kind of constricted consciousness," Bill Richards, who also led the experiments at Johns Hopkins, told me. "You could say people have forgotten who they are, what they're capable of, have gotten stuck . . . Many depressed people can only see their pains, and their hurts, and their resentments, and their failures. They can't see the blue sky and the yellow leaves, you know?" This process of opening consciousness up again can disrupt that—and so it disrupts depression. It takes down the walls of your ego and opens you to connecting with what matters.

And "in spite of the fact that the [drug] experience fades," Roland told me, "the memory of that experience endures," and it can become a new guide through life.

～

But there are two catches, I learned, and they're important ones.

The first is that while some people find it liberating to be released from their ego, some people find it absolutely terrifying. Around 25 percent of people in the Johns Hopkins studies had at least some moments of real terror. For most, like Mark, that sensation was fleeting, but for a handful, it was a horrible six hours. One woman described feeling she was wandering through a desolate wasteland where everyone had died. Lots of the claims about psychedelics made back in the sixties—like the idea that they'll make you stare at the sun until your burn out your corneas—weren't true; but the "bad trip" wasn't a myth. It happened to a lot of people.

As I learned more about all this, I remembered something. Back on a mountain in Canada, Isabel Behncke had taught me about how our disconnection from nature is increasing our depression and anxiety. She told me that often, in the natural world, we realize how small we are. The stories our egos tell us—You're so important! Your worries are so urgent!—seem suddenly trivial. You experience a shrinking of your ego, and that sets a lot of people free. When she told me this, I recognized it as true, and I felt it happening on the mountainside—except I didn't see it as liberating. I saw it as a threat. I wanted to resist it. But I was puzzled about why. Isabel was telling me it would reduce my depression and anxiety, and I could see all the scientific evidence suggesting she was right.

After studying the evidence about meditation and psychedelics—and especially after talking to Mark about how it helped him overcome his grief for his father—I felt I now understood my resistance. I had built up my ego—my sense of importance in the world—to protect me, sometimes in dangerous circumstances. When you see a person under the influence of psychedelics, you see why we need an ego. Their ego is switched off—and they are literally defenseless; you wouldn't leave them alone to walk down the street. Our egos protect us. They guard us. They are necessary. But when they grow too big, they cut us off from the possibility of connection. Taking them down, then, isn't something to be done casually. To people who feel safe only behind walls, dismantling their walls won't feel like a jail break; it will feel like an invasion.

I wasn't ready, in that natural landscape, on that day, to let down the ego walls that I felt I needed.

That's why none of the people I spoke with thought it was a good idea for depressed or anxious people to just go and get some psychedelics and take these drugs, unprepared and unsupported. They're powerful. Bill Richards told me it's like downhill skiing: doing it without guidance is foolish. What they think people might want to do is fight to change the current laws so these drugs can be administered medically, in the right circumstances, to people who could benefit.

The goal in the long term isn't, Bill told me, to annihilate the ego, but to return us to a healthy relationship with our egos. For that, people have to feel secure enough to let down their deepest walls for a time, in a safe space, with people they trust.

∼

The second catch is—I think—even more important. Dr. Robin Carhart-Harris was one of the scientists who ran the experiment giving psilocybin to severely depressed people in London. As we sat for hours discussing it in a café in Notting Hill, he described something they noticed as the experiment went on. The psychedelics had a remarkable effect in the first three months or so: most people felt radically more connected, and so they felt radically better. But he described one patient in particular who seemed to represent a wider trend.

After this extraordinary experience, she went back to her life. She was a receptionist, in a quite degrading job, in a horrible little English town. She'd had this awakening—that materialism doesn't matter, that we're all equal, that our status distinctions are pointless. And now she was back in a world that teaches us all, all the time, that materialism is the most important thing, that we're not equal, and that you'd better bloody respect status distinctions. It was a return to the cold bath of disconnection. And slowly she became depressed again—because the insights she had gained through the psychedelic experience couldn't be maintained in the outside world as it currently exists.

I spent a long time thinking about this. It was only when I spoke with Dr. Andrew Weil, who did some of the 1960s research in this field, that I saw what it really meant. Nobody claims that psychedelics work in the way we were told antidepressants did in the 1990s: they don't change your brain chemistry and therefore "fix" you. No. What they do is give you—when the experience goes well—a remarkable sense of connection, for a very short period. "The value of the experience," Andrew told me, is to "show you the possibility"—how connection can make you feel. Then, he says, "it's up to you to find other ways to maintain the experience." Its value is not as a drug experience but as a learning experience. And you need to keep practicing the lesson, one way or another.

If you have this intense experience, and then return to disconnection, it won't last. But if you use it to build a deeper, longer sense of connection—beyond materialism and ego—it might. It shows you what we've lost, and what we still need.

That's the lesson that Mark, who had such vivid insights as part of the Johns Hopkins study, took from the experience. After his third and final experience with psilocybin, he asked the professor in charge: "Roland, what the hell do I do with this now? . . . I need something in my life to ground this." And Roland—who had once been so lost in workaholism that he hadn't been able to meditate for more than a few minutes—now knew the answer. He introduced Mark to a center that studies the deep techniques of meditation. Mark now goes there often, and he had been doing this for nearly five years by the time I interviewed him. Mark knows he can't live entirely in the space he found using psilocybin, and he wouldn't want to—but he wants to integrate its insights into everyday life. "I didn't want to lose this sense of what I had taken in," he told me.

Roland never expected to be the guy recommending meditation and psychedelics, and Mark never expected to be eagerly receiving those recommendations. To both of them, this seemed like an improbable turn in their life stories—but they had been moved by the sheer weight of the evidence, and the profundity of what they'd seen.

～

Mark is a guide himself in the meditation classes now. Using these techniques, he doesn't feel the social anxiety that used to plague him. He feels open to what the world wants to offer. At the end of our final interview, he told me he feels he now has "some kind of connection that never goes away," a deep sense of sympathetic joy. He's never thought about chemical antidepressants since. They never worked for him, and now he doesn't need them, he says.

～

Not everyone has to follow his path to get here, Mark told me. You can pull the plug on the things that are fragmenting us—the junk values and the egotism they create—in many ways. Some people will do it with psychedelics; more people will do it with loving-kindness meditation— and we need to look at exploring many other techniques too. But whatever way you choose, he says, "it's not a trick of the mind. It's an opening of the mind that allows you to see . . . [the] things that are inside you already."

"All it's doing," he said to me, looking back on this long journey, "is opening the gate" to what we have known—at some level—we needed all along.

CHAPTER 21

Reconnection Six: Acknowledging and Overcoming Childhood Trauma

Vincent Felitti didn't want to discover just a sad fact—he wanted to discover a solution. He was the doctor who—as I described before—uncovered the startling evidence about the role childhood trauma plays in causing depression and anxiety later in life. He proved that childhood trauma makes you far more likely to be depressed or severely anxious as an adult. He traveled across the United States explaining the science—and there is now a broad scientific consensus that he was right. But for Vincent, that wasn't the point. He didn't want to tell people who'd survived trauma that they were broken and doomed to a diminished life because they were not properly protected as kids. He wanted to help them out of this pain. But how?

As I explained before—it's over a hundred pages ago, so don't worry if you need a refresher—he had established these facts partly by sending a questionnaire to every single person who received health care from the insurance company Kaiser Permanente. It asked about ten traumatic things that can happen to you as a kid, and then matched them against your current health. It was only after he had been doing this for more than a year, and the data was clear, that Vincent had an idea.

What if, when a patient checked that they had suffered a trauma in childhood, the doctor waited until they next came in for health care of any kind, and asked the patient about it? Would that make any difference?

So they began an experiment. Every doctor providing help to a Kaiser Permanente patient—for anything from hemorrhoids to eczema to schizophrenia—was told to look at the patient's trauma questionnaire, and if the patient had suffered a childhood trauma, the doctors were given a simple instruction. They were told to say something like: "I see you had to survive X or Y in your childhood. I'm sorry that happened to you—it shouldn't have. Would you like to talk about those experiences?" If the patient said she did, the doctor was told to express sympathy, and to ask: Do you feel it had negative long-term effects on you? Is it relevant to your health today?

The goal was to offer the patient two things at the same time. The first was an opportunity to describe the traumatic experience—to craft a story about it, so the patient could make sense of it. As this experiment began, one of the things they discovered almost immediately is that many of the patients had literally never before acknowledged what happened to them to another human being.

The second—just as crucial—was to show them that they wouldn't be judged. On the contrary, as Vincent explained to me, the purpose was for them to see that an authority figure, who they trusted, would offer them real compassion for what they'd gone through.

So the doctors started to ask the questions. While some patients didn't want to talk about it, many of them did. Some started to explain about being neglected, or sexually assaulted, or beaten by their parents. Most, it turned out, had never asked themselves if these experiences were relevant to their health today. Prompted in this way, they began to think about it.

What Vincent wanted to know was—would this help? Or would it be harmful, stirring up old traumas? He waited anxiously for the results to be compiled from tens of thousands of these consultations.

Finally, the figures came in. In the months and years that followed, the patients who had their trauma compassionately acknowledged by an authority figure seemed to show a significant reduction in their illnesses— they were 35 percent less likely to return for medical help for any condition.

At first, the doctors feared that this might be because they had upset the patients and they had felt shamed. But literally nobody complained; and in follow-ups, a large number of patients said they were glad to have been asked. For example, one elderly woman—who had described being raped as a child for the first time—wrote them a letter: "Thank you for asking," it said simply. "I feared I would die, and no one would ever know what had happened."

In a smaller pilot study, after being asked these questions, the patients were given the option of discussing what had happened in a session with a psychoanalyst. Those patients were *so percent* less likely to come back to the doctor saying they felt physically ill, or seeking drugs, in the following year.

So it appeared that they were visiting the doctor less because they were actually getting less anxious, and less unwell. These were startling results. How could that be? The answer, Vincent suspects, has to do with shame. "In that very brief process," he told me, "one person tells somebody else who's important to them . . . something [they regard as] deeply shameful about themselves, typically for the first time in their life. And [she] comes out of that with the realization—'I still seem to be accepted by this person.' It's potentially transformative."

What this suggests is it's not just the childhood trauma in itself that causes these problems, including depression and anxiety—it's hiding away the childhood trauma. It's not telling anyone because you're ashamed. When you lock it away in your mind, it festers, and the sense of shame grows. As a doctor, Vincent can't (alas) invent time machines to go back and prevent the abuse. But he can help his patients to stop hiding, and to stop feeling ashamed.

There is a great deal of evidence—as I discussed before—that a sense of humiliation plays a big role in depression. I wondered whether this was relevant here, and Vincent told me: "I believe that what we're doing is very efficiently providing a massive reduction in humiliation and poor self-concept." He started to see it as a secular version of confession in the Catholic Church. "I'm not saying this as a religious person—because I'm not [religious]—but confession has been in use for eighteen hundred years. Maybe it meets some basic human need if it's lasted that long." You need to tell somebody what has happened to you, and you need to know they don't regard you as being worth less than them. This evidence suggests that by reconnecting a person with his childhood trauma, and showing him that an outside observer doesn't see it as shameful, you go a significant way toward helping to set him free from some of its negative effects. "Now, is that all that needs to be done?" Vincent asked me. "No. But it's a hell of a big step forward."

Can this be right? There is evidence—from other scientific studies—that shame makes people sick. For example, closeted gay men, during the AIDS crisis, died on average two to three years earlier than openly gay men, even when they got health care at the same point in their illness. Sealing off a part of yourself and thinking it's disgusting poisons your life. Could the same dynamic be at work here?

The scientists involved are the first to stress that more research needs to be done to find out how to build on this encouraging first step. This should only be the start. "Right now, I think that is waiting to happen, in terms of the science of it," Vincent's scientific partner, Robert Anda, told me. "What you've asked about is going to require a whole new thinking, and a generation of studies that has to put all this together. It hasn't been done yet."

~

I didn't talk at all about the violence and abuse I survived as a child until I was in my midtwenties, when I had a brilliant therapist. I was describing the course of my childhood to him, and I told him the story I had told myself my whole life: that I had experienced these things because I had done something wrong, and therefore I deserved it.

"Listen to what you're saying," he said to me. At first I didn't understand what he meant. But then he repeated it back to me. "Do you think any child should be treated like that? What would you say if you saw an adult saying that to a ten-year-old now?"

Because I had kept these memories locked away, I had never questioned the narrative I had developed back then. It seemed natural to me. So I found his question startling.

At first I defended the adults who had behaved this way. I attacked the memory of my childhood self. It was only slowly—over time—that I came to see what he was saying.

And I felt a real release of shame.

CHAPTER 22

Reconnection Seven:
Restoring the Future

There was one more obstacle hanging over these attempts to overcome depression and anxiety—and it seemed larger than anything I had addressed up to now. If you're going to try to reconnect in the ways I've been describing—if you're going to (say) develop a community, democratize your workplace, or set up groups to explore your intrinsic values— you will need time, and you need confidence.

But we are being constantly drained of both. Most people are working all the time, and they are insecure about the future. They are exhausted, and they feel as if the pressure is being ratcheted up every year. It's hard to join a big struggle when it feels like a struggle to make it to the end of the day. Asking people to take on more—when they're already run down— seems almost like a taunt.

But as I researched this book, I learned about an experiment that is designed to give people back time, and a sense of confidence in the future.

~

In the middle of the 1970s, a group of Canadian government officials chose—apparently at random—a small town called Dauphin in the rural province of Manitoba. It was, they knew, nothing special to look at. The nearest city, Winnipeg, was a four-hour drive away. It lay in the middle of the prairies, and most of the people living there were farmers growing a crop called canola. Its seventeen thousand people worked as hard as they could, but they were still struggling. When the canola crop was good, everyone did well—the local car dealership sold cars, and the bar sold booze. When the canola crop was bad, everyone suffered.

And then one day the people of Dauphin were told they had been chosen to be part of an experiment, due to a bold decision by the country's Liberal government. For a long time, Canadians had been wondering if the welfare state they had been developing, in fits and starts over the years, was too clunky and inefficient and didn't cover enough people. The point of a welfare state is to establish a safety net below which nobody should ever be allowed to fall: a baseline of security that would prevent people from becoming poor and prevent anxiety. But it turned out there was still a lot of poverty, and a lot of insecurity, in Canada. Something wasn't working.

So somebody had what seemed like an almost stupidly simple idea. Up to now, the welfare state had worked by trying to plug gaps—by catching the people who fell below a certain level and nudging them back up. But if insecurity is about not having enough money to live on, they wondered, what would happen if we just gave everyone enough, with no strings attached? What if we simply mailed every single Canadian citizen— young, old, all of them—a check every year that was enough for them to live on? It would be set at a carefully chosen rate. You'd get enough to survive, but not enough to have luxuries. They called it a universal basic income. Instead of using a net to catch people when they fall, they proposed to raise the floor on which everyone stands.

This idea had even been mooted by right-wing politicians like Richard Nixon, but it had never been tried before. So the Canadians decided to do it, in one place. That's how for several years, the people of Dauphin were given a guarantee: Each of you will be unconditionally given the equivalent of $19,000 U.S. (in today's money) by the government. You don't have to worry. There's nothing you can do that will take away this basic income. It's yours by right.

And then they stood back to see what would happen.

~

At that time, over in Toronto, there was a young economics student named Evelyn Forget, and one day, one of her professors told the class about this experiment. She was fascinated. But then, three years into the experiment, power in Canada was transferred to a Conservative government, and the program was abruptly shut down. The guaranteed income vanished. To everyone except the people who got the checks—and one other person—it was quickly forgotten.

Thirty years later, that young economics student, Evelyn, had become a professor at the medical school of the University of Manitoba, and she kept bumping up against some disturbing evidence. It is a well-established fact that the poorer you are, the more likely you are to become depressed or anxious—and the more likely you are to become sick in almost every way. In the United States, if you have an income below $20,000, you are more than twice as likely to become depressed as somebody who makes $70,000 or more. And if you receive a regular income from property you own, you are ten times less likely to develop an anxiety disorder than if you don't get any income from property. "One of the things I find just astonishing," she told me, "is the direct relationship between poverty and the number of mood-altering drugs that people take—the antidepressants they take just to get through the day." If you want to really treat these problems, Evelyn believed, you need to deal with these questions.

And so Evelyn found herself wondering about that old experiment that had taken place decades earlier. What were the results? Did the people who were given that guaranteed income get healthier? What else might have changed in their lives? She began to search for academic studies written back then. She found nothing. So she began to write letters and make calls. She knew that the experiment was being studied carefully at the time—that mountains of data were gathered. That was the whole point: it was a study. Where did it go?

After a lot of detective work, stretching over five years, she finally got an answer. She was told that the data gathered during the experiment was hidden away in the National Archives, on the verge of being thrown in the trash. "I got there—and found most of it in paper. It was actually sitting in boxes," she told me. "There were eighteen hundred cubic feet. That's eighteen hundred bankers' boxes, full of paper." Nobody had ever added up the results. When the Conservatives came to power, they didn't want anyone to look further—they believed the experiment was a waste of time and contrary to their moral values.

So Evelyn and a team of researchers began the long task of figuring out what the basic income experiment had actually achieved, all those years before. At the same time, they started to track down the people who had lived through it, to discover the long-term effects.

~

The first thing that struck Evelyn, as she spoke to the people who'd been through the program, was how vividly they remembered it. Everyone had a story about how it had affected their lives. They told her that, primarily, "the money acted as an insurance policy. It just sort of removed the stress of worrying about whether or not you can afford to keep your kids in school for another year, whether or not you could afford to pay for the things that you had to pay for."

This had been a conservative farming community, and one of the biggest changes was how women saw themselves. Evelyn met with one woman who had taken her check and used it to become the first female in her family to get a postsecondary education. She trained to be a librarian and rose to be one of the most respected people in the community. She showed Evelyn pictures of her two daughters graduating, and she talked about how proud she was she had been able to become a role model for them.

Other people talked about how it lifted their heads above constant insecurity for the first time in their lives. One woman had a disabled husband and six kids, and she made a living by cutting people's hair in her front room. She explained that the universal income meant for the first time the family had "some cream in the coffee"—small things that made life a little better.

These were moving stories—but the hard facts lay in the number crunching. After years of compiling the data, here are some of the key effects Evelyn discovered. Students stayed at school longer, and performed better there. The number of low-birth-weight babies declined, as more women delayed having children until they were ready. Parents with newborn babies stayed at home longer to care for them, and didn't hurry back to work. Overall work hours fell modestly, as people spent more time with their kids, or learning.

But there was one result that struck me as particularly important.

~

Evelyn went through the medical records of the people taking part—and she found that, as she explained to me, there were "fewer people showing up at their doctor's [office] complaining about mood disorders." Depression and anxiety in the community fell significantly. When it came to severe depression and other mental health disorders that were so bad the patient had to be hospitalized, there was a drop of 9 percent in just three years.

Why was that? "It just removed the stress—or reduced the stress—that people dealt with in their everyday lives," Evelyn concludes. You knew you'd have a secure income next month, and next year, so you could create a picture of yourself in the future that was stable.

~

It had another unanticipated effect, she told me. If you know you have enough money to live on securely, no matter what happens, you can turn down a job that treats you badly, or that you find humiliating. "It makes you less of a hostage to the job you have, and some of the jobs that people work just in order to survive are terrible, demeaning jobs," she says. It gave you "that little bit of power to say—I don't need to stay here." That meant that employers had to make work more appealing. And over time, it was poised to reduce inequality in the town—which we would expect to reduce the depression caused by extreme status differences.

For Evelyn, all this tells us something fundamental about the nature of depression. "If it were just a brain disorder," she told me, "if it was just a physical ailment, you wouldn't expect to see such a strong correlation with poverty," and you wouldn't see such a significant reduction from granting a guaranteed basic income. "Certainly," she said, "it makes the lives of individuals who receive it more comfortable—which works as an antidepressant."

As Evelyn looks out over the world today, and how it has changed from the Dauphin of the mid-1970s, she thinks the need for a program like this—across all societies—has only grown. Back then, "people still expected to graduate from high school and to go get a job and work at the same company [or] at least in the same industry until they'd be sixty-five, and then they'd be retired with a nice gold watch and a nice pension." But "people are struggling to find that kind of stability in labor today . . . I don't think those days are ever coming back. We live in a globalized world. The world has changed, fundamentally." We won't regain security by going backward, especially as robots and technology render more and more jobs obsolete—but we can go forward, to a basic income for

everyone. As Barack Obama suggested in an interview late in his presi-
dency, a universal income may be the best tool we have for recreating
security, not with bogus promises to rebuild a lost world, but by doing
something distinctively new.

Buried in those dusty boxes of data in the Canadian national archives,
Evelyn might have found one of the most important antidepressants for
the twenty-first century.

~

I wanted to understand the implications of this more, and to explore my
own concerns and questions about it, so I went to see a brilliant Dutch
economic historian named Rutger Bregman. He is the leading European
champion of the idea of a universal basic income. We ate burgers and
inhaled caffeinated drinks and ended up talking late into the night,
discussing the implications of all this. "Time and again," he said, "we
blame a collective problem on the individual. So you're depressed? You
should get a pill. You don't have a job? Go to a job coach—we'll teach you
how to write a résumé or [to join] LinkedIn. But obviously, that doesn't
go to the root of the problem . . . Not many people are thinking about
what's actually happened to our labor market, and our society, that these
[forms of despair] are popping up everywhere."

Even middle-class people are living with a chronic "lack of certainty"
about what their lives will be like in even a few months' time, he says. The
alternative approach—a guaranteed income—is partly about removing
this humiliation and replacing it with security. It has now been tried in
many places on a small scale, as he documents in his book *Utopia for Realists*. There's always a pattern, he shows. When it's first proposed, people
say—what, just give out money? That will destroy the work ethic. People
will just spend it on alcohol and drugs and watching TV. And then the
results come in.

For example, in the Great Smoky Mountains, there's a Native American tribal group of eight thousand people who decided to open a casino. But they did it a little differently. They decided they were going to split the profits equally among everyone in the group—they'd all get a check for (as it turned out) $6,000 a year, rising to $9,000 later. It was, in effect, a universal basic income for everyone. Outsiders told them they were crazy. But when the program was studied in detail by social scientists, it turned out that this guaranteed income triggered one big change. Parents chose to spend a lot more time with their children, and because they were less stressed, they were more able to be present with their kids. The result? Behavioral problems like ADHD and childhood depression fell by 40 percent. I couldn't find any other instance of a reduction in psychiatric problems in children by that amount in a comparable period of time. They did it by freeing up the space for parents to connect with their kids.

All over the world—from Brazil to India—these experiments keep finding the same result. Rutger told me: "When I ask people—'What would you [personally] do with a basic income?' about 99 percent of people say—'I have dreams, I have ambitions, I'm going to do something ambitious and useful.'" But when he asks them what they think *other* people would do with a basic income, they say—oh, they'll become lifeless zombies, they'll binge-watch Netflix all day.

This program *does* trigger a big change, he says—but not the one most people imagine. The biggest change, Rutger believes, will be in how people think about work. When Rutger asks people what they actually *do* at work, and whether they think it is worthwhile, he is amazed by how many people readily volunteer that the work they do is pointless and adds nothing to the world. The key to a guaranteed income, Rutger says, is that it empowers people to say no. For the first time, they will be able to leave jobs that are degrading, or humiliating, or excruciating. Obviously, some boring things will still have to be done. That means those employers will have to offer either better wages, or better working conditions. In one swoop, the worst jobs, the ones that cause the most depression and anxiety, will have to radically improve, to attract workers.

People will be free to create businesses based on things they believe in, to run Kotti-style projects to improve their community, to look after their kids and their elderly relatives. Those are all real work—but much of the time, the market doesn't reward this kind of work. When people are free to say no, Rutger says, "I think the definition of work would [become] to add something of value—to make the world a little more interesting, or a bit more beautiful."

This is, we have to be candid, an expensive proposal—a real guaranteed income would take a big slice of the national wealth of any developed country. At the moment, it's a distant goal. But every civilizing proposal started off as a utopian dream—from the welfare state, to women's rights, to gay equality. President Obama said it could happen in the next twenty years. If we start to argue and campaign for it now—as an antidepressant; as a way of dealing with the pervasive stress that is dragging so many of us down—it will, over time, also help us to see one of the factors that are causing all this despair in the first place. It's a way, Rutger explained to me, of restoring a secure future to people who are losing the ability to see one for themselves; a way of restoring to all of us the breathing space to change our lives, and our culture.

~

I was conscious, as I thought back over these seven provisional hints at solutions to our depression and anxiety, that they require huge changes—in our selves, and in our societies. When I felt that way, a niggling voice would come into my head. It said—nothing will ever change. The forms of social change you're arguing for are just a fantasy. We're stuck here. Have you watched the news? You think positive changes are a-coming?

When these thoughts came to me, I always thought of one of my closest friends.

In 1993, the journalist Andrew Sullivan was diagnosed as HIV-positive. It was the height of the AIDS crisis. Gay men were dying all over the world. There was no treatment in sight. Andrew's first thought was: I deserve this. I brought it on myself. He had been raised in a Catholic family in a homophobic culture in which, as a child, he thought he was the only gay person in the whole world, because he never saw anyone like him on TV, or on the streets, or in books. He lived in a world where if you were lucky, being gay was a punchline, and if you were unlucky, it got you a punch in the face.

So now he thought—I had it coming. This fatal disease is the punishment I deserve.

For Andrew, being told he was going to die of AIDS made him think of an image. He had once gone to see a movie and something went wrong with the projector, and the picture went all wrong—it displayed at a weird, unwatchable angle. It stayed like that for a few minutes. His life now, he realized, was like sitting in that cinema, except this picture would never be right again.

Not long after, he left his job as editor of one of the leading magazines in the United States, the *New Republic*. His closest friend, Patrick, was dying of AIDS—the fate Andrew was now sure awaited him.

So Andrew went to Provincetown, the gay enclave at the tip of Cape Cod in Massachussetts, to die. That summer, in a small house near the beach, he began to write a book. He knew it would be the last thing he ever did, so he decided to write something advocating a crazy, preposterous idea—one so outlandish that nobody had ever written a book about it before. He was going to propose that gay people should be allowed to get married, just like straight people. He thought this would be the only way to free gay people from the self-hatred and shame that had trapped Andrew himself. It's too late for me, he thought, but maybe it will help the people who come after me.

When the book—*Virtually Normal*—came out a year later, Patrick died when it had only been in the bookstores for a few days, and Andrew was widely ridiculed for suggesting something so absurd as gay marriage. Andrew was attacked not just by right-wingers, but by many gay left-wingers, who said he was a sellout, a wannabe heterosexual, a freak, for believing in marriage. A group called the Lesbian Avengers turned up to protest at his events with his face in the crosshairs of a gun. Andrew looked out at the crowd and despaired. This mad idea—his last gesture before dying—was clearly going to come to nothing.

When I hear people saying that the changes we need to make in order to deal with depression and anxiety can't happen, I imagine going back in time, to the summer of 1993, to that beach house in Provincetown, and telling Andrew something:

Okay, Andrew, you're not going to believe me, but this is what's going to happen next. Twenty-five years from now, you'll be alive. I know; it's amazing; but wait—that's not the best part. This book you've written— it's going to spark a movement. And this book—it's going to be quoted in a key Supreme Court ruling declaring marriage equality for gay people. And I'm going to be with you and your future husband the day after you receive a letter from the president of the United States telling you that this fight for gay marriage that you started has succeeded in part because of you. He's going to light up the White House like the rainbow flag that day. He's going to invite you to have dinner there, to thank you for what you've done. Oh, and by the way—that president? He's going to be black.

It would have seemed like science fiction. But it happened. It's not a small thing to overturn two thousand years of gay people being jailed and scorned and beaten and burned. It happened for one reason only. Because enough brave people banded together and demanded it.

Every single person reading this is the beneficiary of big civilizing social changes that seemed impossible when somebody first proposed them. Are you a woman? My grandmothers weren't even allowed to have their own bank accounts until they were in their forties, by law. Are you a worker? The weekend was mocked as a utopian idea when labor unions first began to fight for it. Are you black, or Asian, or disabled? You don't need me to fill in this list.

So I told myself: if you hear a thought in your head telling you that we can't deal with the social causes of depression and anxiety, you should stop and realize—that's a symptom of the depression and anxiety itself. Yes, the changes we need now are huge. They're about the size of the revolution in how gay people were treated. But that revolution happened.

There's a huge fight ahead of us to really deal with these problems. But that's because it's a huge crisis. We can deny that—but then we'll stay trapped in the problem. Andrew taught me: The response to a huge crisis isn't to go home and weep. It's to go big. It's to demand something that seems impossible—and not rest until you've achieved it.

～

Every now and then, Rutger—the leading European campaigner for a universal basic income—will read a news story about somebody who has made a radical career choice. A fifty-year-old man realizes he's unfulfilled as a manager so he quits, and becomes an opera singer. A forty-five-year-old woman quits Goldman Sachs and goes to work for a charity. "It is always framed as something heroic," Rutger told me, as we drank our tenth Diet Coke between us. People ask them, in awe: "Are you really going to do what you want to do?" Are you really going to change your life, so you are doing something that fulfills you?

It's a sign, Rutger says, of how badly off track we've gone, that having fulfilling work is seen as a freakish exception, like winning the lottery, instead of how we should all be living. Giving everyone a guaranteed basic income, he says "is actually all about making [it so we tell everyone]—'Of course you're going to do what you want to do. You're a human being. You only live once. What would you want to do [instead]—something you don't want to do?' "

Conclusion: Homecoming

After my research had ended and I had written most of this book, I went out walking aimlessly for hours one afternoon in London, when I realized I was only a short walk away from the shopping center where I had collected and swallowed my first antidepressant as a teenager nearly twenty years before. I wandered over and I stood in that doorway, and I remembered the story I had believed on that day, and for so long after. I had been told it by my doctor, and by Big Pharma, and by the bestselling books of the day: The problem is in your head. It's a chemical imbalance. Your broken machinery needs to be fixed, and this is the answer.

People were walking in and out of the pharmacy past me, and given how common antidepressants are, I knew it was likely that some of them were going in to collect their own pills. Maybe one of them was about to swallow a pill for the first time, and this whole tale would begin all over again.

I started to wonder what I would say now—after all I had learned—to that teenage version of myself, if I could go back in time and talk with him before he swallowed that first pill on this spot.

I would try, I hope, to tell that teenager a story about his distress that was more honest. What they've been telling you up to now is false, I'd say.

That doesn't mean all chemical antidepressants are bad: some credible scientists argue they give some temporary relief to a minority of users, and that shouldn't be dismissed. The false story is the claim that depression is caused by a chemical imbalance in the brain and that the primary solution for most people is a chemical antidepressant. That story has made Big Pharma over $100 billion, which is one of the crucial reasons why it persists.

The real story, I would explain, has been known to scientists for decades. Depression and anxiety have three kinds of causes—biological, psychological, and social. They are all real, and none of these three can be described by something as crude as the idea of a chemical imbalance. The social and psychological causes have been ignored for a long time, even though it seems the biological causes don't even kick in without them.

These causes aren't some kooky fringe theory, I would explain. They are the official conclusion of the world's leading medical institutions. The World Health Organization—the leading medical body in the world—summarized the evidence well in 2011 when they explained: "Mental health is produced socially: the presence or absence of mental health is above all a social indicator and therefore requires social, as well as individual, solutions."

The United Nations—in its official statement for World Health Day in 2017—explained that "the dominant biomedical narrative of depression" is based on "biased and selective use of research outcomes" that "cause more harm than good, undermine the right to health, and must be abandoned." There is a "growing evidence base," they state, that there are deeper causes of depression, so while there is some role for medications, we need to stop using them "to address issues which are closely related to social problems." We need to move from "focusing on 'chemical imbalances' to focusing on 'power imbalances.'"

So I would want to tell that teenage boy that the implications of these findings for his pain are massive.

You aren't a machine with broken parts. You are an animal whose needs are not being met. You need to have a community. You need to have meaningful values, not the junk values you've been pumped full of all your life, telling you happiness comes through money and buying objects. You need to have meaningful work. You need the natural world. You need to feel you are respected. You need a secure future. You need connections to all these things. You need to release any shame you might feel for having been mistreated.

Every human being has these needs, and in our culture, we're relatively good at meeting physical needs—almost nobody actually starves, for example, which is an extraordinary achievement. But we've become quite bad at meeting these psychological needs. That's a crucial reason why you—and so many of the people around you—are depressed and anxious.

You are not suffering from a chemical imbalance in your brain. You are suffering from a social and spiritual imbalance in how we live. Much more than you've been told up to now, it's not serotonin; it's society. It's not your brain; it's your pain. Your biology can make your distress worse, for sure. But it's not the cause. It's not the driver. It's not the place to look for the main explanation, or the main solution.

Because you have been given the wrong explanation for why your depression and anxiety are happening, you are seeking the wrong solution. Because you are being told depression and anxiety are misfirings of brain chemicals, you will stop looking for answers in your life and your psyche and your environment and how you might change them. You will become sealed off in a serotonin story. You will try to get rid of the depressed feelings in your head. But that won't work unless you get rid of the causes of the depressed feelings in your life.

No, I would say to my younger self—your distress is not a malfunction. It is a signal—a necessary signal.

I know this is going to be hard to hear, I'd tell him, because I know how deep your suffering cuts. But this pain isn't your enemy, however much it hurts (and Jesus, I know how much it hurts). It's your ally—leading you away from a wasted life and pointing the way toward a more fulfilling one.

Then I would tell him—you are at a fork in the road now. You can try to muffle the signal. That will lead you to many wasted years when the pain will persist. Or you can listen to the signal and let it guide you—away from the things that are hurting and draining you, and toward the things that will meet your true needs.

~

Why did nobody tell me all this back then? That $100 billion in sales is a good start when you're looking for an explanation. But it's not enough; we can't put all the blame on Big Pharma. It succeeded, I see now, only because it combined with a deeper trend in our culture.

For decades, long before these new antidepressants were developed, we have been disconnecting—from each other, and from what matters. We have lost faith in the idea of anything bigger or more meaningful than the individual, and the accumulation of more and more stuff. When I was a child, Margaret Thatcher said, "There's no such thing as society, only individuals and their families"—and, all over the world, her viewpoint won. We believed it—even those of us who thought we rejected it. I know this now, because I can see that when I became depressed, it didn't even occur to me, for thirteen years, to relate my distress to the world around me. I thought it was all about me, and my head. I had entirely privatized my pain—and so had everyone I knew.

In a world that thinks there's no such thing as society, the idea that our depression and anxiety have social causes will seem incomprehensible. It's like talking in ancient Aramaic to a twenty-first-century kid. Big Pharma was offering the solution that an isolated, materialistic culture thought it needed—one you can buy. We had lost the ability to understand that there are some problems that can't be solved by shopping.

But it turns out we are all still living in a society, even if we pretend we aren't. The longing for connection never goes away.

So instead of seeing your depression and anxiety as a form of madness, I would tell my younger self—you need to see the sanity in this sadness. You need to see that it makes sense. Of course it is excruciating. I will always dread that pain returning, every day of my life. But that doesn't mean the pain is insane, or irrational. If you touch your hand to a burning stove, that, too, will be agony, and you will snatch your hand away as quickly as possible. That's a sane response. If you kept your hand on the stove, it would burn and burn until it was destroyed.

Depression and anxiety might, in one way, be the sanest reaction you have. It's a signal, saying—you shouldn't have to live this way, and if you aren't helped to find a better path, you will be missing out on so much that is best about being human.

~

That afternoon, I found myself thinking again about so many of the people I got to know on this journey—and one, in particular. Joanne Cacciatorre lost her baby daughter, and she felt the deep sorrow that is natural and right when you have felt deep love and it has been taken from you. Yet she watched as grieving people were told—officially, by psychiatrists—that if their profound distress persisted after a short window, they were mentally ill and needed to be drugged.

Joanne told me that grief is necessary. We grieve because we have loved. We grieve because the person we have lost mattered to us. To say that grief should disappear on a neat timetable is an insult to the love we have felt.

Deep grief and depression, she explained to me, have identical symptoms for a reason. Depression, I realized, is itself a form of grief—for all the connections we need, but don't have.

And now I realized—just like it is an insult to Joanne to say that her ongoing grief for her daughter is a form of mental dysfunction, it was an insult to my teenage self to say that his pain was just the result of bad brain chemistry. It was an insult to what he had been through, and to what he needed.

All over the world today, people's pain is being insulted. We need to start throwing that insult back in their faces—and demanding they engage with the real problems that need to be solved.

~

As I have absorbed all this evidence over the past few years, I have tried to apply what I learned to my own life. I've put into practice some of the psychological tools I talked about in this book: I learned to spend less time puffing up my ego, seeking material possessions, seeking a superior status—they were all, I see now, drugs that left me feeling worse in the end. I learned to spend far more time on pursuits that feed my intrinsic values. I used techniques like meditation to be more calm. I released my trauma.

I began to use some of the environmental tools I've talked about too. I have tried to tie myself more deeply into collectives—with friends, with family, with causes bigger than myself. I changed my own environment so I'm not surrounded by triggers that get me thinking about things that depress me—I've radically cut back on social media, I've stopped watching any TV with advertising. Instead, I spend much more time face-to-face with the people I love, and pursuing causes I know really matter. I am more deeply connected—to other people, and to meaning—than I have ever been before.

As I changed my life in this way, my depression and anxiety have massively reduced. It isn't a straight line. I still have bad days—because of personal challenges, and because I still live in a culture where all the forces we've been talking about are running rampant. But I no longer feel pain leaking out of me uncontrollably. That's gone.

But I am really wary of ending this book with a simplistic cry of "I did it, and you can too." Because that wouldn't be honest. I was able to make these changes because I am really fortunate. I have a job that is compatible with living very differently; I had a lot of time; I had money from my last book so I could make space in my life; I didn't have dependents I have to look after, like kids. Many of the people reading this who are depressed and anxious are—because of the culture we live in—operating within much more narrow parameters than I was.

This is why I believe we should not—must not—talk about solving depression and anxiety only through individual changes. To tell people that the solution lies solely or primarily in tweaking your own life would be a denial of so much of what I learned on this journey. Once you understand that depression is to a significant degree a collective problem caused by something that's gone wrong in our culture, it becomes obvious that the solutions have to be—to a significant degree—collective, too. We have to change the culture so that more people are freed up to change their lives.

Up to now, we have put the onus for solving depression and anxiety solely on depressed and anxious individuals. We lecture or cajole them by saying they have to do better (or swallow the pills). But if the problem doesn't originate with them alone, it can't be solved by them alone. As a group, together, we have to change our culture—to strip out the causes of depression and anxiety that are causing such deep unhappiness.

This, then, is the main thing I would want to tell my younger self. You're not going to be able to deal with this problem alone. It's not a flaw in you. The hunger for this change is out there all around you, waiting just beneath the surface. Look at the people opposite you on the subway as you read this. Many of them are depressed and anxious. Many more are unnecessarily unhappy, feeling lost in the world we have made. If you stay broken up and isolated, you will likely stay depressed and anxious. But if you band together, you can change your environment.

In Kotti, the housing project where I spent so much time in Berlin, that change started with something as prosaic as demanding a rent freeze, but in that fight, they realized that there were many connections that they had been missing for a long time. I thought a lot about what one of the women at Kotti said to me. She had—as I mentioned before—grown up in a village in Turkey, and she thought of the whole village as her home. But when she came to Europe, she learned that you are supposed to think of home as just your own apartment, and she felt alone there. But when the protest began, she started to think of the whole housing project and everyone in it as her home. She realized she had felt homeless for more than thirty years, and now she had a home once again.

Many of us are homeless in the West today. It only took a small impetus—a moment of connection—for the people at Kotti to see that, and to find a way to fix it. But it required somebody to be the first to reach out.

This is what I would want to tell my teenage self. You have to turn now to all the other wounded people around you, and find a way to connect with them, and build a home with these people—a place where you are bonded to one another and find meaning in your lives together.

We have been tribeless and disconnected for so long now.

It's time for us all to come home.

~

In that moment, I finally understood for the first time why—throughout this journey—I kept thinking about that day when I got terribly sick in rural Vietnam. When I yelled for drugs to stop my worst symptom—the extreme room-spinning nausea—the doctor told me: "You need your nausea. It is a message, and we must listen to the message. It will tell us what is wrong with you." If I had ignored or silenced that symptom, my kidneys would have failed, and I would have died.

You need your nausea. You need your pain. It is a message, and we must listen to the message. All these depressed and anxious people, all over the world—they are giving us a message. They are telling us something has gone wrong with the way we live. We need to stop trying to muffle or silence or pathologize that pain. Instead, we need to listen to it, and honor it. It is only when we listen to our pain that we can follow it back to its source—and only there, when we can see its true causes, can we begin to overcome it.

To be kept up to date on new developments in depression and anxiety, you can

(a) Follow this book's Facebook page:
www.facebook.com/thelostconnections

(b) Follow Johann on Twitter:
www.twitter.com/johannhari101

(c) Sign up to receive occasional e-mail updates at
www.thelostconnections.com/updates

To read some of the additional interviews that were carried out for this book, and to find out what Johann is working on now and how you can help him, go to
www.patreon.com/johannhari

ACKNOWLEDGMENTS

You can't write a book like this without being helped by a huge number of people. I want to thank first of all Eve Ensler, who is not just an extraordinary friend and the best person to explore ideas with that you could hope for, but an inspiration for how to fight against injustice with joy rather than rage. In the same vein, I thank my friend Naomi Klein, who is the greatest model I know for how to think deeply about complex questions without diluting or betraying their complexity.

The people I owe the greatest debt to, when it comes to this book, are the social scientists who conducted the research on which it is based, and who patiently answered all my questions and endless requests to see if I had really understood what they were saying. The social sciences are one of the most underappreciated ways in which the world is made better. In that vein, I want to thank the professors who trained me in this subject at Cambridge, especially David Good, Patrick Baert, and John Dunn.

Wherever I've summarized somebody's work or aspects of their life in this book, I've worked really hard to make sure it's accurate. I want to stress these are *my* accounts of their ideas and findings, and they may differ in interpreting aspects of it: this shouldn't be read as their take on it. For that, I recommend reading their own work, which is referenced extensively throughout the endnotes.

This book originated in a conversation with my brilliant U.S. agent, Richard Pine, and without his urging, I wouldn't have written it. My editor at Bloomsbury, Anton Mueller, also made this a radically better book. I also thank my amazing UK literary agent, Peter Robinson, my film agent, Roxana Ardle, and my speaking agent, Charles Yao. Thanks also to Alexa von Hirschberg, Grace McNamee, Sara Kitchen, and Hermione Lawton at Bloomsbury.

My friends tolerated my endlessly discussing this subject, and their questions and thoughts changed how I approached it. I thank especially Alex Higgins, Dorothy Byrne, Jake Hess, Decca Aitkenhead (who made some especially brilliant editing suggestions), Rachel Shubert, Rob Blackhurst, Ammie al-Whatey, Judy Counihan, Harry Woodlock, Josepha Jacobson, Matt Getz, Jay Luxembourg, Noam Chomsky, Chris Wilkinson, Harry Quilter-Pinner, Peter Marshall, Sarah Punshon, Dan Bye, Dot Punshon, Alex Ferreira, Andrew Sullivan, Imtiaz Shams, Anna Powell-Smith, Jemima Khan, Lucy Johnstone, Avi Lewis, Zeynep Gurtin, Jason Hickel, Stuart Rodger, Deborah Orr, Stanton Peele, Peter Marshall, Jacquie Grice, Patrick Strudwick, Ben Stewart, Jamie Byng, Crispin Somervile, and Joss Garman.

Over the years, since I was a teenager, I've discussed depression and anxiety with—and learned a lot about it from—Emily De Peyer, Rosanne Levine, Mike Legg, John Williams, Alex Broadbent, Ben Cranfield, David Pearson, Zoe Ross, Lawrence Morley, Laura Carey, Jeremy Morgale, Matt Rowland Hill, and Eve Greenwood.

Perhaps most of all, the questions and thoughts of Stephen Grosz have helped shape my thinking on these questions: I recommend his remarkable book *The Examined Life* to everyone.

The TED team invited me to a conference in Banff, Canada, where I met some of the key figures in this book: I'm especially grateful to Bruno Giussani and Helen Walters. My friends Martin Kirk and Alnoor Ladha at the campaigning group The Rules brought me to Montreal and infused me with their wisdom all through the writing of this book—to find out more about their brilliant work, go to www.therules.org.

Everyone at Kotti, the ongoing protest in Berlin, was amazing: I particularly thank Matthias Clausen, who helped me so much.

Jim Cates gave me a lot of his time and insight when he took me to an Amish community in Indiana (and showed me the world's greatest manhole). Kate McNaughton gave me a place to stay—and her wisdom—in Berlin, and Jacinta Nandi filled me with joy, as she always does. Stephen Fry talked to me about E. M. Forster in Los Angeles and helped to clarify my thinking about connection. CarolLee Kidd transcribed my interviews: if you need an excellent transcription service, e-mail her at carollee@clktranscription.com. In Denmark, Kim Norager helped me arrange interviews. In Sydney, the Festival of Dangerous Ideas made it possible for me to interview lots of people, and I am also very grateful to Emanuel Stamatakis for suggestions regarding fact checking and scientific accuracy. In Mexico City, Sofia Garcia and Tania Rojas Garcia helped me to think about all of this in their own amazing way. In Vancouver, Gabor Maté introduced me to the work of Vincent Felitti and taught me so much besides. In Toronto, Heather Mallick gave me very useful pointers. In Norway, Sturla Haugsjerd and Oda Julie helped me enormously. In São Paulo, Rebeca Lerer helped me make sense of everything. And in Vietnam, my wonderful fixer, Dang Hoang Linh, prevented me from vomiting myself to death, for which I'll always be grateful.

The wonderful, humane psychologist Bruce Alexander spurred me to think differently about mental health in the first place through his life-changing "Rat Park" experiment, which I discussed in my previous book, *Chasing the Scream*, Jake and Joe Wilkinson helped to shape this book and gave me a lot of joy while they did it. My parents, Violet McRae and Eduard Hari, my siblings, Elisa and Steven, my sister-in-law, Nicola, my nephews, Josh, Aaron, and Ben, and my niece, Erin, all did the same.

If you want to be taught sympathetic joy meditation by the person who taught me—either in person in Illinois, or online—go to rachelshubert.com; she also does work in prisons and kindergartens. If you want to buy a bike anywhere in the United States (they can ship across the country), order it from Baltimore Bicycle Works and support democratic workplaces: www.baltimorebicycleworks.com

Although they'll never get to read this, three writers I love helped me to think—in their different ways—about this question: James Baldwin, E. M. Forster (who everyone misreads on the question of connection—ask me how sometime), and Andrea Dworkin. One writer who might get to read it, because she's still alive—and whose work helped me to think more deeply on these subjects—is Zadie Smith, who I think of as the great poet of our contemporary forms of disconnection.

And a final and special thank-you goes to my friend Lizzie Davidson, whose ability to track down the personal contact details of anyone I need to interview is literally terrifying. Her technical support and ability to hunt down a fact once it's stumped me were essential to this book, and will probably guarantee she'll be running the NSA in ten years. (Don't put me in Gitmo, Lizzie.)

Any and all errors in this book are entirely my responsibility. It's very important to me to make sure all the facts in this book are correct. If our extensive fact-checking process has missed any errors, please e-mail me at chasingthescream@gmail.com and we'll get them corrected in later editions—go to this book's website for a full list of any I have been made aware of.

NOTES

PROLOGUE

4   **"We have learned . . ."** The quotes in this introduction are from memory, in notes taken shortly after the event. Dang Hoang Linh, my translator and fixer, was present the whole time, and he has confirmed in writing that this matches the best of his recollections too. Since he wasn't vomiting at the time, his memory is probably better than mine!

INTRODUCTION

7   **Better than well** This formulation started with Peter D. Kramer, *Listening to Prozac* (New York: Penguin, 1997).

8   **It was a story I was already sold on** Mark Rapley, Joanna Moncrieff, and Jacqui Dillon, eds., *De-Medicalizing Misery: Psychiatry, Psychology and the Human Condition* (London: Palgrave Macmillan, 2011), 7.

11 **"Well," he said** This is from memory, written years later; I checked with my therapist, and he confirmed to the editors of this book that it matched his recollection too.

12 **Some one in five** Allen Frances, *Saving Normal: An Insider's Revolt against Out-of-Control Psychiatric Diagnosis, DSM-5, Big Pharma, and the Medicalization of Ordinary Life* (New York: William Morrow, 2014), xiv.

12 **Nearly one in four** http://www.health.harvard.edu/blog/astounding
-increase-in-antidepressant-use-by-americans-201110203624, as
accessed January 8, 2016; Edward Shorter, *How Everyone Became
Depressed: The Rise and Fall of the Nervous Breakdown* (New York:
Oxford University Press, 2013), 2, 172.

12 **Around one in ten** Carl Cohen and Sami Timimi, eds., *Liberatory
Psychiatry: Philosophy, Politics and Mental Health* (Cambridge:
Cambridge University Press, 2008); Alan Schwarz and Sarah Cohen,
"A.D.H.D. Seen in 11% of U.S. Children as Diagnoses," *New York Times*,
March 31, 2013, http://www.nytimes.com/2013/04/01/health/more
-diagnoses-of-hyperactivity-causing-concern.html; Ryan D'Agostino,
"The Drugging of the American Boy," *Esquire*, March 27, 2014, http://
www.esquire.com/news-politics/a32858/drugging-of-the-american
-boy-0414/; Marilyn Wedge, Ph.D., "Why French Kids Don't Have
ADHD," *Psychology Today*, March 8, 2012, https://www.psychology
today.com/blog/suffer-the-children/201203/why-french-kids-dont
-have-adhd; Jenifer Goodwin, "Number of U.S. Kids on ADHD Meds
Keeps Rising," USNews.com, September 28, 2011, http://health.usnews
.com/health-news/family-health/brain-and-behavior/articles/2011
/09/28/number-of-us-kids-on-adhd-meds-keeps-rising, all as accessed
January 8, 2016.

12 **one in three French people** "France's drug addiction: 1 in 3 on psycho
tropic medication," France24, May 20, 2014, http://www.france24.
com/en/20140520-france-drug-addiction-1-3-psychotropic-medica
tion, as accessed January 8, 2016.

12 **While the UK** Dan Lewer et al, "Antidepressant use in 27 European
countries: associations with sociodemographic, cultural and economic
factors," *British Journal of Psychiatry* 207, no. 3 (July 2015): 221–6,
doi: 10.1192/bjp.bp.114.156786, as accessed June 1, 2016.

12 **the water we drink every day** Matt Harvey, "Your tap water is probably
laced with antidepressants," *Salon*, March 14, 2013, http://www.salon
.com/2013/03/14/your_tap_water_is_probably_laced_with_anti
_depressants_partner/; "Prozac 'found in drinking water,'" BBC News,

August 8, 2004, http://news.bbc.co.uk/1/hi/health/3545684.stm, both accessed January 8, 2016.

13 **when I was thirty-one years old** Like most people who take antidepressants for a long time, I had periods of several months in which I briefly stopped before, and I wrote about this in various places; but this was when I stopped definitively.

13 **I would begin to research** I wrote newspaper articles about this over ten years, mainly in the *Independent* and *Evening Standard*. On some aspects of these questions—as I explain in this introduction—I would do some early steps toward the research in this book, change my thinking a little—and then back off, because I was too alarmed by being forced to rethink these questions. In this book, I haven't described every small shift in my thinking. I occasionally had fragments of the insights I develop in this book, but never for long, and they never prevented my belief in the chemical-imbalance theory from resurfacing in my mind and eclipsing the other more complex thoughts I sometimes had.

By the time I started work on this book, I was however settled in my mind on my belief in the chemical-imbalance theory: I believed it at the start of my period taking antidepressants, most of the time through it, and I believed it again at the very end of the last period I took them. This book is an attempt to think through these different insights.

15 **has stopped funding** https://www.nimh.nih.gov/about/directors /thomas-insel/blog/2013/transforming-diagnosis.shtml, as accessed January 10, 2017.

15 **but they are twinned** For some further context, see Edward Shorter, *How Everyone Became Depressed: The Rise and Fall of the Nervous Breakdown* (New York: Oxford University Press, 2013). I would draw an exception in what I'm saying here for phobias caused by a traumatic experience: like if you're on a plane that crashes, and develop a fear of flying. These are also classed as "anxiety disorders," but they are not what I am discussing in this book. There is a different science studying them, and they largely do have a different set of causes to depression or what most people regard as generalized anxiety problems.

16 **It was a fight** Throughout this book I draw on two different kinds of experiences I have accumulated over the years.

  The first is that I was given a rigorous training in the social sciences when I studied at Cambridge University. The social sciences are where you apply the scientific method not to what's happening in a test tube or a particle collider, but to how you and I live every day—to social life. It's the scientific study of how people live. It ranges from psychology to sociology to anthropology. This training meant, I hope, that I knew how to sift the evidence I was going to have to pore over, and to see what was legit.

  The second is in storytelling. I've been a journalist for fifteen years, and I've learned that we all absorb information far better if it's told through the story of another human being. So I will tell you about this science through my own story and that of some pretty amazing people I got to know. But an individual story isn't evidence of much. The plural of anecdotes is not evidence. That's why I've tried to only write up personal stories that *illustrate* the scientific evidence, or drive us toward it. The science comes first.

  If I'm telling you a story in this book that goes beyond the evidence, or where scientists seriously disagree about what it means, I'll flag it up, to warn you.

CHAPTER 1: THE WAND

23 **What could possibly be going on?** John Haygarth, *Of the Imagination as a Cause And as a Cure of Disorders of the Body, Exemplified by Fictitious Tractors and Epidemical Convulsions* (London: R. Crutwell, 1800); Stewart Justman, "Imagination's Trickery: The Discovery of the Placebo Effect," *The Journal of the Historical Society* 10, no. 1 (March 2010): 57–73, doi: 10.1111/j.1540-5923.2009.00292.x, as accessed January 1, 2016; Joel Falack and Julia M. Wright, eds., *A Handbook of Romanticism Studies* (Chichester, West Sussex, UK; Malden, MA: Wiley, 2012), 31–2; Heather R. Beatty, *Nervous Disease in Late Eighteenth-Century*

Britain: The Reality of a Fashionable Disorder (London; Vermont: Pickering and Chatto, 2011).

24 **Irving Kirsch sat** Irving Kirsch, *The Emperor's New Drugs: Exploding the Antidepressant Myth* (London: Bodley Head, 2009), 1.

25 **A placebo can cure** Dylan Evans, *Placebo: The Belief Effect* (New York: HarperCollins, 2003), 35.

25 **An American anesthetist named** Ibid., 1–2; Ben Goldacre, *Bad Science: Quacks, Hacks, and Big Pharma Flacks* (London: Harper, 2009), 64.

26 **The third group, Irving says** Kirsch, *Emperor's New Drugs*, 7.

27 **The numbers showed that 50 percent** Ibid., 9–11. For this and the next chapter, I also drew on (amongst many other studies): Irving Kirsch and Guy Sapirstein, "Listening to Prozac but Hearing Placebo: A Meta-Analysis of Antidepressant Medication," *Prevention & Treatment* 1, no. 2 (June 1998); Kirsch, "Anti-depressants and the Placebo Effect," *Z Psychol* 222, no 3 (2014): 128–134, doi: 10.1027/2151-2604/a000176; Kirsch, "Challenging Received Wisdom: Antidepressants and the Placebo Effect," *MJM* 11, no. 2 (2008): 219–222, PMCID: PMC2582668; Kirsch et al., "Initial Severity and Antidepressant Benefits: A Meta-Analysis of Data Submitted to the Food and Drug Administration," http://dx.doi.org/10.1371/journal.pmed.0050045; Kirsch et al., "The emperor's new drugs: An analysis of antidepressant medication data submitted to the U.S. Food and Drug Administration," *Prevention & Treatment* 5, no. 1 (July 2002), http://dx.doi.org/10.1037/1522-3736.5.1.523a; Kirsch, ed., "Efficacy of antidepressants in adults," *BMJ* (2005): 331, doi: https://doi.org/10.1136/bmj.331.7509.155; Kirsch, ed., *How Expectancies Shape Experience* (Washington, DC: American Psychological Association, 1999), xiv, 431, http://dx.doi.org/10.1037/10332-000; Kirsch et al., "Antidepressants and placebos: Secrets, revelations, and unanswered questions," *Prevention & Treatment* 5, no. 1 (July 2002): No Pagination Specified Article 33, http://dx.doi.org/10.1037/1522-3736.5.1.533r; Irving Kirsch and Steven Jay Lynn, "Automaticity in clinical psychology," *American Psychologist* 54, no. 7 (July 1999): 504–515, http://dx.doi.org/10.1037/0003-066X.54.7.504;

Arif Khan et al., "A Systematic Review of Comparative Efficacy of Treatments and Controls for Depression," http://dx.doi.org/10.1371/journal. pone.0041778; Kirsch, "Yes, there *is* a placebo effect, but is there a powerful antidepressant drug effect?" *Prevention & Treatment* 5, no. 1 (July 2002): No Pagination Specified Article 22, http://dx.doi. org/10.1037/1522-3736.5.1.522i; Ben Whalley et al., "Consistency of the placebo effect," *Journal of Psychosomatic Research* 64, no. 5 (May 2008): 537–541; Kirsch et al., "National Depressive and Manic-Depressive Association Consensus Statement on the Use of Placebo in Clinical Trials of Mood Disorders," *Arch Gen Psychiatry* 59, no. 3 (2002): 262–270, doi:10.1001/archpsyc.59.3.262; Kirsch, "St John's wort, conventional medication, and placebo: an egregious double standard," *Complementary Therapies in Medicine* 11, no. 3 (Sept. 2003): 193–195; Kirsch, "Antidepressants Versus Placebos: Meaningful Advantages Are Lacking," *Psychiatric Times*, September 1, 2001, 6, Academic OneFile, as accessed Nov. 5, 2016; Kirsch, "Reducing noise and hearing placebo more clearly," *Prevention & Treatment* 1, no. 2 (June 1998): No Pagination Specified Article 7r, http:// dx.doi.org/10.1037/1522-3736.1.1.17r; Kirsch et al., "Calculations are correct: reconsidering Fountoulakis & Möller's re-analysis of the Kirsch data," *International Journal of Neuropsychopharmacology* 15, no. 8 (August 2012): 1193–1198, doi: https://doi.org/10.1017/S1461145711001878; Erik Turner et al., "Selective Publication of Antidepressant Trials and Its Influence on Apparent Efficacy," *N Engl J Med* 358 (2008): 252–260, doi: 10.1056/NEJMsa065779.

28   **This is called "publication bias."** Kirsch, *Emperor's New Drugs*, 25. My friend Dr. Ben Goldacre has done outstanding work on publication bias. See http://www.badscience.net/category/publication-bias/ for some background.

28   **Intrigued, Irving joined** Kirsch, *Emperor's New Drugs*, 26–7.

29   **Those twenty-seven patients** Ibid., 41.

30   **"dirty little secret"** Ibid., 38.

31   **In the end, in court,** Ibid., 40; http://web.law.columbia.edu/sites /default/files/microsites/career-services/Driven%20to%20Settle.pdf;

http://www.independent.co.uk/news/business/news/drug-firm
-settles-seroxat-research-claim-557943.html; http://news.bbc.co.uk/1
/hi/business/3631448.stm; http://www.pharmatimes.com/news/gsk
_to_pay_$14m_to_settle_paxil_fraud_claims_995307; http://www
.nbcnews.com/id/5120989/ns/business-us_business/t/spitzer-sues
-glaxosmithkline-over-paxil/; http://study329.org/; http://science
.sciencemag.org/content/304/5677/1576.full?sid=86b4a57d-2323
-41a5-ae9e-e6cbf406b142; http://www.nature.com/nature/journal
/v429/n6992/full/429589a.html; all as accessed January 3, 2017; Wayne
Kondro and Barb Sibbald, "Drug company experts advised staff to with
hold data about SSRI use in children," *Canadian Medical Association
Journal* 170, no. 5 (March 2004): 783.

31   **The journal concluded they shouldn't be prescribed to teenagers any
more.** Andrea Cipriani et al., "Comparative efficacy and tolerability of
antidepressants for major depressive disorder in children and adolescents: a network meta-analysis," *The Lancet* 338, no. 10047 (Aug. 2016):
881–890, doi: http://dx.doi.org/10.1016/S0140-6736(16)30385-3, as
accessed November 1, 2016.

32   **but they were going to carry on promoting it anyway** To understand
the wider context for how this could have happened, I'd recommend
three really terrific books: Ben Goldacre, *Bad Pharma: How Drug
Companies Mislead Doctors and Harm Patients* (London: Fourth Estate,
2012); Marcia Angell, *The Truth About Drug Companies: How They
Deceive Us and What We Can Do About It* (New York: Random House,
2004); Harriet A. Washington, *Deadly Monopolies: the Shocking Corporate Takeover of Life Itself* (New York: Anchor, 2013).

CHAPTER 2: IMBALANCE

33   **Tipper Gore** David Healy, *Let Them Eat Prozac* (New York; London:
New York University Press, 2004), 263.

33   **What's the evidence, he began to wonder, that depression is caused
primarily by an imbalance** John Read and Pete Saunders, *A*

Straight-Taking Introduction to The Causes of Mental Health Problems (Ross-on-Wye, Hertfordshire, UK: PCCS Books, 2011), 43–45.

33   **The serotonin story began** Katherine Sharpe, *Coming of Age on Zoloft: How Anti-depressants Cheered Us Up, Let Us Down, and Changed Who We Are* (New York: Harper, 2012), 31; Untitled article, *Popular Science*, November 1958, 149–152. See also: https://deepblue.lib.umich.edu /bitstream/handle/2027.42/83270/LDH%20science%20gender .pdf?sequence=1, as accessed September 20, 2016; "TB Milestone," *Life* magazine, March 3, 1952, 20–1; Scott Stossell, *My Age of Anxiety: Fear, Hope, Dread, and the Search for Peace of Mind* (London: William Heinemann, 2014), 171.

34   **Not long after that, other drugs came along that also seemed** Kirsch, *Emperor's New Drugs*, 83–5.

34   **"It's hard to overstate"** Gary Greenberg, *Manufacturing Depression: The Secret History of a Modern Disease* (London: Bloomsbury, 2010), 167–8. See also Gary Greenberg, *The Noble Lie: When Scientists Give the Right Answers for the Wrong Reasons* (Hoboken, NJ: Wiley, 2008). I also interviewed Dr. Greenberg.

34   **"at best a reductionist"** James Davies, *Cracked: Why Psychiatry Is Doing More Harm Than Good* (London: Icon Books, 2013), 29.

34   **they didn't become depressed** Kirsch, *Emperor's New Drugs*, 91–2.

35   **There wasn't ever any evidence** Edward Shorter: *How Everyone Became Depressed: The Rise and Fall of the Nervous Breakdown* (New York: Oxford University Press, 2013), 4–5; Davies, *Cracked*, 125; Gary Greenberg: *The Book of Woe: The DSM and the Unmasking of Psychiatry* (Victoria, Australia: Scribe, 2013), 62–4; Gary Greenberg, *Manufacturing Depression: The Secret History of a Modern Disease* (London: Bloomsbury, 2010), 160–8, 274–6.

35   **it found no direct relationship** H. G. Ruhé, et al., "Mood is indirectly related to serotonin, norepinephrine, and dopamine levels in humans: a meta-analysis of monoamine depletion studies," *Mol Psychiatry* 8, no. 12 (April 2007): 951–73.

35 **"deeply misleading and unscientific"** Davies, *Cracked*, 128; John Read and Pete Saunders, *A Straight-Talking Introduction to the Causes of Mental Health Problems* (Ross-on-Wye, Hertfordshire: PCCS Books, 2011), 45.

35 **Okay, they said, if it's not low serotonin** Shorter, *How Everyone Became Depressed*, 156–9.

35 **If one chemical turns out** Lawrence H. Diller: *Running on Ritalin: A Physician Reflects on Children, Society, and Performance in a Pill* (New York: Bantam Books, 1999), 128.

37 **Professor Joanna Moncrieff** I recommend her excellent books. Joanna Moncrieff, *The Myth of the Chemical Cure: A Critique of Psychiatric Treatment* (London: Palgrave Macmillan, 2009); and Mark Rapley, Joanna Moncrieff, and Jacqui Dillon, eds., *De-Medicalizing Misery: Psychiatry, Psychology and the Human Condition* (London: Palgrave Macmillan, 2011), all of which helped to shape my thinking.

37 **The clinical psychologist Dr. Lucy Johnstone** I recommend her terrific books. *A Straight-Talking Guide To Psychiatric Diagnosis* (London: PCCS, 2014); *Formulation In Psychology and Psychotherapy* (London: Routledge, 2006), and *Users and Abusers of Psychiatry* (London: Routledge, 1989).

37 **only to be told that the plane had been flown by a monkey** This is an adaptation of a metaphor the great California journalist Robert Scheer used to describe the dismantling of bank regulation that led to the home foreclosure crisis.

38 **one of the most influential scientists alive** David H. Freedman, "Lies, Damned Lies, and Medical Science," *The Atlantic*, November 2010, http://www.theatlantic.com/magazine/archive/2010/11/lies-damned-lies-and-medical-science/308269/, as accessed March 20, 2016.

38 **"Typically, it's the company people"** Professor Ioannidis asked me to make some minor alterations to his comments when I sent them to him—so there's a small difference between the audio of these quotes you can hear on the website, and the statements here.

39   **"In young people, they increase the risk"** H. Edmund Pigott et al.,
     "Efficacy and Effectiveness of Antidepressants: Current Status of
     Research," *Psychotherapy and Psychosomatics* 79 (2010): 267–279, doi:
     10.1159/000318293; Yasmina Molero et al., "Selective Serotonin Reup-
     take Inhibitors and Violent Crime: A Cohort Study," *PLOS Medicine*
     12 no. 9 (Sept. 2015), doi:10.1371/journal.pmed.1001875; Paul W.
     Andrews, "Primum non nocere: an evolutionary analysis of whether
     antidepressants do more harm than good," *Frontiers in Psychology* 3,
     no. 177 (April 2012), https://doi.org/10.3389/fpsyg.2012.00117; A. D.
     Domar, "The risks of selective serotonin reuptake inhibitor use in infer-
     tile women: a review of the impact on fertility, pregnancy, neonatal
     health and beyond," *Human Reproduction* 28, no. 1 (2013): 160–171;
     Dheeraj Rai, "Parental depression, maternal antidepressant use during
     pregnancy, and risk of autism spectrum disorders: population based
     case-control study," *BMJ* 346 (April 2013); doi: https://doi.org/10.1136
     /bmj.f2059; André F. Carvalho et al., "The Safety, Tolerability and Risks
     Associated with the Use of Newer Generation Antidepressant Drugs:
     A Critical Review of the Literature," *Psychotherapy and Psychosomatics*
     85 (2016): 270–88, https://doi.org/10.1159/000447034.

40   **serious withdrawal symptoms** Kirsch, *Emperor's New Drugs*, 153.

40   **This message angered almost everyone.** John Haygarth, *Of the Imagi-
     nation as a Cause And as a Cure of Disorders of the Body, Exemplified by
     Fictitious Tractors and Epidemical Convulsions* (London: R. Crutwell,
     1800), 25.

41   **In the 1990s,** Peter D. Kramer, *Listening To Prozac: The Landmark
     Book About Antidepressants and the Remaking of the Self* (New York:
     Penguin, 1993), vi–vii.

41   **So he started taking apart Irving's critique of antidepressants** This
     is my best attempt to summarize Peter Kramer's work. From reading his
     pieces, I have noticed he seems to respond aggressively to anyone who
     describes his work in anything other than laudatory terms. Here, I have
     tried to fairly and dispassionately summarize the core of his argument—
     he may well disagree. If you want to read his arguments in his own

words, I recommend his book: Peter D. Kramer. *Ordinarily Well: The Case for Anti-Depressants* (New York: Farrar, Straus and Giroux, 2016).

42 **the placebo did *better*** Kirsch, *Emperor's New Drugs*, 63–7; Davies, *Cracked*, 143.

42 **So when Irving adds up an average for everyone** Peter D. Kramer, *Ordinarily Well: The Case For Anti-Depressants*, (New York: Farrar, Straus and Giroux, 2016), 127.

42 **studies of people classed as having very severe depression** Joanna Moncrieff, *The Myth of the Chemical Cure: A Critique of Psychiatric Treatment* (London: Palgrave Macmillan, 2009), 143.

43 **The trials themselves are fraudulent** Kramer, *Ordinarily Well*, 132–3, 138–146.

44 **"does anyone really know about what fourteen years of use"** I used them for thirteen years with some short gaps. I misspoke in the interview and told him I'd used them for fourteen years, which is why he used this figure.

45 **Only one in three of the people who stayed on the pills** Kirsch, *Emperor's New Drugs*, 58–062, 73, 94; Healy, *Let Them Eat Prozac*, 29.

45 **Now I was reading the Star-D Trial's results** Diane Warden et al., "The STAR*D Project Results: A Comprehensive Review of Findings," *Current Psychiatry Reports* 9, no. 6 (2007): 449–459; A. John Rush et al., "Acute and Longer-Term Outcomes in Depressed Outpatients Requiring One or Several Treatment Steps: A STAR*D Report," *American Journal of Psychiatry* 163 (2006): 1905–1917; Bradley Gaynes et al., "What Did STAR*D Teach Us? Results from a Large-Scale, Practical, Clinical Trial for Patients With Depression," *Psychiatric Services* 60, no. 11 (November 2009), http://dx.doi.org/10.1176/ps.2009.60.11.1439; Mark Sinyor et al., "The Sequenced Treatment Alternatives to Relieve Depression (STAR*D) Trial: A Review," *Canadian Journal of Psychiatry* 55, no. 3 (March 2010): 126–135, doi: 10.1177/070674371005500303; Thomas Insel at al., "The STAR*D Trial: Revealing the Need for Better Treatments" *Psychiatric Services* 60 (2009): 1466–1467. Warden et al., "The STAR*D project results: A comprehensive review of findings,"

Current Psychiatry Reports 9, no. 6 (Dec. 2007): 449–459. The Star-D trial evidence is disputed by Peter Kramer, in a way I found unpersuasive: Anyone who wants to look it up can find his critique in *Ordinarily Well*, 192–3. See also Robert Whitaker, "Mad in America: History, Science, and the Treatment of Psychiatric Disorders," *Psychology Today*, https://www.psychologytoday.com/blog/mad-in-america/201008/the-stard-scandal-new-paper-sums-it-all; https://www.nimh.nih.gov/funding/clinical-research/practical/stard/allmedicationlevels.shtml, as accessed November 1, 2016.

45 **This evidence has been followed up several times since** Corey-Lisle, P. K. et al., "Response, Partial Response, and Nonresponse in Primary Care Treatment of Depression," *Archives of Internal Medicine* 164 (2004): 1197–1204; Trivedi et al., "Medication Augmentation after the Failure of SSRIs for Depression," *New England Journal of Medicine* 354 (2006): 1243–1252; Stephen S. Ilardi, *The Depression Cure: The Six-Step Programme to Beat Depression Without Drugs* (London: 2010, Ebury Publishing), 44–5. They also point out that you can remain depressed and still feel some benefit—i.e., some movement on the Hamilton scale. To say you remained depressed is not the same as saying there was no benefit at all—just that it's not enough, and can't be regarded as a full solution.

CHAPTER 3: THE GRIEF EXCEPTION

47 **Somebody once told me** I was told this by the terrific clinical psychologist Lucy Johnstone. It wasn't her quote originally and I haven't been able to track down the original source—if anyone knows it, please contact me so I can give full credit here.

49 **Over the years that followed, Joanne** In this chapter I draw on much of Joanne's published work. See Joanne Cacciatore and Kara Thieleman, "When a Child Dies: A Critical Analysis of Grief-Related Controversies in DSM-5," *Research on Social Work Practice* 24, no. 1 (Jan. 2014): 114–122; Cacciatore and Thieleman, "The DSM-5 and the Bereavement Exclusion: A Call for Critical Evaluation," *Social Work* (2013), doi:

10.1093/sw/swt021; Jeffrey R. Lacasse and Joanne Cacciatore, "Prescribing of Psychiatric Medication to Bereaved Parents Following Perinatal/Neonatal Death: An Observational Study," *Death Studies* 38, no. 9 (2014); Cacciatore, "A Parent's Tears: Primary Results from the Traumatic Experiences and Resiliency Study," *Omega: Journal of Death and Dying* 68, no. 3 (Oct. 2013–2014): 183–205; Cacciatore and Thieleman, "Pharmacological Treatment Following Traumatic Bereavement: A Case Series," *Journal of Loss and Trauma* 17, no. 6 (July 2012): 557–579.

50 **"became known as the 'grief exception' "** I first learned about the grief exception from the brilliant work of Gary Greenberg, which I recommend strongly. See: *Book of Woe* (New York: Penguin, 2013), 6, 158–60; *Manufacturing Depression: The Secret History of a Modern Disease* (London: Bloomsbury, 2010), 246–8; John Read and Pete Sanders, *A Straight-Talking Introduction to the Causes of Mental Health Problems* (Herefordshire, UK: PCCS Books, 2013), 60, 88–91.

51 **But once you've conceded that** One of the leading authors of the fourth edition of the *DSM*, Robert Spitzer, tacitly admitted this. See *The Therapy Trap*, p. 49, and my friend Adam Curtis's BBC documentary *The Trap*.

52 **"we don't consider context."** Other key figures in writing the *DSM* have admitted this. See William Davies, *The Happiness Industry: How the Government and Big Business Sold Us Well-Being* (New York: Verso, 2016), 174.

53 **There's just the checklist of symptoms** See American Psychiatric Association, *Diagnostic and Manual of Mental Disorders, 5th Edition* (Washington, DC: American Psychiatric Publishing, 2013), 155–189. The vague footnote is on p. 126.

CHAPTER 4: THE FIRST FLAG ON THE MOON

55 **a young woman in her early twenties** I have, at George's request, made some minor changes to details about this woman in order to preserve her anonymity.

56 **About to make a remarkable discovery** For this chapter I have drawn on many of George and Tirril's scientific papers. They include: George

W. Brown et al., "Social Class and Psychiatric Disturbance Among Women in An Urban Population," *Sociology* 9, no. 2 (May 1975): 225–254; Brown, Harris et al., "Social support, self-esteem and depression," *Psychological Medicine* 16, no. 4 (November 1986): 813–831; George W. Brown et al., "Life events, vulnerability and onset of depression: some refinements," *The British Journal of Psychiatry* 150, no. 1 (Jan. 1987): 30–42; George W. Brown et al., "Loss, humiliation and entrapment among women developing depression: a patient and non-patient comparison," *Psychological Medicine* 25, no. 1 (Jan. 1995): 7–21; George W. Brown et al., "Depression and loss," *British Journal of Psychiatry* 130, no. 1 (Jan. 1977): 1–18; George W. Brown et al., "Life events and psychiatric disorders Part 2: nature of causal link," *Psychological Medicine* 3, no. 2 (May 1973): 159–176; George W. Brown et al., "Life Events and Endogenous Depression: A Puzzle Reexamined," *Arch Gen Psychiatry* 51, no. 7 (1994): 525–534; Brown and Harris, "Aetiology of anxiety and depressive disorders in an inner-city population. 1. Early adversity," *Psychological Medicine* 23, no. 1 (Feb. 1993): 143–154; Brown et al., "Life stress, chronic subclinical symptoms and vulnerability to clinical depression," *Journal of Affective Disorders* 11, no. 1 (July–August 1986): 1–19; Harris et al., "Befriending as an intervention for chronic depression among women in an inner city. 1: Randomised controlled trial," *British Journal of Psychiatry* 174, no. 3 (March 1999): 219–224; Brown et al., "Depression: distress or disease? Some epidemiological considerations," *British Journal of Psychiatry* 147, no. 6 (Dec 1985): 612–622; Brown et al., "Depression and anxiety in the community: replicating the diagnosis of a case," *Psychological Medicine* 10, no. 3 (Aug. 1980): 4445–454; Brown et al., "Aetiology of anxiety and depressive disorders in an inner-city population. 2. Comorbidity and adversity," *Psychological Medicine* 23, no. 1 (Feb. 1993): 155–165; Brown and Harris, "Stressor, vulnerability and depression: a question of replication," *Psychological Medicine* 16, no. 4 (Nov. 1986): 739–74; Harris et al., "Mourning or early inadequate care?

Reexamining the relationship of maternal loss in childhood with adult depression and anxiety," *Development and Psychopathology* 4, no. 3 (July 1992): 433–449; Brown et al., "Psychotic and neurotic depression Part 3. Aetiological and background factors," *Journal of Affective Disorders* 1, no. 3 (Sept 1979): 195–211; Brown et al., "Psychiatric disorder in a rural and an urban population: 2. Sensitivity to loss," *Psychological Medicine* 11, no. 3 (Aug. 1981): 601–616; "Psychiatric disorder in a rural and an urban population: 3. Social integration and the morphology of affective disorder," *Psychological Medicine* 14, no. 2 (May 1984): 327–345; Brown and Harris, "Disease, Distress and Depression," *Journal of Affective Disorders* 4, no. 1 (March 1982): 1–8.

I have also drawn on George and Tirril's 1989 book *Life Events and Illness* (Sydney, Australia: Unwin Hyman, 1989) and the excellent Festschrift for George edited by Tirril called *Where Inner and Outer Worlds Meet: Psychosocial Research in the Tradition of George Brown* (London: Routledge, 2000).

56 **When depression was discussed by professionals** George Brown and Tirril Harris, *Social Origins of Depression: A Study of Psychiatric Disorder in Women* (London: Tavistock Publications, 1978), 19; Edward Shorter: *How Everyone Became Depressed: The Rise and Fall of the Nervous Breakdown* (New York: Oxford University Press, 2013) 152–5.

57 **"two warring factions"** John Read and Pete Saunders, *A Straight-Taking Introduction to the Causes of Mental Health Problems* (Ross-on-Wye, Hertfordshire, UK: PCCS Books, 2011), 32–41.

57 **"endogenous depression"** Shorter, *How Everyone Became Depressed*, 80, 89, 112, 122, 135–9, 171.

57 **You had to conduct a proper scientific investigation** Harris, *Where Inner and Outer Worlds Meet*, 7–10.

58 **comparing these two groups** Harris and Brown, *Social Origins of Depression*, 49.

59 **Mrs. Trent** This is a pseudonym they gave her to preserve her medical confidentiality.

61 **They called the first category "difficulties"** Harris, *Where Inner and Outer Worlds Meet*, 14–16; Harris and Brown, *Social Origins of Depression*, 174–5.

62 **It was a gap of 48 percent** Harris and Brown, *Social Origins of Depression*, 63, 136.

62 **75 percent** Ibid., 180.

63 **"a quantum leap ahead"** Harris and Brown, *Where Inner and Outer Worlds Meet*, 123.

63 **understandable response to adversity** Harris, *Social Origins of Depression*, 46.

63 **the "fault" for her depression lay "in the environment"** Ibid., 83.

64 **It spreads over your whole life** Ibid., 82, 234.

64 **places as radically different as the Basque country and rural Zimbabwe** I. Gaminde et al., "Depression in three populations in the Basque Country—A comparison with Britain," *Social Psychiatry and Psychiatric Epidemology* 28 (1993): 243–51; J. Broadhead et al., "Life events and difficulties and the onset of depression amongst women in an urban setting in Zimbabwe," *Psychological Medicine* 28 (1998): 29–30. See also Harris and Brown, *Where Inner and Outer Worlds Meet*, 22–5.

65 **This distinction, they concluded, was meaningless** Harris, *Social Origins of Depression* 217–8.

65 **to carry out a study of anxiety** R. Finlay-Jones and G. W. Brown, "Types of stressful life event and the onset of anxiety and depressive disorders," *Psychological Medicine* 11, no. 4 (1981): 803–815; R. Prudo, et al., "Psychiatric disorder in a rural and an urban population: 3. Social integration and the morphology of affective disorder," *Psychological Medicine* 14 (May 1984): 327–345; G. W. Brown et al., "Aetiology of anxiety and depressive disorders in an inner-city population. 1. Early adversity," *Psychological Medicine*, 23 (1993):143–154. Brown et al., "Aetiology of anxiety and depressive disorders in an inner-city population. 2. Comorbidity and adversity," *Psychological Medicine* 23 (1993): 155–165.

66 **three kinds of cause: biological, psychological, and social** Harris, *Social Origins of Depression*, 235. See Harris, *Where Inner and Outer Worlds Meet*, 25–27, for more on this.

66   **Bio-psycho-social model.** The history of this concept is outlined in Nassir Ghaemi, *The Rise and Fall of the Biopsychosocial Model: Reconciling Art and Science in Psychiatry* (Baltimore: Johns Hopkins University Press, 2010)—although I don't agree with some of his conclusions about it. See also: Nassir Ghaemi, *On Depression: Drugs, Diagnosis and Despair in the Modern World* (Baltimore: Johns Hopkins University Press, 2013); John Read and Pete Saunders, *A Straight-Taking Introduction to the Causes of Mental Health Problems* (Ross-on-Wye, Hertfordshire, UK: PCCS Books, 2011), 36–7, 53–5.

66   **"paying attention to a person's environment"** Harris, *Social Origins of Depression*, 266.

67   **I pictured his neighbor, drowning herself** George stressed to me he does not see a direct connection between that suicide and the research into depression he later did—he only began to think about it again years later.

CHAPTER 5: PICKING UP THE FLAG
(AN INTRODUCTION TO PART TWO)

71   **all across the world, there are social scientists and psychologists who had been picking up** Tirril Harris, *Where Inner and Outer Worlds Meet: Psychosocial Research in the Tradition of George Brown* (London: Routledge, 2000), 27–8.

CHAPTER 6: CAUSE ONE: DISCONNECTION
FROM MEANINGFUL WORK

73   **Joe Phillips** Joe is not his real name; he asked me to use a pseudonym. No other details have been changed, and his real identity and the audio of our interview were verified by Bloomsbury, the publisher of this book.

76   **Between 2011 and 2012** William Davies, *The Happiness Industry: How the Government and Big Business Sold Us Well-Being* (New York: Verso, 2016), 106.

77   **And a further 23 percent** Peter Fleming, *The Mythology of Work* (London: Pluto Press, 2015), 41–3; Daniel Pink, *Drive: The Surprising*

Truth About What Motivates Us (London: Canongate, 2011), 111. There's
an excellent discussion of how we are prepared for this in the unfairly
forgotten book by Joel Spring, *A Primer On Libertarian Education*
(Toronto: Black Rose Books, 1999).

77 **One professor who has studied this** Fleming, *Mythology of Work*, 35.
Other shocking stats about this in Rutger Bregman, *Utopia For Realists*
(London: Bloomsbury, 2017), 41.

77 **"derealization"** Matt Haig, *Reasons to Stay Alive* (London: Canongate,
2016), 157.

78 **people would come in with problems in their lives** Michael Marmot,
The Health Gap: The Challenge of an Unequal World (London: Bloomsbury, 2015), 2.

78 **One day in the late 1960s** Ibid., 3. For this chapter I've drawn on lots
of studies by Michael and his colleagues. They include: Marmot
et al., "Health inequalities among British civil servants: the Whitehall II study," *The Lancet* 337, no. 8745 (June 1991): 1387–1393;
Marmot et al., "Low job control and risk of coronary heart disease in
Whitehall II (prospective cohort) study," *BMJ* 314 (1997): 558, doi:
http://dx.doi.org/10.1136/bmj.314.7080.558; Marmot et al., "Work
characteristics predict psychiatric disorder: prospective results from
the Whitehall II Study," *Occup Environ Med* 56 (1999): 302–307,
doi:10.1136/oem.56.5.302; Marmot et al., "Subjective social status: its
determinants and its association with measures of ill-health in the
Whitehall II study," *Social Science & Medicine* 56, no. 6 (March
2003): 1321–1333; Marmot et al., "Psychosocial work environment
and sickness absence among British civil servants: the Whitehall II
study," *American Journal of Public Health* 86, no. 3 (March 1996):
332–340, doi: 10.2105/AJPH.86.3.332; Marmot et al., "Explaining
socioeconomic differences in sickness absence: the Whitehall II
Study," *BMJ* 306, no. 6874 (Feb. 1993): 361–366, doi: http://dx.doi
.org/10.1136/bmj.306.6874.361; Marmot et al., "When reciprocity
fails: effort–reward imbalance in relation to coronary heart disease

and health functioning within the Whitehall II study," *Occupational and Environmental Medicine* 59 (2002): 777–784, doi:10.1136/oem .59.11.777; Marmot et al., "Effects of income and wealth on GHQ depression and poor self rated health in white collar women and men in the Whitehall II study," *J Epidemiol Community Health* 57 (2003): 718–723, doi:10.1136/jech.57.9.718; M. Virtanen et al., "Long working hours and symptoms of anxiety and depression: a 5-year follow-up of the Whitehall II study," *Psychological Medicine* 41, no. 12 (December 2011): 2485–2494.

81   *four times less* likely Michael Marmot, *Status Syndrome: How Your Place on the Social Gradient Affects Your Health* (London: Bloomsbury, 2004), 1.

82   **If you worked in the civil service and you had a higher degree of control** Ibid., 130–1, 157.

82   **"We were not allowed to talk,"** Ibid., 126.

82   **"Imagine a typical Tuesday morning"** Ibid., 129.

83   **affected your whole life.** Michael points out he was building on the research of other social scientists. The idea that stress comes from the balance between demand and control was especially influenced by R. A. Karasek and T. Theorell. The insights are the relationship between effort and reward built on work by J. Siegrist—see especially "Adverse health effects of high-effort/low-reward conditions," *J Occup Health Psychol* 1, no. 1 (Jan. 1996): 27–41.

83   **"Disempowerment," Michael told me, "is at the heart** This also helps to explain why the evidence shows people who are unemployed feel even worse than people in meaningless jobs. The primary way in which meaningless work causes depression is through a lack of control—and unemployed people have even *less* control over their lives. They have no financial resources, no social status, and no choices about their lives.

84   **"Holidays made them unhappy,"** Marmot, *The Health Gap*, 180.

84   **a "lack of balance between efforts and rewards."** Marmot, *Status Syndrome*, 125.

CHAPTER 7: CAUSE TWO: DISCONNECTION
FROM OTHER PEOPLE

87 **When John and his colleagues added up the data** For this chapter I
have drawn on many published studies by John and his colleagues. They
include: Y. Luo et al., "Loneliness, health, and mortality in old age: A
national longitudinal study," *Social Science & Medicine* 74, no. 6 (March
2012): 907–914; Cacioppo et al., "Loneliness as a specific risk factor for
depressive symptoms: Cross-sectional and longitudinal analyses,"
Psychology and Aging 21, no. 1 (March 2006): 140–151; L. C. Hawkley
and J. T. Cacioppo, "Loneliness Matters: A Theoretical and Empirical
Review of Consequences and Mechanisms," *Ann Behav Med* 40, no. 2
(2010): 218; Cacioppo et al., "Loneliness and Health: Potential Mechanisms," *Psychosomatic Medicine* 64, no. 3 (May/June 2002): 407–417;
J. T. Cacioppo et al., "Lonely traits and concomitant physiological
processes: the MacArthur social neuroscience studies," *International
Journal of Psychophysiology* 35, no. 2–3 (March 2000): 143–154;
Cacioppo et al: "Alone in the crowd: The structure and spread of loneliness in a large social network," *Journal of Personality and Social
Psychology* 97, no. 6 (Dec. 2009): 977–991; Cacioppo et al., "Loneliness
within a nomological net: An evolutionary perspective," *Journal of
Research in Personality* 40, no. 6 (Dec. 2006): 1054–1085; Cacioppo
et al., "Loneliness in everyday life: Cardiovascular activity, psychosocial
context, and health behaviors," *Journal of Personality and Social
Psychology* 85, no. 1 (July 2003): 105–120; Cacioppo and Ernst, "Lonely
hearts: Psychological perspectives on loneliness," *Applied and Preventive
Psychology* 8, no. 1 (1999): 1–22; Cacioppo et al., "Loneliness is a unique
predictor of age-related differences in systolic blood pressure,"
Psychology and Aging 21, no. 1 (March 2006): 152–164; Cacioppo et al.,
"A Meta-Analysis of Interventions to Reduce Loneliness," *Personality
and Social Psychology Review* 15, no. 3 (2011); Hawkley and Cacioppo,
"Loneliness and pathways to disease," *Brain, Behavior, and Immunity*
17, no. 1 (Feb. 2003): 98–105; Cacioppo et al., "Do Lonely Days Invade

the Nights? Potential Social Modulation of Sleep Efficiency," *Psychological Science* 13, no. 4 (2002); Hawkley et al., "From Social Structural Factors to Perceptions of Relationship Quality and Loneliness: The Chicago Health, Aging, and Social Relations Study," *J Gerontol B Psychol Sci Soc Sci* 63, no. 6 (2008): S375–S384; Cacioppo et al., "Loneliness. Clinical Import and Interventions Perspectives on Psychological Science," 10, no. 2 (2015); Cacioppo et al., "Social Isolation," *Annals of the New York Academy of Sciences* 1231 (June 2011): 17–22; Cacioppo et al., "Evolutionary mechanisms for loneliness," *Cognition and Emotion* 28, no 1 (2014); Cacioppo et al., "Toward a neurology of loneliness," *Psychological Bulletin* 140, no. 6 (Nov. 2014): 1464–1504; Cacioppo et al., "In the Eye of the Beholder: Individual Differences in Perceived Social Isolation Predict Regional Brain Activation to Social Stimuli," *Journal of Cognitive Neuroscience* 21, no. 1 (Jan. 2009): 83–92; Cacioppo et al., "Objective and perceived neighborhood environment, individual SES and psychosocial factors, and self-rated health: An analysis of older adults in Cook County, Illinois," *Social Science & Medicine* 63, no. 10 (Nov. 2006): 2575–2590; Jarameka et al., "Loneliness predicts pain, depression, and fatigue: Understanding the role of immune dysregulation," *Psychoneuroendocrinology* 38, no. 8 (Aug. 2013): 1310–1317; Cacioppo et al., "On the Reciprocal Association Between Loneliness and Subjective Well-being," *Am J Epidemiol* 176, no. (2012): 777–784; Mellor et al., "Need for belonging, relationship satisfaction, loneliness, and life satisfaction," *Personality and Individual Differences* 45, no. 3 (Aug. 2008): 213–218; Doane and Adam, "Loneliness and cortisol: Momentary, day-to-day, and trait associations," *Psychoneuroendocrinology* 35, no. 3 (April 2010): 430–441; Cacioppo et al., "Social neuroscience and its potential contribution to psychiatry," *World Psychitary* 13, no. 2 (June 2014): 131–139; Shanakar et al., "Loneliness, social isolation, and behavioral and biological health indicators in older adults," *Health Psychology* 30, no. 4 (July 2011): 377–385; Cacioppo et al., "Day-to-day dynamics of experience-cortisol associations in a population-based sample," *PNAS* 103, no. 45 (Oct. 2006): 17058–17063; Cacioppo et al., "Loneliness and Health: Potential Mechanisms," *Psychosomatic Medicine* 64 (2002): 407–417.

90 **Becoming acutely lonely, the experiment found** John T. Cacioppo and William Patrick, *Loneliness: Human Nature and the Need for Social Connection* (New York: W. W. Norton, 2008), 94–5.

90 **A professor named Sheldon Cohen** Marmot, *Status Syndrome*, 164–5.

90 **Another scientist, Lisa Berkman** Susan Pinker, *The Village Effect: Why Face-to-Face Contact Matters* (London: Atlantic Books, 2015), 67–8.

90 **the same effect on your health as being obese** Cacioppo, *Loneliness*, 5, 94; George Monbiot, "The age of loneliness is killing us," *Guardian*, October 14, 2014, https://www.theguardian.com/commentisfree/2014/oct/14/age-of-loneliness-killing-us, as accessed September 16, 2016.

91 **a psychiatrist called David Spiegel to hypnotize each group** Cacioppo et al., "Loneliness within a nomological net: An evolutionary perspective," *Journal of Research in Personality* 40 (2006): 1054–1085.

92 **"the starring role"** Cacioppo, *Loneliness*, 88.

93 **loneliness *preceded* depressive symptoms** Cacioppo et al., "Perceived Social Isolation Makes Me Sad: 5-Year Cross-Lagged Analyses of Loneliness and Depressive Symptomatology in the Chicago Health, Aging, and Social Relations Study," *Psychology and Aging* 25, no. 2 (2010): 453–463.

94 **Nature *is* connection** Cacioppo, *Loneliness*, 61.

94 **You would be right to feel terrible** Bill McKibben, *Deep Economy: The Wealth of Communities and the Durable Future* (New York: Henry Holt, 2007), 109, 125.

94 **It was an urgent signal** Cacioppo, *Loneliness*, 7.

94 **Humans need tribes** There's a brilliant discussion of this in Sebastian Junger, *Tribe: One Homecoming and Belonging* (New York: Twelve, 2016), especially p. 1–34. See also Hugh MacKay, *The Art of Belonging: It's Not Where You Live, It's How You Live* (Sydney: Pan Macmillan, 2016), especially p. 27–8.

94 **"Evolution fashioned us not"** Cacioppo, *Loneliness*, 15.

94 **The Hutterites** They are not, of course, nomads, so they don't live in the way most humans did in history. But they are closer to that model than we are.

95 **It turned out they had barely any.** Cacioppo et al., "Loneliness Is Associated with Sleep Fragmentation in a Communal Society," *Sleep* 34, no. 11 (Nov, 2011): 1519–1526. See also Junger, *Tribe*, 19.

95 **For decades now, a Harvard professor** Robert Putnam, *Bowling Alone: The Collapse and Revival of American Community* (New York: Simon and Schuster, 2001), 111–2.

96 **"In the ten short years between 1985 and 1994"** Putnam, *Bowling Alone*, 60.

96 **By 2004, the most common answer was none** Cacioppo, *Loneliness*, 247; M. McPherson et al., "Social isolation in America: Changes in core discussion networks over two decades," *American Sociological Review* 71 (2006): 353–375.

96 **"Virtually all forms of family togetherness,"** Putnam, *Bowling Alone*, 101.

98 **She said this to the interviewer, Terry Gross** http://www.npr.org/sections/health-shots/2015/10/22/450830121/sarah-silverman-opens-up-about-depression-comedy-and-troublemaking, as accessed September 16, 2016.

98 **For example, Professor Martha McClintock** Pinker, *Village Effect*, 26; McClintock et al., "Social isolation dysregulates endocrine and behavioral stress while increasing malignant burden of spontaneous mammary tumors," *Proc Natl Acad Sci USA* 106, no. 52 (Dec. 2009): 22393–22398.

101 **We have started to believe that doing things alone** McKibben, *Deep Economy*, 96–104.

102 **"social neuroscience"** There's an excellent discussion of this field in *The Village Effect*, pp. 4–18. See also William Davies, *The Happiness Industry: How the Government and Big Business Sold Us Well-Being* (New York: Verso, 2016), 212–4.

103 **James was from a small town** James is not his real name: Hilarie asked me to use a pseudonym to protect his identity.

NOTES

105 **the first dedicated rehabilitation center for Internet and gaming addicts** Hilarie discussed some of this in her book *Video Games and Your Kids: How Parents Stay in Control* (New York: Issues Press, 2008).

105 **At first, I was shown around by two of the patients** I have changed their first names but no other identifying details.

106 **If you're a typical Westerner** Sherry Turkle, *Reclaiming Conversation: The Power of Talk in a Digital Age* (New York: Penguin, 2015), 42.

107 **The comedian Marc Maron** Marc Maron, *Attempting Normal* (New York, Spiegel and Grau, 2014), 161.

CHAPTER 8: CAUSE THREE: DISCONNECTION
FROM MEANINGFUL VALUES

112 **When Tim was a teenager** Tim writes about his relationship to Lennon's music in his book *Lucy in the Mind of Lennon* (New York: OUP, 2013).

113 **For thousands of years, philosophers** R. W. Belk, "Worldly possessions: Issues and criticisms," *Advances in Consumer Research* 10 (1983): 514–9; Tim Kasser and Allen Kanner, eds., *Psychology and Consumer Culture: The Struggle for a Good Life in a Materialistic World* (Washington, DC: American Psychological Association, 2003), 3–6.

113 **He called it the Aspiration Index** Tim Kasser, *The High Price of Materialism* (Cambridge: MIT Press, 2003), 6–8; Kasser and Ryan, "A dark side of the American dream: Correlates of financial success as a central life aspiration," *Journal of Personality and Social Psychology* 65, no 2 (1993): 410–422.

114 **When the results came back** Kasser, "A dark side . . ." 410–422; Kasser, *High Price of Materialism*, 10.

114 **The more the kids valued getting things** Kasser and Ryan, "Further examining the American dream: Differential correlates of intrinsic and extrinsic goals," *Personality and Social Psychology Bulletin*, 31, 907–914.

114 **"Something about a strong desire for materialistic"** Kasser, *High Price of Materialism*, 11–2, 14.

115 **The first are called *intrinsic* motives** Pink, *Drive*, 1–11, 37–46; Junger, *Tribe*, 21–2.

115 **At the same time, there's a rival set of values** I first learned about this distinction in a brilliant article by George Monbiot: see http://www.monbiot.com/2010/10/11/the-values-of-everything/, as accessed December 1, 2016. For a good guide to how intrinsic and extrinsic motivations were first discovered, I recommend pp. 1–11 of Pink, *Drive*.

116 **The results, when he calculated them out** Kasser and Sheldon, "Coherence and Congruence: Two Aspects of Personality Integration," *Journal of Personality and Social Psychology* 68, no. 3 (1995): 531–543.

116 **Twenty-two different studies have** Helga Dittmar et al., "The Relationship Between Materialism and Personal Well-Being: A Meta-Analysis," *Journal of Personality and Social Psychology* 107, no. 5 (Nov. 2014): 879–924; Kasser, *High Price of Materialism*, 21.

117 **He teamed up again with another professor, Richard Ryan** Kasser and Ryan, "Be careful what you wish for: Optimal functioning and the relative attainment of intrinsic and extrinsic goals," in *Life Goals and Well-Being: Towards a Positive Psychology of Human Striving*, ed. by P. Schmuck and K. Sheldon (New York: Hogrefe & Huber Publishers, 2001), 116–131. See also Kasser, *High Price of Materialism*, 62.

118 **You will have fewer friends and connections** Sherry Turkle, *Reclaiming Conversation: The Power of Talk in a Digital Age* (New York: Penguin, 2015), 83. See also Robert Frank, *Luxury Fever: Weighing the Cost of Excess* (Princeton: Princeton University Press, 2010); William Davies, *The Happiness Industry: How the Government and Big Business Sold Us Well-Being* (New York: Verso, 2016), 143.

118 **what are called "flow states"** Mihály Csíkszentmihály, *Creativity: the Power of Discovery and Invention* (London: Harper, 2013).

118 **they experience significantly fewer flow states** Tim Kasser, "Materialistic Values and Goals," *Annual Review of Psychology* 67 (2016): 489–514, doi: 10.1146/annurev-psych-122414-033344.

119 **chasing a way of life that does a bad job** Tim Kasser, "The 'what' and 'why' of goal pursuits," *Psychol Inqu* 11, no. 4 (2000) 227–268; Ryan and

Deci, "On happiness and human potential," *Annu Rev Psychol* 52 (2001): 141–66.

120 **"Each value" you have, he explained, "is like a slice of that pie."** Kasser, *Materialistic Values*; S. H. Schwartz, "Universals in the structure and content of values: theory and empirical tests in 20 countries," *Advances in Experimental Social Psychology* 25 (Dec. 1992): 1–65.

120 **The I-Want-Golden-Things Rule** I was very conscious—as Tim has been throughout his work—that evidence of correlation is not evidence of causation. The fact that two things happen at the same time is not proof that one causes the other. The cock crows and the sun rises—but that's not proof that the cock crowing causes the sun to rise.

So I discussed with Tim (and with all the social scientists I interviewed) whether this could be merely a correlation, and we were surmising too much from it. Tim said: "The first thing I would say is it's very difficult to prove it, because the only way to prove causation is to randomly assign people to groups. Which would mean I'd have to randomly assign people to become materialistic or to not become materialistic, and then test whether or not they've become more depressed. So first off that's impossible, second off it's probably unethical."

However, he said, there is a whole range of techniques which suggest there is a deeper relationship than coincidence here. He explained to me—and in his published research—that (1) In experimental settings, you can make people more materialistic or less materialistic in the moment. This is called "priming"—you get people to unconsciously think about money, and then you see if their mood changes afterward.

(2) You can do longitudinal studies, which track changes in people's materialism, and see the relationship with depression.

(3) You can look at the evidence about what happens when people do become more materialistic—and it demonstrates that when this happens, it "sets up a lifestyle for themselves which does a relatively bad job of meeting their psychological needs, and the research bears that out pretty well. So they end up feeling less free, they end up feeling less

competent, they end up with worse interpersonal relationships, and that in turn is associated with lower levels of well-being." This is called "a path model or a structural equation model" and it "goes from extrinsic materialistic values to low need satisfaction, to low levels of well-being."

When we take all these pieces of evidence together, I believe we can draw some fairly robust conclusions—but it is important to state that you simply can't do a randomized control trial, so this doesn't meet the very highest bar of evidence.

He also pointed to evidence he has gathered that causation also appears to run the other way—depression and insecurity (especially in childhood) seem to trigger more materialism. The causation does not only run in one direction: It runs both ways.

121 **There's an experiment, by a different group of social scientists, that gives us one early clue.** Marvin E. Goldberg and Gerald J. Gorn, "Some Unintended Consequences of TV Advertising to Children," *Journal of Consumer Research* 5, no. 1 (June 1978), 22–29; Kasser, *High Price of Materialism*, 66; Kasser, *Materialistic Values*, 499; S. E. G. Lea et al., *The Individual in the Economy: A Textbook of Economic Psychology* (New York: Cambridge University Press, 1987), 397; Kasser, ed., *Psychology and Consumer Culture*, 16–18.

122 **More eighteen-month-olds can recognize the McDonald's M** Neal Lawson, *All Consuming: How Shopping Got Us into This Mess and How We Can Find Our Way Out* (London: Penguin, 2009), 143.

122 **By the time an average child is thirty-six months old** Martin Lindstrom, *Brandwashed: Tricks Companies Use to Manipulate Our Minds and Persuade Us to Buy* (New York: Kogan Page, 2012), 10.

122 **So with another social scientist named Jean Twenge** Twenge and Kasser, "Generational changes in materialism," *Personal Soc Psychol Bull* 39 (2013): 883–97. I also interviewed Twenge.

122 **A few years ago, an advertising agency head named Nancy Shalek** Kasser, *High Price of Materialism*, 91.

122 **That would—from the perspective of the advertising industry** Gary Greenberg, *Manufacturing Depression: The Secret History of a Modern Disease* (London: Bloomsbury, 2010), 283.

123 **"The way I understand the intrinsic values,"** Kasser, *Materialistic Values*, 499, gives a good overview of the scientific evidence for this.

125 **three stop signs on my way to my office** In the audio, it says two stop signs—this has been corrected because Tim told me, as part of my fact-checking process, that he misspoke.

CHAPTER 9: CAUSE FOUR: DISCONNECTION
FROM CHILDHOOD TRAUMA

128 **When the women first came into Dr. Vincent Felitti's office** I was first told about Dr. Felitti's work by Dr. Gabor Mate when I interviewed him in Vancouver, and through Gabor's writing, especially his wonderful book *In The Realm of Hungry Ghosts* (Toronto: Random House Canada, 2013). I have briefly referenced Dr. Felitti's work before in *Chasing the Scream* and a few pieces spun off from it.

129 **For years, in Northern Ireland** http://www.bbc.co.uk/history/events/republican_hunger_strikes_maze, as accessed September 17, 2016.

130 **you'll lose three hundred pounds a year.** Vincent Felitti et al., "Obesity: Problem, Solution, or Both?" *Premanente Journal* 14, no. 1 (2010): 24; Vincent Felitti et al., "The relationship of adult health status to childhood abuse and household dysfunction," *American Journal of Preventive Medicine* 14 (1998): 245–258.

130 **The people who did best, and lost the most weight** Vincent Felitti, "Ursprünge des Suchtverhaltens—Evidenzen aus einer Studie zu belastenden Kindheitserfahrungen," *Praxis der Kinderpsychologie und Kinderpsychiatrie* 52 (2003): 547–559.

130 **They felt unbelievably vulnerable** Vincent Felitti et al., *Chadwick's Child Maltreatment: Sexual Abuse and Psychological Maltreatment,* Volume 2 of 3, Fourth edition, (2014): 203; Vincent Felitti et al., "The

relationship of adult health status to childhood abuse and household dysfunction," *American Journal of Preventive Medicine* 14 (1998): 245–258.

132 **"Overweight is overlooked"** Felitti et al., *Chadwick's Child Maltreatment*, 203.

132 **Vincent began to wonder if the anti-obesity programs** Felitti, *Obesity: Problem, Solution, or Both?*, 24.

134 **This survey was then given to seventeen thousand people** Felitti, *Chadwick's Child Maltreatment*, 204.

135 **If you had six categories of traumatic events in your childhood, you were *five times*** Vincent Feliiti, "Adverse childhood experiences and the risk of depressive disorders in childhood," *Journal of Affective Disorders* 82 (Nov. 2004): 217–225.

135 **If you had seven categories of traumatic event as a child, you were 3,100 percent** Felitti, *Chadwick's Child Maltreatment*, 209.

135 **You just don't get figures like this in medicine very often.** Felitti, *Chadwick's Child Maltreatment*, 206; Vincent Felitti, "Ursprünge des Suchtverhaltens—Evidenzen aus einer Studie zu belastenden Kindheitserfahrungen," *Praxis der Kinderpsychologie und Kinderpsychiatrie*, 52 (2003): 547–559. Vincent Felitti, "Childhood Sexual Abuse, Depression, and Family Dysfunction in Adult Obese Patients," *Southern Medical Journal* 86: (1993): 732–736.

135 **Curiously, it turned out emotional abuse was more likely** Felitti, "Adverse childhood experiences," 223. There's a good graph of antidepressant prescriptions in relation to ACE scores too in Vincent Felitti, *Chadwick's Child Maltreatment*, 208.

136 **In the years that followed, the study has been replicated many times** For some meta-analyses, see for example: A. Danese and M. Tan, "Childhood maltreatment and obesity: systematic review and meta-analysis," *Molecular Psychiatry* 19 (May 2014): 544–554; Nanni et al., "Childhood Maltreatment Predicts Unfavorable Course of Illness and Treatment Outcome in Depression: A Meta-Analysis," *American Journal of Psychiatry* 169, no. 2 (Feb. 2012): 141–151.

136 **There's a house fire inside many of us** George Brown and Tirril Harris did some interesting research with similar—but not identical—findings. For an overview see *Where Inner and Outer Worlds Meet*, 16–20, 227–40.

136 **he learned that Allen Barbour, an internist at Stanford University** Felitti, *Chadwick's Child Maltreatment*, 209.

137 **Once that was in place, far more people became able to keep going** Felitti, *Obesity: Problem, Solution, or Both?*, 24.

137 **After I met with him, I went to the beach** I had known about the ACE studies for some time, and I thought I had absorbed their insights, especially when it came to addiction. It was only there that I realized I hadn't properly assimilated their insights—not for myself, anyway—and this is why I reacted with such strong emotion, I think.

CHAPTER 10: CAUSE FIVE: DISCONNECTION FROM STATUS AND RESPECT

141 I couldn't have written this chapter without the guidance of Kate Pickett and Richard Wilkinson. I met Kate years ago when we both addressed the Green Party conference, and they are two of the social scientists I most admire in the world. I first learned about Robert Sapolsky's work from their writings, and they discussed the subjects and themes of this chapter in detail with me. They have a forthcoming book discussing similar themes—as I am writing it has not gone to press, so I don't know the title, but I strongly recommend reading everything they write.

141 **One afternoon in the late 1960s** Robert Sapolsky: *A Primate's Memoir* (London: Vintage, 2002), 13. It was Richard Wilkinson and Kate Pickett who first suggested I look at the work of Robert Sapolsky and explained how this is linked to depression and anxiety: I'm very grateful to them. A key source for this account is *A Primate's Memoir*, and in the introduction, Robert says that he has amalgamated some minor characters in the book for the sake of clarity. I don't refer to any of the minor characters, so I don't think that is relevant here, but I wanted to offer it

as a point of clarity. Unlike the other social scientists I discuss in this book, I was only able to interview Robert briefly, by e-mail.

142 **Just over a decade later, Robert made it** Sapolsky, *Primate's Memoir*, 65; Robert Sapolsky, *Why Zebras Don't Get Ulcers* (New York: Henry Holt, 2004), 312.

142 **All five women clucked with relief** Sapolsky, *Primate's Memoir*, 240.

142 **Back in New York, Robert had the first of his depressions.** Ibid., 302–3.

142 **He suspected that a key to understanding depression might lie out here** Ibid., 14–15.

142 **there was a king of the swingers, a jungle VIP** Ibid., 16–21.

143 **Robert saw a scrawny, feeble creature who he named Job** Ibid., 21–2.

143 **This blood sample would then be tested for several key factors** Ibid., 38, 105; Sapolsky *Why Zebras Don't*, 355–6.

144 **It turned out—when his blood samples were tested** Robert Sapolsky, "Cortisol concentrations and the social significance of rank instability among wild baboons," *Psychoneuroendochrinology* 17, no. 6 (Nov. 1992): 701–709; Robert Sapolsky, "The endocrine stress-response and social status in the wild baboon," *Hormones and Behavior* 16, no. 3 (September 1982): 279–292. Robert Sapolsky, "Adrenocortical function, social rank, and personality among wild baboons," *Biological Psychiatry* 28, no. 10 (Nov. 1990): 862–878.

144 **To avoid getting savaged, the baboons with the lowest status** Sapolsky, *Primate's Memoir*, 97; Sapolsky, *Why Zebras Don't*, 300–4, 355–359.

144 **One day, after Solomon had been at the top of the hierarchy** Sapolsky, *Primate's Memoir*, 23.

145 **One day, Solomon was so despairing** Ibid., 95.

145 **As Robert investigated these questions further** Ibid., 177.

145 **So some other scientists began** See for example Carol Shivley et al., "Behavior and physiology of social stress and depression in female cynomolgus monkeys," *Biological Psychiatry* 41, no. 8 (April 1997): 871–882.

146 **With baboons, their hierarchies are fairly fixed** Some cultural evolution is possible even with baboons. See Natalie Angier, "No Time for Bullies: Baboons Retool Their Culture," *New York Times*, April 13, 2004, http://www.nytimes.com/2004/04/13/science/no-time-for-bullies-baboons-retool-their-culture.html for the fascinating story, as accessed December 23, 2016.

147 **Other social scientists then broke this down to look at depression specifically** Erick Messias et al., "Economic grand rounds: Income inequality and depression across the United States: an ecological study," *Psychiatric Services* 62, no. 7 (2011): 710–2. See also http://csi.nuff.ox .ac.uk/?p=642, as accessed December 10, 2016.

147 **This is true if you compare different countries** Richard Wilkinson and Kate Pickett, *The Spirit Level: Why Equality Is Better for Everyone* (London: Penguin, 2009), 31–41, 63–72, 173–196.

148 **"We're extraordinarily sensitive to these things,"** Paul Moloney, *The Therapy Industry* (London: Pluto Press, 2013), 109.

148 **If you work for a company, in living memory** http://www.hrreview .co.uk/hr-news/ftse-100-bosses-earn-average-5-5m-year-report-says /100790, as accessed January 10, 2017; Sebastian Junger, *Tribe: One Homecoming and Belonging* (New York: Twelve, 2016), 31.

148 **The six heirs to the Walmart fortune** http://www.vanityfair.com /news/2012/05/joseph-stiglitz-the-price-on-inequality, as accessed December 10, 2016.

148 **Eight billionaires own more wealth** http://www.bbc.co.uk/news /business-38613488, as accessed April 1, 2017.

148 **After he had returned from living with his troop of wild baboons** I am not arguing that Robert Sapolsky shares all of the analysis in this chapter (or the rest of this book). This is a dimension of thinking about depression and anxiety that was opened up by his early research into baboons, and has later been developed by social scientists in ways he may not entirely agree with. He clearly believes depression is multi-causal. Anyone wanting a short intro to his wider approach should watch this excellent lecture by him: https://www.youtube.com/watch?v=NOAgplgTxfc (as accessed

February 3, 2017). Anyone who wants a longer guide should read his superb book *Why Zebras Don't Get Ulcers.*

148 **Robert Sapolsky had a recurring dream** Sapolsky, *Primate's Memoir,* 127.

149 **I think this is a dream about how we can be** This is my interpretation of the dream; Robert may disagree.

CHAPTER 11: CAUSE SIX: DISCONNECTION FROM THE NATURAL WORLD

151 **"the nature of human nature."** She used this phrase in a talk at FutureFest in London that I attended in September 2016.

153 **Some elephants in captivity are so traumatized** John Sutherland, *Jumbo: The Unauthorized Biography of a Victorian Sensation* (London: Aurum Press, 2014), 9–10 26–7, 46, 58–60, 127.

153 **Many animals in captivity lose the desire to have sex** Sutherland, *Jumbo,* 62.

153 **the landscape they evolved to live in** Edmund Ramsden and Duncan Wilson, "The nature of suicide: science and the self-destructive animal," *Endeavour* 34, no. 1 (March 2010): 21–24.

154 **It's been known for a long time that all sorts of mental health problems** Ian Gold and Joel Gold, *Suspicious Minds: How Culture Shapes Madness* (New York: Free Press, 2015). I also interviewed both of the authors. For a good quick summary, see also: T. M. Luhrmann, "Is the World More Depressed?" *New York Times,* March 24, 2014, https://www.nytimes.com/2014/03/25/opinion/a-great-depression .html

154 **the people who moved to green areas saw a big reduction in depression** Ian Alcock et al., "Longitudinal Effects on Mental Health of Moving to Greener and Less Green Urban Areas," *Environmental Science and Technology* 48, no. 2 (2014): 1247–1255. See also William Davies, *The Happiness Industry: How the Government and Big Business Sold Us Well-Being* (New York: Verso, 2016), 245–7.

154 **This was just one of many studies with similar findings** e.g., David G. Pearson and Tony Craig: "The great outdoors? Exploring the mental health benefits of natural environments," *Front Psychol* 5 (2014): 1178; Kirsten Beyer et al., "Exposure to Neighborhood Green Space and Mental Health: Evidence from the Survey of the Health of Wisconsin," *Int J Environ Res Public Health* 11, no. 3 (March 2014): 3452–3472. See also Richard Louv, *The Nature Principle* (New York: Algonquin Books, 2013), 29, 33–4; Richard Louv, *Last Child in The Woods* (New York: Atlantic Books, 2010), 50.

155 **But it turned out there was less stress and despair in the greener neighborhood.** Catherine Ward Thompson et al., "More green space is linked to less stress in deprived communities," *Landscape and Urban Planning* 105, no 3 (April 2012): 221–229.

155 **Their improvement was *five times* greater** Marc Berman et al., "Interacting with Nature Improves Cognition and Affect for Individuals with Depression," *Journal of Affective Disorders* 140, no. 3 (Nov. 2012): 300–305.

156 **It's hard for a hungry animal moving** Louv, *Last Child*, 32.

156 **exercise significantly reduces depression and anxiety** Andreas Ströhle, "Physical activity, exercise, depression and anxiety disorders," *Journal of Neural Transmission* 116 (June 2009): 777.

156 **When scientists have compared people who run on treadmills in the gym** Natasha Gilbert, "Green Space: A Natural High," *Nature* 531 (March 2016): S56–S57.

157 **"biophilia"** E. O. Wilson: *Biophilia* (Cambridge: Harvard University Press, 1984).

157 **The social scientists Gordon Orians and Judith Heerwagen** Louv, *The Nature Principle*, 54.

158 **But a range of scientists have shown that a common reaction** A good summary is at https://www.psychologytoday.com/articles/201603/its -not-all-about-you, as accessed September 3, 2016.

159 **In the State Prison of Southern Michigan in the 1970s** This is from Howard Frumkin's brilliant review paper (which I really recommend

reading in full) "Beyond Toxicity: Human Health and the Natural Environment," *Am J Prev Med* 20, no. 3 (2001): 237. See also: David Kidner, "Depression and the Natural World," *International Journal of Critical Psychology* 19 (2007).

CHAPTER 12: CAUSE SEVEN: DISCONNECTION FROM
A HOPEFUL OR SECURE FUTURE

162 **Not long before he died, a Native American named Chief Plenty Coups** Jonathan Lear, *Radical Hope: Ethics in the Face of Cultural Devastation* (New York: Harvard University Press, 2006), 1–4. I learned about all this material from Lear's wonderful book—I really recommend it.

162 **When he was young, he explained** Ibid., 10.

162 **These were at the core of their moral vision.** Ibid., 13–14.

163 **"After this, nothing happened."** Ibid., 2.

163 **the philosopher Jonathan Lear explained when he wrote about this** Ibid., 40–1.

164 **A century later, a psychology professor named Michael Chandler** Michael J. Chandler and Christopher Lalonde, "Cultural continuity as a hedge against suicide in Canada's First Nations," *Transcultural Psychiatry* 35, no. 2 (1998): 191–219; Marc Lewis, *The Biology of Desire: Why Addiction Is Not a Disease* (Victoria, Australia: Scribe, 2015), 203–4.

165 **So Michael and his colleagues spent years carefully gathering** Along with interviewing Michael Chandler and reading his scientific work, my writing in this section was also informed by my interview with Laurence Kirmayer, who edited Michael's study for the brilliant academic journal the *Journal of Transcultural Psychiatry*. He also helped to place it in a wider context for me.

167 **Asked to describe themselves five or ten or twenty years from now** Lorraine Ball and Michael Chandler, "Identity formation in suicidal and nonsuicidal youth: The role of self-continuity," *Development and*

Psychopathology I, no. 3 (1989): 257–275; Michael C. Boyes and Michael Chandler, "Cognitive development, epistemic doubt, and identity formation in adolescence," *Journal of Youth and Adolescence* 21, no. 3 (1992): 277–304; Michael Chandler et al., "Assessment and training of role-taking and referential communication skills in institutionalized emotionally disturbed children," *Developmental Psychology* 10, no. 4 (July 1974): 546; Michael Chandler, "The Othello Effect," *Human Development* 30, no. 3 (Jan. 1970): 137–159; Chandler et al., "Aboriginal language knowledge and youth suicide," *Cognitive Development* 22, no. 3 (2007): 392–399; Michael Chandler, "Surviving time: The persistence of identity in this culture and that," *Culture & Psychology* 6, no. 2 (June 2000): 209–231.

167 **It was like a muscle they couldn't work** The observation that depression involves despair about the future specifically precedes this study. For example, in the 1960s the psychologist Aaron Beck named it as part of the "depressive triad"—the three cognitive characteristics of all depressed people. For a good exposition of this, see Brown and Harris, *Where Inner and Outer Worlds Meet: Psychosocial Research in the Tradition of George Brown* (London: Routledge, 2000), 10–11.

169 **the story of her life since we last met** The audio of this conversation and her identity were verified by the publisher.

172 **The Italian philosopher Paolo Virno says** Ivor Southwood, *Non-Stop Inertia* (Arlesford, Hants: Zero Books, 2011), 15–6 (which, by the way, is a terrific book); Nick Srnicek and Alex Williams, *Inventing the Future: Postcapitalism and a World Without Work* (London: Verso, 2015), 93; Mark Fisher, *Capitalist Realism: Is There No Alternative?* (Winchester, UK: O Books, 2009), 32–37.

CHAPTER 13: CAUSES EIGHT AND NINE: THE REAL ROLE
OF GENES AND BRAIN CHANGES

175 **Marc Lewis's friends thought he was dead.** Marc Lewis, *Memoirs of an Addicted Brain: A Neuroscientist Examines His Former Life on Drugs*

(Toronto: Doubleday Canada, 2011), 139–42. I also discussed these events with Marc in detail.

176 **He wanted to know—how does your brain change when you are deeply distressed?** Marc Lewis, *The Biology of Desire: Why Addiction Is Not a Disease* (Victoria, Australia: Scribe, 2015), xv.

176 **a crucial concept called neuroplasticity** Some good guides: Norman Doidge, *The Brain That Changes Itself* (London: Penguin, 2008); Moheb Costandi, *Neuroplasticity* (Cambridge: MIT Press, 2016); Lewis, *Memoirs of an Addicted Brain*, 154–6; Lewis, *Biology of Desire*, 32–3, 163–5, 194–7.

177 **If you do a brain scan of a London taxi driver** Eleanor A. Maguire et al., "London taxi drivers and bus drivers: A structural MRI and neuropsychological analysis," *Hippocampus* 16, no. 12 (2006): 1091–1101.

177 **if you raise a baby in total darkness** Gabor Mate, *In the Realm of Hungry Ghosts* (Toronto: Random House Canada, 2013), 183.

177 **the brain "is always changing,"** The audio of the quote in this paragraph that you can hear on the website is slightly different because Marc asked me to change it very slightly, to make it more factually accurate.

178 **You couldn't figure out the plot of *Breaking Bad*** This analogy was first said to me by the brilliant clinical psychologist Lucy Johnstone, and by the wonderful child psychiatrist Sami Tamimi; they weren't sure who first said it, and I haven't been able to track down the original source. If anyone knows it, please e-mail me and I'll include it in future editions of this book.

179 **But telling depressed people that it was simply caused by their brains** John Read and Pete Saunders, *A Straight-Taking Introduction to the Causes of Mental Health Problems* (Ross-on-Wye, Hertfordshire, UK: PCCS Books, 2011), 34.

180 **"Ask not what's inside your head,"** http://cspeech.ucd.ie/Fred/docs/Anthropomorphism.pdf; http://www.trincoll.edu/~wmace/publications/Ask_inside.pdf, as accessed June 8, 2016.

180 **You take large groups of identical twins** There's some dispute about the legitimacy of this technique. I don't have space to go into it here,

but if you want a skeptical take on it, read Sami Timimi, *Rethinking ADHD: From Brain to Culture* (London: Palgrave Macmillan, 2009), 63.

181 **This has been done with depression and anxiety** Falk W. Lohoff, "Overview of the Genetics of Major Depressive Disorder," *Curr Psychiatry Rep* 12, no. 6 (Dec. 2010): 539–546, as accessed June 12, 2016—this is the best overview.

181 http://coping.us/images/Hettema_et_al_2001_OCD_Meta_analysis .pdf, as accessed June 12, 2016.

181 **To give you a comparison, how tall you are is 90 percent inherited** Michael Marmot, *Status Syndrome: How Your Place on the Social Gradient Affects Your Health* (London: Bloomsbury, 2004), 50.

182 **If those bad things *hadn't* happened to you** Robert Sapolsky, *Monkeyluv: And Other Lessons on Our Lives as Animals* (New York: Vintage, 2006), 55–6; A. Caspi et al., "Influence of Life Stress on Depression: moderation by a polmorphism in the 5-HTT gene," *Science* 301 (2003): 386; Brown and Harris, *Where Inner and Outer Worlds Meet: Psychosocial Research in the Tradition of George Brown* (London: Routledge, 2000), 131–6.

182 **The first kind of depression was called "reactive"** Sometimes scientists used different names, and there were some variations in definition, but at its core was a consistent belief there was an inherent biological form of depression distinct from one with causes in the person's social or psychological life. Their definitions were not, however, identical.

183 **It might just mean that doctors weren't good at spotting the difference back then.** Initially, after his research in the 1970s, George Brown concluded that endogenous depression does not exist. But when I interviewed him more than thirty years after this conclusion, he said he had changed his mind—while he hadn't conducted further research into this question, he believed by then that some small fraction of depression must be endogenous.

184 **several studies have found that the social causes of depression and anxiety will still affect** See for example Brown and Harris, *Where Inner*

and Outer Worlds Meet, 263–72; S. Malkoff-Schwartz et al., "Stressful Life events and social rhythm disruption in the onset of manic and depressive bipolar episodes: a preliminary investigation," *Archives of General Psychiatry* 55, no. 8 (Aug. 1998): 702–9.

185 **to read some of the early feminist classics from the 1960s** Betty Freidan's book *The Feminine Mystique* (London: Penguin, 2010) particularly helped me with this.

185 **Picture a 1950s housewife living before feminism.** As I hope is clear from the context, this is a hypothetical conversation, of the kind that happened then, not a literal quotation from one.

185 **that doesn't fit with what you *actually* need.** It might seem odd to suggest that human beings are not good at understanding our own needs and wants, and can be misinformed about what we are actually feeling, or why. In fact there's a huge scientific literature about how poor we are at understanding our own feelings or interpreting why they happen. If you are interested I'd strongly recommend reading the extraordinary book *Strangers to Ourselves* by Tim Wilson (Cambridge: Harvard University Press, 2010) as a good introduction to this whole field of science.

186 **The right-wing British pundit Katie Hopkins recently said depression** Zoe Shenton, "Katie Hopkins comes under fire for ridiculing depression in series of tweets," *Mirror*, March 30, 2015, http://www.mirror.co.uk/3am/celebrity-news/katie-hopkins-comes-under-fire-5427934, as accessed April 28, 2015.

187 **What Sheila and the other experimenters wanted to know was** Sheila Mehta and Amerigo Farina, "Is Being 'Sick' Really Better? Effect of the Disease View of Mental Disorder on Stigma," *Journal of Social and Clinical Psychology* 16, no. 4 (1997): 405–419. I first learned about this experiment in James Davies, *Cracked: Why Psychiatry Is Doing More Harm Than Good* (London: Icon Books, 2013), 222. See also Ethan Watters, "The Americanization of Mental Illness," *New York Times Magazine*, January 8, 2010, http://www.nytimes.com/2010/01/10/magazine/10psyche-t.html, as accessed June 10, 2016.

188 **for decades, psychiatrists have—in their training—been taught something called the bio-psycho-social model** The history of this concept is outlined in *The Rise and Fall of the Biopsychosocial Model* by S. Nassir Ghaemi. See also: John Read and Pete Saunders, *A Straight-Taking Introduction to the Causes of Mental Health Problems* (Ross-on-Wye, Hertfordshire, UK: PCCS Books, 2011), 36–7, 53–5.

188 **depression and anxiety have three kinds of causes** Another key reason leading me to these broader insights was my research into the social causes of addiction, for my book *Chasing the Scream: The First and Last Days of the War on Drugs* (New York: Bloomsbury, 2015). I don't want to repeat that material here, but if you're interested in how I came to these insights, check out chapters twelve and thirteen of that book in particular, and the work of one of my heroes, Bruce Alexander, especially *The Globalization of Addiction: A Study in Poverty of the Spirit* (New York: Oxford University Press, 2008).

189 **"Things have changed in psychiatry,"** For more background on this see Roberto Lewis-Fernandez, "Rethinking funding priorities in mental health research," *British Journal of Psychiatry* 208 (2016): 507–509.

189 **it is "much more politically challenging"** This thesis is discussed further, and brilliantly, in Mark Rapley, Joanna Moncrieff, and Jacqui Dillon, eds., *De-Medicalizing Misery: Psychiatry, Psychology and the Human Condition* (London: Palgrave Macmillan, 2011).

190 **He sometimes quotes the Eastern philosopher Jiddu Krishnamurti** Merrill Singer and Hans A. Baer, *Introducing Medical Anthropology: A Discipline in Action* (Lanham, MD: AltaMira Press, 2007), 181. The academic David Mechanic summarized George Brown's work as "bringing meaning back into social psychiatric research"—see *Where Inner and Outer Worlds Meet*, 61–77.

CHAPTER 14: THE COW

193 **Old land mines left behind by the U.S.** For more info on the unexploded ordinance in Southeast Asia, see Michaela Haa, "The

Killing Fields of Today: Landmine Problem Rages On," *Huffington Post*, June 2, 2013, http://www.huffingtonpost.com/michaela-haas/the -killing-fields-of-tod_b_2981990.html, as accessed December 21, 2016.

194 **He thought about the people he worked with there** Derek also discusses this argument in "Global Mental Health Is an Oxymoron and Medical Imperialism," *British Medical Journal* 346 (May 2013): f3509.

195 **"How different would it be," she said,** Lucy asked me this particular question via e-mail, which is why there's no audio for it on the website.

198 **An elderly woman named Regina Schwenke** There's a good article about her: Sara Wilde, "Life inside the bunkers," *Exberliner*, September 17, 2013, http://www.exberliner.com/features/people/inside-we-felt -safe/, as accessed December 10, 2016.

CHAPTER 15: WE BUILT THIS CITY

199 **We Built This City** For this chapter, these are some of the news reports I drew on: https://kottiundco.net/; https://www.flickr.com/photos /79930329@N08/; https://www.neues-deutschland.de/artikel /228214.mieter-protestieren-gegen-verdraengung.html; http://www .tagesspiegel.de/berlin/kreuzberg-protest-aus-der-huette/6686496 .html; http://www.taz.de/Protestcamp-am-Kotti/!5092817/; http:// needleberlin.com/2010/10/31/when-youre-from-kotti/; http://jungle -world.com/artikel/2012/24/45631.html; http://www.tagesspiegel.de /berlin/mietenprotest-am-kotti-opposition-will-mietobergrenze-fuer -soziale-wohnungen/6772428.html; as accessed September 30, 2016. (With thanks to my father, Eduard Hari, for helping me to make sense of the German). I interviewed dozens of people at Kotti stretched over several years. As with any complex event, there were some minor discrepancies in how people remembered specific events. I have not reflected these minor disagreements in the text itself: I went with whichever explanation was backed by the most people, or seemed to have been remembered most strongly by the individuals in question.

Separately, to describe the wider situation with rents in Berlin, I also drew on the book by Peter Schneider *Berlin Now: The Rise of the City and the Fall of the Wall* (London: Penguin, 2014).

214 **the ludicrous contracts that had been drawn up so long ago** The complexities of this are described in the book *Abschoeibongs Dschungel Buch* by Mischa and Susan Claasen (Berlin: LitPol, 1982).

CHAPTER 16: RECONNECTION ONE: TO OTHER PEOPLE

219 **They wanted to know: Does trying consciously to make yourself happier actually work?** https://eerlab.berkeley.edu/pdf/papers/Ford _etal_inpress_JEPG.pdf, as accessed November 1, 2016; B. Q. Ford et al., "Culture Shapes Whether the Pursuit of Happiness Predicts Higher or Lower Well-Being," *Journal of Experimental Psychology: General. Advance* online publication 144, no. 6 (2015), http://dx.doi .org/10.1037/xge0000108.

220 **For Asians, it's the other way around** Richard Nisbett, *The Geography of Thought: How Asians and Westerners Think Differently . . . and Why* (New York: Nicholas Brealey Publishing, 2005) is a really interesting discussion of this whole field of science. See also Paul Moloney, *The Therapy Industry: The Irresistible Rise of the Talking Cure, and Why It Doesn't Work* (London: Pluto Press, 2013), 118.

222 **Don't be yourself.** John Gray, *The Silence of Animals: On Progress and Other Modern Myths* (London: Penguin, 2014), 108–112.

225 **I saw them as crazy anachronisms** I stress I am talking here about how I felt as a teenager about ultra-Orthodox Jews and any other apparently extreme religious group, like fundamentalist Christians or Muslims. I felt the opposite about secular or moderate Jewish people: I grew up in an area that was overwhelmingly secular-Jewish, and my family intermarried with a local Jewish family, and it is a culture I felt very close to.

226 **Around 80 percent choose to join the Church.** http://www.npr.org /templates/story/story.php?storyId=5455572, as accessed December 10, 2016.

228 **But a major scientific study carried out into Amish mental health in the 1970s** J. A. Egeland et al., "Amish Study: I. Affective disorders among the Amish, 1976–1980," *American Journal of Psychiatry* 140 (1983): 56–61, https://www.ncbi.nlm.nih.gov/pubmed/6847986; E. Diener et al., "Beyond money: Toward an economy of well-being." *Psychological Science in the Public Interest* 5, no. 1 (July 2004): 1–31; Tim Kasser, "Can Thrift Bring Well-being? A Review of the Research and a Tentative Theory," *Social and Personality Psychology Compass* 5, no. 11 (2011): 865–877, doi:10.1111/j.1751-9004.2011.00396.x. See also Brandon H. Hidaka, "Depression as a disease of modernity: explanations for increasing prevalence," *Journal of Affective Disorders* 140, no. 3 (Nov. 2013): 205–214, https://www.ncbi.nlm.nih.gov/pmc/articles /PMC3330161/; and Kathleen Blanchard, "Depression symptoms may come from modern living," Emaxhealth.com, August 13, 2009, http:// www.emaxhealth.com/1020/25/32851/depression-symptoms-may -come-modern-living.html. See also Sebastian Junger, *Tribe: One Homecoming and Belonging* (New York: Twelve, 2016), 22.

CHAPTER 17: RECONNECTION TWO: SOCIAL PRESCRIBING

230 **So he was part of a team who helped to turn this doctor's office suite** The other key figures included Lord Andrew Mawson, Rob Trimble, Karen McGee, Sheenagh McKinlay, and Dr. Julia Davis.

235 **She met a white working-class man** Both Phil and Mr. Singh are pseudonyms to protect the medical confidentiality of the individuals I'm describing.

241 **Sam calls this approach "social prescribing"** There's a good summary of the debate at Janet Brandling and William House, "Social prescribing in general practice: adding meaning to medicine," *Br J Gen Pract* 59, no. 563 (June 2009): 454–456, doi: 10.3399/bjgp0 9X421085. See also: Peter Cawston, "Social prescribing in very deprived areas," *Br J Gen Pract* 61, no. 586 (May 2011): 350, doi: 10.3399/ bjgp11X572517.

241 **There has, however, been a series of scientific studies of "therapeutic horticulture"** Marianne Thorsen Gonzalez et al., "Therapeutic
horticulture in clinical depression: a prospective study of active
components," *Journal of Advanced Nursing* 66, no. 9 (Sept. 2010):
2002–2013, doi: 10.1111/j.1365-2648.2010.05383.x; Y. H. Lee et al.,
"Effects of Horticultural Activities on Anxiety Reduction on Female
High School Students," *Acta Hortic* 639 (2004): 249–251, doi:
10.17660/ActaHortic.2004.639.32; P. Stepney et al., "Mental health,
social inclusion and the green agenda: An evaluation of a land based
rehabilitation project designed to promote occupational access and
inclusion of service users in North Somerset, UK," *Soc Work Health
Care* 39, no. 3–4 (2004): 375–97; M. T. Gonzalez, "Therapeutic Horticulture in Clinical Depression: A Prospective Study," *Res Theory Nurs
Pract* 23, no. 4 (2009): 312–28; Joe Sempik and Jo Aldridge, "Health,
well-being and social inclusion: therapeutic horticulture in the UK,"
https://dspace.lboro.ac.uk/2134/2922; V. Reynolds, "Well-being
Comes Naturally: an Evaluation of the BTCV Green Gym at Port-
slade, East Sussex," Report no. 17, Oxford: Oxford Brookes University;
Caroline Brown and Marcus Grant, "Biodiversity and Human Health:
What Role for Nature in Healthy Urban Planning?" *Built Environment
(1978-)* 31, no. 4, Planning Healthy Towns and Cities (2005): 326–338.
There's also a treasure trove of interesting research on this in the *Journal
of Therapeutic Horticulture*, which you can access at http://ahta.org
/ahta-the-journal-of-therapeutic-horticulture, as accessed September
10, 2016. See also William Davies, *The Happiness Industry: How the
Government and Big Business Sold Us Well-Being* (New York: Verso,
2016), 246.

242 **This suggests, at the very least, that it is a good place to start** Paul
Moloney, *The Therapy Industry: The Irresistible Rise of the Talking Cure,
and Why It Doesn't Work* (London: Pluto Press, 2013), 61.

242 **Until the 1850s, nobody knew what caused cholera** http://www.bbc
.co.uk/history/historic_figures/bazalgette_joseph.shtml, as accessed
December 10, 2016.

CHAPTER 18: RECONNECTION THREE: TO MEANINGFUL WORK

246 **It felt like a karaoke life** I think I first heard this metaphor from the British writer Dennis Potter, in an interview where he was talking about his TV series *Lipstick on Your Collar*.

246 **On Sunday nights, she'd feel her heart pounding in her chest** Paul Verhaeghe, *What About Me? The Struggle for Identity in a Market-Based Society* (Victoria, Australia: Scribe, 2014), 199, explains how common this is as a reaction to the way we work.

249 **Some of them, Josh learned, had proposed organizing our work on totally different principles.** I am grateful to Noam Chomsky—who inspired Josh and Meredith—for talking me through this history. He has written about it throughout his work.

252 **This way of living and working is, he explains, an attempt to deal with that problem.** I didn't have space here to go into the evidence for how workplaces where you can use your intrinsic motivation are also more efficient. To learn about that I'd recommend *Drive: The Surprising Truth About What Motivates Us* by Daniel Pink, pp. 28–31, and p. 51, and Thomas Georghegan's excellent explanation of German democratic workplaces in his book *Were You Born on the Wrong Continent? How the European Model Can Help You Get a Life*. See also Paul Rogat Loeb, *Soul of a Citizen: Living with Conviction in Challenging Times* (New York: St. Martin's Press, 2010), 100–4.

254 **"Everybody wants to feel useful, and have purpose."** Pink, *Drive*, 76.

254 **The businesses closer to the democratic model grew, on average, four times more than the others.** Pink, *Drive*, 91; Paul Baard et al., "Intrinsic Need Satisfaction: A Motivational Basis of Performance and Well-Being in Two Work Settings," *Journal of Applied Social Psychology* 34 (2004).

254 **Several distinguished social scientists have tried to get grants to study** For example—Kate Pickett and Richard Wilkinson.

255 **But there is a large amount of evidence—as I discussed before** William Davies, *The Happiness Industry: How the Government and Big Business Sold Us Well-Being* (New York: Verso, 2016) 108, 132–3. See also:

Robert Karasek and Tores Theorell, *Healthy Work: Stress, Productivity and the Reconstruction of Working Life* (New York: Basic Books, 1992).

CHAPTER 19: RECONNECTION FOUR: TO MEANINGFUL VALUES

257 **For example, the city of São Paulo, in Brazil, was being slowly smothered by billboards.** I first learned about this from the excellent documentary *This Space Available* at the New York Documentary Film Festival. See also Justin Thomas, "Remove billboards for the sake of our mental health," *The National*, January 25, 2015, http://www.the national.ae/opinion/comment/remove-billboards-for-the-sake-of-our -mental-health; Amy Curtis, "Five Years After Banning Outdoor Ads, Brazil's Largest City Is More Vibrant Than Ever," NewDream.org, https://www.newdream.org/blog/sao-paolo-ad-ban; Arwa Mahdawi, "Can cities kick ads? Inside the global movement to ban urban billboards," *The Guardian*, August 12, 2015, https://www.theguardian.com /cities/2015/aug/11/can-cities-kick-ads-ban-urban-billboards, as accessed August 25, 2016.

257 **there was a controversy after a company marketing diet products put advertisements in the London Underground** Rose Hackman, "Are you beach body ready? Controversial weight loss ad sparks varied reactions," *The Guardian*, June 27, 2015, https://www.theguardian.com/us -news/2015/jun/27/beach-body-ready-america-weight-loss-ad-insta gram, as accessed January 10, 2017.

263 **It was a big and measurable effect** Tim Kasser et al., "Changes in materialism, changes in psychological well-being: Evidence from three longitudinal studies and an intervention experiment," *Motivation and Emotion* 38 (2014): 1–22.

CHAPTER 20: RECONNECTION FIVE: SYMPATHETIC JOY, AND OVERCOMING ADDICTION TO THE SELF

265 Dr. Miguel Farias and Catherine Wilkholm, *The Buddha Pill: Can Meditation Change You?* (New York: Watkins, 2015), 108–9; T. Toneatta and

L Nguyen: "Does mindfulness meditation improve anxiety and mood symptoms? A review of the evidence," *Canadian Journal of Psychiatry* 52, no. 4 (2007): 260–266; J. D. Teasdale et al., "Prevention of relapse/ recurrence in major depression by mindfulness-based cognitive therapy," *Journal of Consulting and Clinical Psychology* 68, no. 4 (Aug. 2000): 615–623; J. D. Creswell et al., "Brief mindfulness meditation training alters psychological and neuroendocrine responses to social evaluative stress," *Psychoneuroendochrinology* 32, no. 10 (June 2014): 1104–9.

271   **Some 58 percent of the control group became depressed again** Miguel Farias and Catherine Wikholm, *The Buddha Pill: Can Meditation Change You?* (London: Watkins Publishing, 2015), 74; C. Hutcherson and E. Seppala, "Loving-kindness meditation increases social connectedness," *Emotion* 8, no. 5 (Oct. 2008): 720–4; J. Mascaro et al., "Compassion meditation enhances empathic accuracy and related neural activity," *Social Cognitive and Affective Neuroscience* 8, no. 1 (Jan. 2013): 48–55; Y. Kang et al., "The non-discriminating heart: Lovingkindness meditation training decreases implicit intergroup bias," *Journal of Experimental Psychology, General* 143, no. 3 (June 2014): 1306–1313; Y. Kang et al., "Compassion training alters altruism and neural responses to suffering," *Psychological Science* 24, no. 7 (July 2013), 1171–1180; Eberth Sedlmeier et al., "The psychological effects of meditation: A meta-analysis," *Psychological Bulletin* 138, no. 6 (Nov. 2012): 1139–1171.

271   **One different study honed this effect a little and found that meditation works particularly well** Farias and Wikholm, *Buddha Pill*, 112; Frank Bures, *The Geography of Madness: Penis Thieves, Voodoo Death and the Search for the Meaning of the World's Strangest Syndromes* (New York: Melville House, 2016), 123.

271   **you could double your compassion through doing this practice** Farias and Wikholm, *Buddha Pill*, 128–131.

272   **there's evidence that people who pray become less depressed** P. A. Boelens et al., "A randomized trial of the effect of prayer on depression and anxiety," *International Journal of Psychiatry Medicine* 39, no. 4 (2009): 377–92.

272 **Another is Cognitive Behavioral Therapy (CBT)** D. Lynch, "Cognitive behavioural therapy for major psychiatric disorder: does it really work? A meta-analytical review of well-controlled trials," *Psychological Medicine* 40, no. 1 (Jan. 2010): 9–24, doi: https://doi.org/10.1017/S00 3329170900590X.

276 **You can make them feel they are transcending their egos and their everyday concerns** Walter Pahnke and Bill Richards, "Implications of LSD and experimental mysticism," *Journal of Religion and Health* 5, no. 3 (July 1966): 175–208; R. R. Griffith et al., "Psilocybin can occasion mystical-type experiences having substantial and sustained personal meaning and spiritual significance," *Psychopharmacology* 187, no. 3 (Aug. 2006): 268–283; Michael Lerner and Michael Lyvers, "Values and Beliefs of Psychedelic Drug Users: A Cross-Cultural Study," *Journal of Psychoactive Drugs* 38, no. 2 (2006): 143–7; Stephen Trichter et al., "Changes in Spirituality Among Ayahuasca Ceremony Novice Participants," *Journal of Psychoactive Drugs* 41, no. 2 (2009): 121–134; Rick Doblin: "Pahnke's 'Good Friday experiment': A long-term follow-up and methodological critique," *Journal of Transpersonal Psychology* 23, no. 1 (Jan. 1991): 1. For a good background on all of this, read the excellent William Richards, *Sacred Knowledge: Psychedelics and Religious Experiences* (New York: Columbia University Press, 2016).

276 **When it was given to chronic alcoholics** Pahnke et al., "LSD In The Treatment of Alcoholics," *Pharmacopsychiatry* 4, no. 2 (1971); 83–94, doi: 10.1055/s-0028-1094301.

276 **When it was given to chronically depressed people** L. Grinspoon and J. Bakalar, "The psychedelic drug therapies," *Curr Psychiatr Ther* 20 (1981): 275–283.

276 **These scientific trials weren't conducted according to the standards that we'd use today** Bill Richards explains why in *Sacred Knowledge: Psychedelics and Religious Experiences* (New York: Columbia University Press, 2015).

276 **there were lots of stories that were invented to demonize the drugs** The best deconstruction of these myths—laying out the evidence—can

be found in the excellent *Saying Yes* by Jacob Sullum (New York: Jeremy Tarcher, 2004).

276 **So Roland applied to conduct the very first clinical trial on a psychedelic since the ban a generation before.** No law was passed banning these drugs. But in practice, the authorities gave no permission for any experiments. It was a de facto ban, not a legal one.

277 **Mark didn't know what to expect as he walked through Roland's lab** Mark is his real name, but he asked me to change some minor identifying details about his life in this account. The audio and details of this interview have been verified by the publisher.

285 **To understand what is happening, I traveled to Los Angeles, Maryland . . .** In Los Angeles, at UCLA, I interviewed Charles Grob and Alicia Danforth. In Baltimore, at Johns Hopkins, I interviewed Albert Garcia, Bill Richards, Fred Barratt, Roland Griffiths, Jim Fadiman, and several participants in their trials who asked not to be named. In London, at UCL, I interviewed David Nutt, Jim Rucker, and Robin Carhart-Harris. In San Francisco, I interviewed Richard Vaughan. In Denmark I interviewed David Eritzoe. In New York I interviewed Elias Dakwar, Andrew Tatarsky, and Katherine Maclean. In Norway I interviewed Teri Krebbs and Pal Johansen. In São Paulo, Brazil, I interviewed Diartiu Silviera. I also interviewed some of the key funders of this research: Rick Doblin, head of MAPS, in Boston; Brad Burge of MAPS in California; and Amanda Fielding, head of the Beckley Foundation, in London. A guide to this research that helped me to identify who to talk to was this superb article by Michael Pollan: "The Trip Treatment," *New Yorker*, February 9, 2015, http://www.newyorker.com/maga zine/2015/02/09/trip-treatment, as accessed December 12, 2016.

285 **After just three sessions—like Mark—80 percent of them quit** Matthew W. Johnson et al., "Pilot study of the 5-HT$_{2A}$R agonist psilocybin in the treatment of tobacco addiction," *Journal of Psychopharmacology* 28, no. 11 (Sept. 2014): 983–992.

285 **A team working at University College London gave psilocybin to people who had severe depression** Robin Carhart-Harris et al.,

"Psilocybin with psychological support for treatment-resistant depression: an open-label feasibility study," *Lancet Psychiatry* 3, no. 7 (July 2016): 619–627.

285 **These positive effects were dependent on one thing.** Matthew W. Johnson et al., "Pilot study of the 5-HT$_{2A}$R agonist psilocybin in the treatment of tobacco addiction," *Journal of Psychopharmacology* 28, no. 11 (Sept. 2014): 983–992.

286 **Fred Barrett, an assistant professor at Johns Hopkins, is running a study with Roland** This study has not yet been published. You can watch Fred discuss it here: https://vimeo.com/148364545, as accessed December 12, 2016.

CHAPTER 21: RECONNECTION SIX: ACKNOWLEDGING AND OVERCOMING CHILDHOOD TRAUMA

294 **Do you feel it had negative long-term effects on you?** Vincent Felitti et al., *Chadwick's Child Maltreatment: Sexual Abuse and Psychological Maltreatment*, Volume 2 of 3, Fourth edition, (2014): 211; V. Felitti et al., "The relationship of adult health status to childhood abuse and household dysfunction," *American Journal of Preventive Medicine* 14 (1998): 245–258.

295 **Finally, the figures came in.** Felitti et al., *Chadwick's Child Maltreatment*, 212; V. Felitti, "Long Term Medical Consequences of Incest, Rape, and Molestation," *Southern Medical Journal* 84 (1991): 328–331.

295 **For example, one elderly woman—who had described being raped as a child for the first time** Felitti et al., *Chadwick's Child Maltreatment*, 205.

295 **Those patients were *50 percent* less likely to come back** Vincent Felitti, "Ursprünge des Suchtverhaltens—Evidenzen aus einer Studie zu belastenden Kindheitserfahrungen," *Praxis der Kinderpsychologie und Kinderpsychiatrie*, 52 (2003): 547–559.

296 **For example, closeted gay men, during the AIDS crisis, died on average two to three years earlier** Judith Shulevitz, "The Lethality of

Loneliness," *New Republic*, May 13, 2013, https://newrepublic.com /article/113176/science-loneliness-how-isolation-can-kill-you, as accessed December 12, 2016. The most important research on how releasing mental burdens has all sorts of extraordinary positive effects has been done by James Pennebaker at the University of Texas at Austin. If you are interested in this subject I recommend reading broadly across his important work.

CHAPTER 22: RECONNECTION SEVEN: RESTORING THE FUTURE

299 **In the middle of the 1970s, a group of Canadian government officials chose** This account is based on interviewing Evelyn Forget and reading her published papers, especially Evelyn Forget, "The Town with No Poverty: The Health Effects of a Canadian Guaranteed Annual Income Field Experiment," *Canadian Public Policy* 37, no. 3 (2011), doi: 10.3138/cpp.37.3.283. I have also drawn on Nick Srnicek and Alex Williams, *Inventing the Future: Postcapitalism and a World Without Work* (London: Verso, 2015), and Rutger Bregman, *Utopia for Realists: The Case for a Universal Basic Income, Open Borders, and a 15-hour Workweek* (Netherlands: Correspondent Press, 2016). I have also drawn on these articles: Zi-Ann Lum, "A Canadian City Once Eliminated Poverty and Nearly Everyone Forgot About It," *Huffington Post*, January 3, 2017, http://www.huffingtonpost.ca/2014/12/23/mincome-in -dauphin-manitoba_n_6335682.html; Benjamin Shingler, "Money for nothing: Mincome experiment could pay dividends 40 years on," *Aljazeera America*, August 26, 2014, http://america.aljazeera.com /articles/2014/8/26/dauphin-canada-cash.html; Stephen J. Dubner, "Is the World Ready for a Guaranteed Basic Income?" *Freakonomics*, April 13, 2016, http://freakonomics.com/podcast/mincome/; Laura Anderson and Danielle Martin, "Let's get the basic income experiment right," TheStar.com, March 1, 2016, https://www.thestar.com/opinion /commentary/2016/03/01/lets-get-the-basic-income-experiment-right

.html; CBC News, "1970s Manitoba poverty experiment called a success," CBC.ca, March 25, 2010, http://www.cbc.ca/news/canada /manitoba/1970s-manitoba-poverty-experiment-called-a-success -1.868562; all as accessed August 20, 2016. I was also helped by interviewing the excellent German economist and thinker Stefan Mekkifer in Berlin, and the American economist Karl Widerquist in Montreal.

300 **In the United States, if you have an income below $20,000** Carl I. Cohen and Sami Timimi, eds., *Liberatory Psychiatry: Philosophy, Politics and Mental Health* (Cambridge: Cambridge University Press, 2008), 132–4; Blazer et al., "The prevalence and distribution of major depression in a national community sample: the National Comorbidity Survey," *Am Psych Assoc* 151, no. 7 (July 1994): 979–986.

302 **here are some of the key effects Evelyn discovered** Rutger Bregman, *Utopia for Realists: The Case for a Universal Basic Income, Open Borders, and a 15-hour Workweek* (Netherlands: Correspondent Press, 2016), 63–4.

304 **He is the leading European champion of the idea of a universal basic income.** https://www.indybay.org/newsitems/2010/07/06/18652754 .php, as accessed December 12, 2016.

305 **Behavioral problems like ADHD and childhood depression fell by 40 percent** E. Jane Costello et al., "Relationships Between Poverty and Psychopathology: A Natural Experiment," *JAMA* 290, no. 15 (2003): 2023–2029. See also Moises Velasquez-Manoff, "What Happens When the Poor Receive a Stipend?" *New York Times*, January 18, 2014, http:// opinionator.blogs.nytimes.com/2014/01/18/what-happens-when-the -poor-receive-a-stipend/, as accessed Jan 1, 2017. Also Bregman and Manton, *Utopia for Realists*, 97–9. See also https://academicminute .org/2014/06/jane-costello-duke-university-sharing-the-wealth/, as accessed Jan 1, 2017.

305 **The biggest change, Rutger believes, will be in how people think about work** http://edoc.vifapol.de/opus/volltexte/2014/5322/pdf /Papers_Basic_Income_Blaschke_2012pdf.pdf, as accessed October 20, 2016; Danny Dorling: *A Better Politics: How Government Can Make Us Happier* (London: London Publishing Partnership, 2016), 98–100.

305 **the key to a guaranteed income** This case is also powerfully made in
     Nick Srnicek and Alex Williams, *Inventing the Future: Postcapitalism
     and a World Without Work* (London: Verso, 2015), 120–1.

306 **President Obama said it could happen in the next twenty years.**
     https://www.wired.com/2016/10/president-obama-mit-joi-ito-inter
     view/, as accessed December 12, 2016.

307 **He had been raised in a Catholic family in a homophobic culture**
     Andrew describes a lot of this in his totally beautiful book *Love Unde-
     tectable* (London: Vintage, 2014).

309 **You don't need me to fill in this list** For a more comprehensive guide
     to how this works, I recommend two amazing books: Rebecca Solnit,
     Hope in the Dark: Untold Histories, Wild Possibilities (London: Canon-
     gate, 2016) and Paul Rogat Loeb, *Soul of a Citizen: Living with Convic-
     tion in Challenging Times* (New York: St Martin's Press, 2010).

CONCLUSION: HOMECOMING

312 **That story has made Big Pharma over $100 billion** http://www
     .researchandmarkets.com/research/p35qmw/u_s, as accessed December
     23, 2016.

312 **The World Health Organization—the leading medical body in the
     world—summarized the evidence well in 2011** Paul Verhaeghe, *What
     About Me? The Struggle for Identity in a Market-Based Society* (Victoria,
     Australia: Scribe, 2014), 191–3.

312 **The United Nations—in its official statement for World Health Day
     in 2017— explained** http://www.ohchr.org/EN/NewsEvents/Pages
     /DisplayNews.aspx?NewsID=21480&LangID=E, as accessed April 16,
     2017. They state that for severe cases medication should remain as an
     option but "the use of psychotropic medications as the first line treat-
     ment for depression and other conditions is, quite simply, unsupported
     by the evidence. The excessive use of medications and other biomedical
     interventions, based on a reductive neurobiological paradigm causes
     more harm than good."

313   **You will become sealed off in a serotonin story** Paul Moloney, *The Therapy Industry: The Irresistible Rise of the Talking Cure, and Why It Doesn't Work* (London: Pluto Press, 2013), 70.

315   **If you kept your hand on the stove, it would burn** This image comes from Stephen Grosz's wonderful book *The Examined Life: How We Lose and Find Ourselves* (London: Vintage, 2015).

315   **Depression and anxiety might, in one way, be the sanest reaction you have.** Mark Fisher talks about this interestingly in his excellent book *Capitalist Realism: Is There No Alternative?* (Winchester, UK: O Books, 2009)—see pp. 18–20.

318   **You have to turn now to all the other wounded people around you, and find a way to connect with them** This idea—that we need to come home—was influenced by Naomi Klein's writing in *This Changes Everything: Capitalism vs. The Climate* (London: Penguin, 2015), and Avi Lewis's film of the same name.

INDEX

Cunningham, Lisa
depression of, 230–32
and non-drug treatments for
depression, 234–38

depression
and anxiety, as paired disorders
with single origin, 14–15
bipolar (manic), biological
component of, 183–84
bowed-down posture
characteristics of, 141, 144
in captive animals, 152–54, 160
chronic, in author's childhood and
youth, 5–6
as form of grief, 54, 315–16
high incidence in Western cultures,
12
measurement of, 29
as once-taboo subject, 56
painfulness of, 5
as type of submission response, 146
and unhappiness, continuum
between, 15–16
depression, causes of
author's reluctance to begin
research into, 13–14, 23
disconnection as common thread
in, 71–72
limited data on, 57
non-chemical, as commonly
ignored, 8
See also bio-psycho-social model of
depression; childhood
trauma; endogenous model of
depression; environmental
causes of depression; future,
hopeful/secure; genetic causes

of depression; natural world,
disconnection from;
neuroplasticity and
depression; people,
disconnection from; reactive
model of depression; status
and respect, disconnection
from; values, meaningful,
disconnection from; work,
meaningful, disconnection
from
derealization, as symptom of
depression, 77
*Diagnostic and Statistical Manual
(DSM)*
and confusion of grief with
depression, 50–53
and "grief exception," 50–53
symptoms of depression in, 50–53
diet, poor, as common problem, 110
dopamine
imbalance of, as cause of
depression, lack of evidence
for, 36, 136
and Internet addiction, 106
drug testing
as corrupt process, 38–39
low threshold for drug approval in,
37
standard format for, 25–26
drug testing of antidepressants
as corrupt process, 38–39
drug companies' suppression of
unfavorable results, 27–29
fundamental problems with,
43–44
Kirsch and Sapirstein review of,
25–30, 41

Kaltnhorn, Uli, 207, 209, 211
Kasser, Tim
  on advertising's power to create
    materialistic desires, 121–23
  childhood of, 111, 112
  and consumer values, experiment
    in changing, 260–64
  on intrinsic vs. extrinsic
    motivations, 115–17
  nonmaterialistic lifestyle adopted
    by, 125–27
  personal realization about link
    between materialism and
    depression, 112–13
  research on link between
    materialism and depression,
    112–17, 256
  research on materialism's
    destructive effects, 118–19
Kavlak, Mehmet, 205, 209, 212,
  214–15, 218
Kirmayer, Laurence, 189
Kirsch, Irving
  credentials of, 24
  experience with prescribing
    antidepressants, 24
  opposition to research conclusions
    of, 41
  research on origin of serotonin
    theory of depression, 33–36
  research on placebo effect, 24–26
  review of antidepressant drug
    testing, 25–30, 31–32, 41
  on side effects of antidepressants,
    39
Kohlenberg, Robert, 14–15
Kotti neighborhood (Berlin)
  experience of residents in, 203

history of, 200
  poverty and crime in, 199
  rising rents in, 200, 208
  tensions between groups in, 200,
    205–7
Kotti neighborhood protest, 199–217,
  318
  accomplishment of rent-freeze
    goals, 214
  attention attracted by, 201, 208, 214
  bonding of residents during, 205,
    206–7, 208, 211–12, 214–15,
    216–17
  camp blocking street, 201
  and connection to other people as
    treatment for depression, 215,
    216–17, 218, 220–21
  demands of, 202
  and expanded sense of "home," 214,
    318
  expansion to city-wide referendum
    effort, 216
  guarding of camp, 202
  marches, 208
  origins of, 199–201
  perseverance of, 213–14
  police efforts to shut down, 202,
    210
  strain on protesters, 209
  and Tuncai (homeless man),
    adoption of, 209
  and Tuncai, freeing from
    psychiatric facility, 210–11
Kramer, Peter
  critiques of drug testing for
    antidepressants, 43–44
  on effectiveness of antidepressants,
    41–44

A NOTE ON THE AUTHOR

JOHANN HARI is the *New York Times* bestselling author of *Chasing the Scream: The First and Last Days of the War on Drugs*, which has been published in eleven languages. It is currently being adapted into a fictional feature film by producer Joe Roth and into a feature-length documentary by Academy Award–nominated producer Jeff Hayes. Hari has written for the *New York Times*, the *Los Angeles Times*, the *Guardian*, *Le Monde*, *Slate*, the *New Republic*, the *Melbourne Age*, and the *Nation*. He has twice been named Newspaper Journalist of the Year by Amnesty International UK for his reporting on the war in the Congo and human rights abuses in Dubai.

He appears regularly as a panelist on the HBO show *Real Time with Bill Maher*.

His TED Talk, "Everything You Think You Know About Addiction Is Wrong," and the animation he scripted based on it have been viewed over twenty million times.